D0225027

*Supreme Court
Decision Making*

Supreme Court Decision Making

David W. Rohde and Harold J. Spaeth
MICHIGAN STATE UNIVERSITY

W. H. Freeman and Company
San Francisco

KF
8742
R63

Library of Congress Cataloging in Publication Data

Rohde, David W.
    Supreme Court decision making.
    Includes bibliographical references and index.
    1.   United States. Supreme Court.   2.   Judicial
process—United States—Research.   I.   Spaeth,
Harold J., joint author.   II.   Title.
KF8742.R63   347'.73'265   75-25645
ISBN 0-7167-0717-9
ISBN 0-7167-0716-0 pbk.

Copyright © 1976 by W. H. Freeman and Company

No part of this book may be reproduced by any
mechanical, photographic, or electronic process, or
in the form of a phonographic recording, nor may it
be stored in a retrieval system, transmitted, or otherwise copied for public or private use, without written
permission from the publisher.

Printed in the United States of America

10   9   8   7   6   5   4   3   2

For my parents and Professor Walter G. Sharrow

D. W. R.

For Jean, Susan, Catherine, and Esther

H. J. S.

12-82 gift

Contents

List of Tables

List of Figures

Preface

The purpose of this book is to offer a theory of decision making in the United States Supreme Court—a theory that is capable of predicting the decisions of the justices and, within the context of these predictions, of explaining why the justices make the decisions they do. Such prediction and explanation require the formulation of a theory sufficiently broad to encompass the full range of Supreme Court activities. This theory, moreover, must of necessity focus upon what the justices actually do, as distinct from what we might like to think they *ought* to do.

Although in this book we depart somewhat from the more familiar paths followed by authors of other works that deal with the Supreme Court, the reader should not assume that this book's utility is thereby lessened. We have, for a number of years, presented the material contained herein in lecture form to large undergraduate classes studying the Supreme Court with, we believe, favorable results. (But it would be false modesty for us to assert that more advanced readers will learn nothing from the pages that follow. We certainly hope they will.) Indeed, our main purpose is to bring together a variety of research results (some of which have appeared elsewhere, most of which have not); place them within a theoretical context; and thereby provide the reader with what we hope is a comprehensible and relatively complete picture of decision making in the Supreme Court.

We are presenting our data and conclusions in such a way that they can be replicated by others. The theory itself is neither technical nor complex. The methodology, though not especially difficult or mathematical, is discussed only briefly in the body of the relevant chapters. For those who may wish a more complete explanation, the details of how we operationalize and test the hypotheses that flow from our theory are presented in appendices at the ends of chapters.

Our theory assumes that decisions are the consequence of three factors: goals, rules, and situations. We assume that people behave purposively; that is, they have goals they wish to achieve and they take action in order to achieve them. In addition, people are continually faced with alternative courses of action among which they must choose. The alternative an individual chooses is, we assume, the one that he or she perceives will best achieve the desired goal.*

Individuals, however, do not make choices in a vacuum. The relationship between a set of alternatives and a person's calculation of which alternative will best achieve his goals is affected by what we term "the rules of the game"—the various structures of formal and informal rules and norms that form the framework within which decisions are made. Depending upon the rule structures, the same individual may behave quite differently in two alternative settings. Also, decisions are affected by the particular configuration of circumstances that constitute the various decision-making situations in which individuals find themselves.

These, then, are the assumptions that form the foundation of our theory. In the first two chapters, we discuss the formal and informal rules that govern the judiciary in the United States generally. In Chapter 3, we present a brief description of the decision-making process of the Supreme Court in order to provide a context within which the reader can place the details in the chapters that follow.

In Chapter 4 we discuss in full our theory of Supreme Court decision making and introduce some of the concepts and methodology that are employed subsequently. In Chapter 5 we consider the process by which justices are appointed and examine how the goals we assume for the justices in our theory affect the decisions of those responsible for appointment (i.e., the President, who nominates, and the members of the Senate, who must confirm or reject nominees).

In the remainder of the book we break down the Court's decision making into four sequential stages, each of which is the subject of a separate chapter. In Chapter 6 we analyze the factors that affect the Court's decision regarding which cases it will consider. In Chapter 7 we focus on the vote on the merits in the cases that the Court agrees to decide. In Chapter 8 we discuss the strategic considerations that affect the decision to whom the assignment of the majority opinion should be made. Chapter 9 concerns the process by which the coalition that joins in the majority opinion is formed. It focuses on the size and composition of that coalition, and how the actions of persons outside the Court sometimes affect the process. In the Epilogue we present some concluding remarks.

---

*Technically, we are assuming here that people are "rational," in the sense employed in a variety of formal approaches to the study of decision making. See William H. Riker and Peter C. Ordeshook, *An Introduction to Positive Political Theory* (Englewood Cliffs, N.J.: Prentice-Hall, 1973), Chapter 2, for an extended discussion.

We should note here that a variety of data from different periods is used to apply the theory and test the predictions based thereon. This is primarily a consequence of the fact that some of the research was completed previously and independently of the writing of this book, and the remainder of it was prepared specifically for this volume. Thus the data in Chapter 8 are limited to civil liberties cases decided during the period 1953–1969, whereas those in Chapter 7 include all cases decided during the period 1958–1974. In addition, and for the same reason, the classification of cases into issue areas in Chapters 7 through 9 varies somewhat. We do not believe that this adversely affects the validity of our conclusions. First, although the overlap of the data is not complete, it is substantial. In addition, where possible (e.g., in Chapter 8), we have drawn on the research of others to help complete the picture.

Although this book is entirely a combined effort, primary responsibility for the writing of each of the chapters was assumed by one of the authors. David Rohde wrote Chapters 3, 5, 8, and 9; Harold Spaeth wrote Chapters 1, 2, 4, 6, and 7.

We believe that our emphasis on prediction and explanation—what the Court will do and why—will minimize the effect of the ravages of time on the contents of this book. It is an unhappy fact of life that few things, other than yesterday's newspaper, become dated more quickly than books dealing with the Supreme Court. As new issues and concerns confront American Society, the Court is expected to resolve them in whole or in part. So too do changing circumstances and conditions, to say nothing of changes in the Court's personnel, alter, often substantially, policies made at an earlier time. The theory presented herein should continue to explain the Court's activities, absent marked changes in the role performed by the Court, or alteration of the rule structures that govern the Court's decision-making processes, even though the data themselves are quickly supplanted by new decisions on old issues and the raising of altogether new issues.

We wish to add a few words about the methods of citation of Supreme Court cases for those unfamiliar with the subject. For convenience we have cited two different sources for cases. The citations of most older cases are taken from the *United States Reports*.† Thus, *Brown* v. *Board of Education* is cited 347 U.S. 483 (1954). This means that the case was decided in 1954, and the opinions may be found in volume 347 of the *United States Reports* beginning on page 483. The citations of more recent cases, including most of those used in our data analysis, are taken from *United States Supreme Court Reports, Lawyers' Edition*.‡ Thus, *United States* v. *Nixon* is cited 41 L Ed 2d 1039 (1974), which means that the case, decided in 1974, may be found in volume 41 of the second series of the

†Published by the Government Printing Office, Washington, D.C.
‡Published by the Lawyers Co-Operative Publishing Company, Rochester, New York.

Lawyers' Edition, starting on page 1039. Any reader who wishes to look up a particular case should go to the bound volume of the Lawyers' Edition for the appropriate year. (These volumes are found in most libraries.) This edition will have not only its own pagination, but also the corresponding volume and page numbers for the *United States Reports*. Thus any case may be quickly and easily found.

Finally, we wish to thank those who assisted us at various stages of this endeavor. Douglas R. Parker, Gregory J. Rathjen, Robert Delgrosso, and John Schuiteman helped us in the collection of some of the data. Charles F. Wrigley, former director of the Michigan State University Computer Institute for Social Science Research, made available his staff and facilities. Scott B. Guthery of the Bell Telephone Laboratories provided valuable assistance to Harold Spaeth in explaining the techniques of data reduction. A grant to Harold Spaeth from the National Institutes of Mental Health supported the theoretical formulation presented in Chapter 4 and the analysis of the justices' voting behavior contained in the first three sections of Chapter 7 and the Appendix to Chapter 7. Special thanks are due Maxim (Bud) Goode of R-Squared, Inc., for suggesting and promoting Harold Spaeth's predictions of some of the Court's more newsworthy decisions, and to the *Los Angeles Herald-Examiner*, which provided space in its Sunday editions for printing these predictions.

Sheldon Goldman of the University of Massachusetts read the entire manuscript twice. His trenchant suggestions improved the readability of the manuscript and kept us from committing many errors of fact. The manuscript was efficiently typed by Iris Richardson, Trudy Carmany, Kathy Bryant, and Judy Hazle. Richard J. Lamb of W. H. Freeman and Company provided editorial guidance and encouragement. It was indeed a pleasure to work with him. Jeanne Singeisen, our manuscript editor, did an excellent job. Also, the cooperation and assistance of the past and present chairpersons of the Michigan State University Political Science Department—Charles Press and Charles Cnudde—is much appreciated.

We wish to gratefully acknowledge the permission of Holt, Rinehart and Winston, the Charles E. Merrill Publishing Company, Oxford University Press, Chandler Publishing Company, and the Macmillan Company, to reprint quotations from works under their copyright. The majority of the material in Chapters 8 and 9 originally appeared in article form in the *American Journal of Political Science* (formerly the *Midwest Journal of Political Science*), Vol. 16 (November 1972), and Vol. 16 (May 1972), respectively.

Last, but by no means least, we wish to express our gratitude to our families, who showed great understanding during this project, the duration of which was much longer than any of us anticipated.

July 1975   David W. Rohde
                                                        Harold J. Spaeth

Supreme Court
Decision Making

The Judiciary and Its Activities

1

The Activities of the Judiciary

What do courts do? To answer this question with any degree of comprehensiveness, it is necessary to focus upon the judiciary as an organization. Human organizations, unlike physical and biological systems, lack an anatomical structure. A rock, a tree, and a human being all share one characteristic: each is held together by its structure—by the fact that it is physically bounded. Human organizations, however, are held together by social, cultural, and psychological factors. These factors define the behavioral pattern expected of each individual member; in other words, they reduce human variability sufficiently to enable an organization to exist and function effectively. The social factors are the roles of an organization; the cultural factors are norms; and the psychological factors are values. Roles, norms, and values, then, are the cement that holds an organization together.

Roles, norms, and values may be distinguished from one another as follows: A *role* is the standardized, distinctive set of activities—the formalized pattern of behavior that is required of each person occupying a position in an organization. A *norm* is a guideline that specifies how an individual is to perform his assigned role in an organization. Whereas roles differentiate an organization's membership, in that each member of an organization may perform a role distinct from that of every other member of that organization, norms integrate the members of an organization, and are therefore more general. *Values*, like norms, also integrate and hold together the members of an organization. Their purpose is to justify, to rationalize, an organization's roles and norms. Unlike norms, however, values are not enforced by sanctions.

1

We may now answer the question with which this chapter began. Courts, in the American governmental system, perform three activities: they administer laws; they resolve conflicts; and they make policy. The role of the courts is the subject of this chapter; norms and values are discussed in Chapter 2.

Administration of the Laws

Administration of the laws pertains to the determination of guilt or innocence and, if guilt is found, the punishment to be inflicted upon the wrongdoer. Society, through its lawmakers, defines certain actions to be criminal. It is the responsibility of the courts to apply these laws in the context of the individual cases that law enforcement officials initiate.

The most basic reason for the enactment of criminal laws is that man is a creature of habit. As such, he is incapable of functioning in an overly dynamic environment. Consider a society with mechanized modes of transportation. Were there no laws regulating traffic flow, chaos would result. The psychic cost—to say nothing of the risk of physical injury—to the individual attempting to go from one place to another would be inordinate. Consequently, to some extent and within certain degrees of freedom, the individual members of a society must be able to demand from others certain regularities of behavior, and they must also accord others the expectation that they, themselves, will behave predictably. To ensure that such predictability obtains, lawmakers enact laws governing important kinds of interpersonal behavior, the violation of which is a crime.

Conflict Resolution

The second activity performed by courts is conflict resolution—the settlement of private disputes. In addition to being a creature of habit, man is also motivated by self-interest. Behavior so motivated often results in conflict with other persons. Although much self-interested behavior may result in violation of the criminal law, there is much that is sufficiently personal that society does not regulate it by means of criminal law. To the affected individual, however, such conflicts may be a matter of major concern, so much so that his well-being may be at stake: for example, a person who is physically injured as a result of another's negligence, or a person who incurs financial loss because of nonfulfillment of a contractual obligation or the nonpayment of a debt owed him. Consequently, society provides a mechanism—civil law—for the resolution of private disputes in a socially acceptable manner.

There are three distinguishable services that American courts provide with regard to conflict resolution.[1] First, a set of procedures and remedies is made available. Second, the settlement of private matters may be legitimized. This occurs, for example, in matters concerning domestic and familial relations. The adoption of a child, the termination of a marriage, and the disposition of the assets of a deceased person are typical. The parties need not utilize the courts in all such matters, but a court's seal of approval upon these private relationships is authoritative against those who would question the arrangement existing among the affected persons. Third, persons may use governmental power for private purposes. A creditor may obtain a court order authorizing him to garnishee a debtor's salary. A landlord may secure an eviction notice against his tenant. At an individual's request, a judge may issue a writ of mandamus or an injunction that orders a specified person to do or not to do certain specified actions.

Judges, of course, are no more free to resolve conflicts without justifying their decisions in these civil actions than they are free to do so when they administer criminal laws. In a recent decision, the Supreme Court addressed itself to the matter of conflict resolution in the following words:

> Perhaps no characteristic of an organized and cohesive society is more fundamental than its erection and enforcement of a system of rules defining the various rights and duties of its members, enabling them to govern their affairs and definitively settle their differences in an orderly, predictable manner. Without such a "legal system," social organization and cohesion are virtually impossible; with the ability to seek regularized resolution of conflicts individuals are capable of interdependent action that enables them to strive for achievements without the anxieties that would beset them in a disorganized society. . . .
> . . . It is to courts, or other quasi-judicial official bodies, that we ultimately look for the implementation of a regularized, orderly process of dispute settlement. Within this framework, those who wrote our original Constitution, in the Fifth Amendment, and later those who drafted the Fourteenth Amendment, recognized the centrality of the concept of due process in the operation of this system. Without this guarantee that one may not be deprived of his rights, neither liberty nor property, without due process of law, the State's monopoly over techniques for binding conflict resolution could hardly be said to be acceptable under our scheme of things. Only by providing that the social enforcement mechanism must function strictly within these bounds can we hope to maintain an ordered society that is also just. . . .
> . . . our society has been so structured that resort to the courts is not usually the only available, legitimate means of resolving private disputes. Indeed, private structuring of individual relationships and repair of their breach is largely encouraged in American life, subject only to the caveat that the formal judicial process, if resorted to, is paramount.[2]

Notwithstanding the impression that may be given by the statements just quoted, due process is not a precisely defined concept. Judges, at all levels of the judicial hierarchy, have great discretion as to how they decide the cases before them. Although juries share decision making with trial court judges, it is the judge who instructs the jury. And though he may (but rarely does) order a jury to bring in a prespecified verdict, his influence nonetheless dominates the entire proceedings.

Policy Making

It is the fact of judicial decision-making discretion, which regard not only to the concept of due process, but to the totality of legal rules and principles, legislative enactments, executive orders, and constitutional provisions, as well, that gives rise to the last of the activities performed by American courts —policy making.

Judicial policy making is rather distinctive to American courts. What is involved here is the ability of judges to resolve authoritatively public policy issues. Because courts are hierarchically structured and because those at the apex of the hierarchy—the appellate courts—generally have a broader jurisdiction than the trial courts at the base of the hierarchy, the appellate courts, especially the state courts and the United States Supreme Court, are the most concerned with policy making. But this does not mean that local trial courts do not make policy; most assuredly they do.[3]

Reasons for Judicial Policy Making

Because policy making is directly related to the purpose of this book— the formulation and application of a theory of Supreme Court decision making—an explanation of the reasons why policy making is an activity of the American judiciary is in order.

Fundamental law. Underlying the development of the American political system was the concept of a fundamental law. Governmental action was to be compatible with the word of God or the dictates of nature as these were interpreted by the founders and the subsequent leaders of most of the American colonies. The overtly religious motivation that led to the establishment of these colonies—especially those in New England— was evidence of this concern. Apart from religious motivation, support for the concept of fundamental law derived from the extremely volatile environment in which Americans found themselves in colonial times, as they do today. Drastic changes in life style and status have characterized the personal history of millions of Americans, past and present. What was religiously homogeneous when viewed from the perspective of a single colony became heterodox when viewed nationally. The westward movement from the Atlantic tidewater to the far reaches of the Pacific produced profound economic and social turbulence. Mass immigration diversified the nation culturally. The industrial and technological revolutions transformed yeoman farmers into urbanized employees. The collective impact of these forces precluded the establishment of a fixed and stable social, economic, religious, or cultural system. Consequently, the only sphere of human activity that could be made subject to effective control and direction was the political. The solution adopted was to replace the hitherto parochial and essentially religious notion of a fundamental law with one that would control all governmental activities. Hence the written Constitution, which is enshrined as American society's secular substitute for Holy Writ.

Distrust of centralized government. A second reason for the existence of judicial policy making is the fear or distrust of centralized governmental power. Opposition to British governmental policies led to the Revolutionary War. Acts of Parliament following the French and Indian War were viewed as inimical to the traditional liberties of British citizens. Concomitant with the onset of the Revolutionary War was an internal struggle for political dominance within the newly formed state governments. This struggle pitted the socioeconomic elite against the yeoman farmers and the urban artisans. It was by no means resolved when the Constitutional Convention convened in 1787. Mindful of the ongoing struggle and the recently concluded war against England, the Framers of the Constitution created a governmental system that neither the "haves" nor the "have nots" were capable of using to completely dominate the other.

The major political concern of the socioeconomic elite was that legislation might be enacted that threatened their vested economic rights. The shifting of taxation from their opponents to themselves, the passage of stay laws that lengthened the time for the payment of private debts, the issuance of cheap paper money as legal tender, and efforts to reapportion state legislatures to allow greater representation to rural and frontier areas exemplify specific policy differences between this elite and the lower strata of American society. Participation in governmental activity was a new experience for the latter group. Lack of experience left them somewhat disadvantaged in the resulting political conflict. Such headway as they did make occurred at the state and local levels of government. Sentiments supportive of states' rights and local self-government heightened their opposition to a strong and efficient central government. Evidence that they did indeed distrust the establishment of a central government was their insistence that a Bill of Rights be added to the Constitution in return for their support of ratification. Furthermore, a substantial proportion of the lower strata lived on the frontier—those sections of the country that were beyond the pale of effective governmental authority. This condition was to prevail for the next hundred years as the nation expanded from the Atlantic tidewater and Appalachia to the far reaches of the Pacific Coast.

Nor was the socioeconomic elite adverse to a governmental system not susceptible to anyone's effective control. As privileged groups, their

5

especial concern was the loss of historically vested rights. So long as governmental power was not used against them, they could successfully perpetuate their position in society, given their possession and control of economic power and the social status that accompanied it. Consequently, the notion that that government is best which governs least quickly became an article of faith for most of those Americans for whom it was not already such.

Two of the three remaining reasons for the existence of judicial policy making concern methods whereby the Framers structured a governmental system that could not be utilized by either the haves or the have nots to attempt to effectively subjugate the other. These methods are federalism and separation of powers.

Federalism.   Federalism is the geographical division of governmental powers between the national level and state levels. The constitutional provisions that specify what powers the national government may exercise, those that the state governments may exercise, and those that are shared by both are vaguely and imprecisely phrased. The result has been a steady stream of litigation; the Supreme Court is responsible for final adjudication of cases bearing on the issue of the relative power of the national government vis-à-vis the states and the resultant degree of centralization/decentralization that is to prevail. An excellent example from recent history—although mooted by the passage of the Twenty-sixth Amendment—was the attempt by Congress in 1970 to lower the voting age in all elections to 18. The Court, by a 5 to 4 vote, held that Congress had power to do so for federal elections, but that Congress lacked such power for state and local elections.[4]

Separation of powers.   Separation of powers is the functional division of governmental powers among autonomous "branches" of government. The branches parallel the classic typology of governmental functions: legislative, executive, and judicial. Autonomy was secured by separately constituting the membership of each branch. To ensure that this autonomy did not become *pro forma*, the Framers of the Constitution gave to each of the branches the authority to exercise certain powers that properly belonged to one of the other branches. Thus, for example, the President has the capacity to check Congress by his power to veto legislation; Congress, on the other hand, checks executive activity by virtue of the constitutional requirement that all the President's major appointees must be confirmed by the Senate.

A further extension of the concept of separation of powers is bicameralism, the division of the legislative branch into two autonomous segments—the House of Representatives and the Senate. For legislation to be enacted, the bill in question must be approved separately by a majority of the members of each house who are present and voting. The bill, moreover, must be worded in identical language when passed by both houses.

The Framers did not provide the judiciary with checks on the legislative and executive branches. Their concern, rather, was that the judiciary not be subject to the dictates of either Congress or the President. Accordingly, all federal judges "hold their offices during good behavior"; that is, for life. They are nominated by the President and must be confirmed by the Senate. In addition, Congress has the power to establish federal courts below the Supreme Court and to determine their jurisdiction, including the cases that litigants may appeal to the Supreme Court. The number of federal judges is similarly within Congress' province.

The Framers' concern that the judiciary be independent of Congress and the executive branch has aided the policy-making capabilities of the federal judiciary in general, and the Supreme Court in particular. If the judges were not autonomous of the President and Congress, their ability to present themselves as objective and impartial decision makers would be much more difficult. As we shall document, the objectivity and impartiality of the justices of the Supreme Court is less than complete. But this does not belie the fact that American society has tenaciously clung to a belief in judicial objectivity. Desire for wish fulfillment is inherent in man's nature. Too much reality is painful. Hence the ostrich posture: let us not be confused by facts. As Justice Holmes once wrote, "we live by symbols." Chief among our symbols are the Constitution[5] and the Supreme Court. They are symbols, as Max Lerner has said, of an ancient sureness, of timelessness, of a comforting stability.[6] But though the reality in which these symbols are rooted is itself a myth, the myth itself to be believed must be plausible. And it is the fact of separation of powers that provides a measure of plausibility. For if federal judges were not autonomous decision makers, the public would likely tar them with the same brush that paints other political actors—that politics is a dirty business and that only persons of minimal abilities and/or virtue occupy governmental office. But because federal judges are autonomous (the most striking manifestation of which is their authority to determine the constitutionality—i.e., the legality—of the actions of other governmental officials and to set the standards that are to govern the subsequent activity of these political actors), they thus have the opportunity—regularly utilized in their opinions—to assert that their sole allegiance is to the Constitution.

Judicial review. Although the judiciary did not formally receive from the Framers any powers that allow it to check the activities of the other branches of government, within fifteen years after the ratification of the Constitution the Supreme Court arrogated to itself such a capability. This resulted from the Court's enunciation of the doctrine of judicial review in the momentous case of *Marbury* v. *Madison*,[7] a case that, incongruously, was nothing more than a "trivial squabble over a few petty political plums."[8]

Marbury had been a political appointee, serving as an aide to the Secretary of the Navy. As an active member of the Federalist Party, he was one of many whom President Adams sought to place in judicial office following the Federalists' overwhelming defeat in the election of 1800. Marbury was commissioned as a justice of the peace for the District of Columbia and, accordingly, became one of Adams' "midnight appointments." Such appointments were commonplace before the passage of the Twentieth Amendment in 1933 whenever one party displaced another from control of the Presidency and both Houses of Congress. The Constitution originally provided that the second session of each Congress would meet *following* the November election during which federal elections were held. Consequently, the second (so-called lame duck) sessions were populated with persons who did not stand for re-election or who had been defeated at the polls. The President, similarly, remained in office after the November election until the following March 4th. Hence, the Congress elected in 1798, controlled by the Federalists, remained in existence until March 4, 1801.

Because of their overwhelming defeat, President Adams, as the leader of the Federalists, had resolved to entrench his party in the federal judiciary, the only branch of government not yet in control of Jefferson and his supporters. Congress willingly enacted the necessary legislation and confirmed the President's nominees. But time was short, and in the flurry of last-minute activities the commissions of several persons to lower judicial offices were not delivered, including that of Marbury. Upon the refusal of the new Secretary of State, James Madison, to deliver his commission, Marbury and several others similarly situated brought an original action in the Supreme Court requesting the Court to order Madison to deliver their commissions. Marbury did so under a provision of the Judiciary Act of 1789 that authorized the Supreme Court to issue writs of mandamus to "persons holding office under the authority of the United States."

Marbury's case came to a Supreme Court presided over by John Marshall. Marshall had been Adams' Secretary of State and had remained in that position until Jefferson's Administration took office. Hence, he was directly involved in the matter that gave rise to the case. Judicial norms mandate that a judge should disqualify himself in such circumstances.[9] Marshall, however, was not about to let a golden opportunity pass. In a brilliant political maneuver, Marshall, speaking for a unanimous Court, held that Madison's refusal to deliver Marbury's commission was illegal. The Supreme Court, however, could provide Marbury no relief. The original jurisdiction of the Supreme Court was specified in the Constitution and covered only cases affecting diplomats and those in which a state was party. Any attempt by Congress to alter the Court's original jurisdiction was consequently unconstitutional. The Court could grant Marbury relief only if his case came to it on appeal.

On the face of the matter, Marshall appeared to rule against his party, not only in the person of Marbury and his associates, but also from the standpoint of Federalist strategy, the aim of which was to make the judiciary a stronghold against the Jeffersonians. But though Marshall appeared to lose the battle, the deeper reality was the establishment of the Supreme Court as a major policy-making body. By rejecting Congress' effort to give the Court an expanded original jurisdiction, Marshall established the principle of *judicial review*—that it is the responsibility of the judiciary to determine whether contested governmental actions are constitutional.

Although no reference to judicial review is found in the Constitution, Marshall's enunciation of the doctrine is fully compatible with the motivations and concerns that led to the drafting and ratification of that document.

If the Constitution is to be the fundamental law because of the felt need of Americans for a measure of stability in an otherwise fluid and dynamic environment, then some decision-making body must authoritatively interpret the provisions of the fundamental law. Congress and/or the President are capable of doing so; however, they are subject to electoral pressures; federal judges are not. Therefore, why not accept judicial interpretation as authoritative?

Marbury v. *Madison* thus asserted the power of the Supreme Court to declare acts of Congress unconstitutional. This power of judicial review is also exercised by the lower federal courts, and by state courts with respect to the laws and ordinances of state and local legislative bodies. The power applies to actions of the executive branch as well. Through the end of 1973, the Supreme Court has ruled unconstitutional, in whole or in part, 103 acts of Congress.[10]

Factors Governing the Activation of Judicial Activities

Having described what it is that courts do, we now turn to the conditions that are necessary to activate these activities. We begin by noting that the activities of courts just described are not mutually distinct. That is to say, a given case may involve either administration of the laws or conflict resolution, but occasionally these two activities will be intertwined, as in a case where the driver of an automobile is adjudged guilty of failure to yield the right of way and subsequently is ordered to pay damages to the person or property damaged as a result of his negligence. Invariably, a case pertaining to conflict resolution or administration of the laws will perforce result in the making of policy. The essential ingredient of policy making is that the decision maker have discretion as to how the matter is to be resolved. No matter what the issue may be, judges always have a range of alternative courses of action from which to choose in deciding the cases before them. Thus, a judge in a criminal case is free to impose one sentence rather than another upon a person found guilty of a crime; he has discretion to order one type of relief rather than another to the plaintiff in a civil case; he can decide that either more or less monetary compensation be paid to the injured party, or that the plaintiff has not proven his case. Of course, if the matter is tried by a jury, the judge's discretion is substantially lessened. In criminal cases, he will impose sentence if the jury finds the accused guilty. He also has the authority to set aside a guilty verdict. In a civil proceeding, the judge does little more than preside if a jury determines the result. Nonetheless, the judge remains involved in a policy-making process. Even though he shares responsibility with the jury, he will rule on disputed procedural points; the jury will look to him for guidance, and he may reverse the jury's verdict if he deems it excessive.

Judicial policy making at the trial court level may thus be mundane and of limited applicability, in comparison with judicial policy made at the state and United States Supreme Court levels. But to the affected individuals and to the local community, this exercise of judicial discretion is by no means inconsequential. Some examples are the rural community that becomes a speed trap for unwary motorists; the college town where the municipal judge suspends sentences for marijuana users; the metropolis where criminal court judges apply one type of justice to residents of the central city and another to those in suburban areas.

Unlike other political actors, judges cannot initiate action. They can only respond to action initiated by others. Not all requests of judges to resolve conflicts and administer laws are automatically accepted, however. In order for a court to decide a matter, two conditions must be met: The court must have jurisdiction, and the party bringing the matter to court must have standing.

Jurisdiction

Jurisdiction is the authority by which judges take cognizance of and decide matters brought to their attention. Courts do not themselves determine their jurisdiction. The state and federal constitutions outline the jurisdictions of courts within their boundaries, and the legislatures are generally responsible for spelling out the specific scope of a given court's jurisdiction. The perimeters of federal court jurisdiction, for example, as outlined in the Constitution, include matters involving the meaning of the provisions of the Constitution itself, acts of Congress, treaties of the United States, controversies between states, and disputes between citizens of different states. The establishment of the lower federal courts and the specification of their jurisdiction and the appellate jurisdiction of the Supreme Court were entrusted to Congress, a task that initially bore fruit with the passage of the Judiciary Act of 1789. Most of the states' constitutions, however, spell out the jurisdiction of their courts in some detail, with the result that state legislatures have much less authority to establish courts and apportion the state's judicial power among them than does Congress.

Because no court determines for itself what its jurisdiction shall be, as an organization the American judicial system is decidely deficient. The typical organization possesses a screening process whereby it determines what characteristics the inputs into the organization must possess before it can or will transform them into outputs. As detailed in Chapter 3, only the Supreme Court has been given authority to determine for itself which input cases it will transform into output decisions. All other courts are at the mercy of their environment in the sense that they have no way to limit the number of cases that they must decide. The result, especially at the trial court level in urban areas, is dockets crowded with cases that are delayed for months and years before they are decided. If justice delayed is indeed justice denied, then American trial courts have reached a point of crisis.[11]

There are three types of jurisdiction: subject matter, geographic, and hierarchical. In its broadest classification, subject matter jurisdiction is divisible into two parts: general jurisdiction and specialized jurisdiction. General jurisdiction applies to all matters within the judicial power of the government creating it, whereas specialized jurisdiction applies only to a portion of the subject matter jurisdiction allotted to the judiciary. The most common basis for specialized jurisdiction is the distinction between civil and criminal matters. When jurisdiction is specialized in this fashion, there will exist one separate set of courts that only resolves conflicts (civil), and another separate set that only administers the laws (criminal).

The major federal courts (the district courts, the courts of appeal, and the Supreme Court) have general jurisdiction. Most of the states, by contrast, have established a system of courts with specialized jurisdiction. The basic division of the state courts is between civil and criminal jurisdiction. Quite commonly, these two types of jurisdiction are also divided. In such states, some courts will hear only minor criminal cases (*misdemeanors*), and others are limited to major criminal cases (*felonies*). When the accused is below the age of majority, regardless of whether the charge is a misdemeanor or a felony, a juvenile court is likely to have jurisdiction. A similar division exists with regard to civil jurisdiction: a court of common pleas hears cases where the sum in controversy is less than a specified dollar amount, and another, more major, court hears cases where the sum exceeds that amount. Independent of criminal and civil subject matter jurisdiction are probate courts, which handle the settlement of estates, wills, and deeds, as well as adoption and guardianship proceedings.

The second type of jurisdiction is geographic. A court may only hear those cases within its subject matter jurisdiction when one or the other of the parties to the litigation, or the subject matter being litigated, resides, or is located within, the geographical area for which the court is responsible. The basic geographic unit of the state judicial systems is the county; the jurisdiction of the municipal and other local courts, as well as that of the justice of the peace, is limited to only a portion of a given county. Obviously, no court of any state has geographic jurisdiction over persons or property not resident or located within the confines of the state in question.

By comparison, the basic geographical unit of the federal judicial system is the state. At present, there are ninety-four federal district courts, no one of which (with one small exception) has jurisdiction in more than one state. If the state is sufficiently populous and engenders enough federal court business, there will be more than one federal district court therein. These courts are identified geographically as, for example, the Federal District Court for the Southern District of New York, or that for the Eastern District of Michigan, or for the Northern District of Illinois. Each of the eleven federal courts of appeals has jurisdiction over a number of contiguous states except the one located in Washington, which has jurisdiction only in the District of Columbia.

The third type of jurisdiction, hierarchical, distinguishes between courts of original jurisdiction and those that hear cases on appeal. Courts of original jurisdiction are the trial courts or, as they are sometimes called, courts of first instance. The subject matter specialization in the state judicial systems is limited almost exclusively to the trial courts. Oddly enough, three of the four specialized federal courts are appellate, rather than trial, courts. These are the Customs Court, which adjudicates appeals from decisions of collectors of customs regarding the duty to be paid on goods imported into the United States; the Court of Customs and Patent Appeals, which hears appeals from the Customs Court and the Patent Office; and the Court of Military Appeals, which reviews decisions of courts martial. The trial court among the specialized federal courts is the Court of Claims, whose jurisdiction is largely limited to suits between the United States and persons holding public contracts.

Appellate courts are divisible into two types: intermediate, or inferior, courts of appeals and supreme courts. Only about half the states have an intermediate court of appeals; in the others, decisions appealed from the trial courts proceed directly to the state supreme court. But those states that do have an intermediate court of appeals tend to give it statewide geographic jurisdiction. This is not true of the intermediate federal courts of appeal, which, as noted, have geographical jurisdiction over only a portion of the United States. That a state or the federal government has an intermediate court of appeals does not necessarily mean that every appealed decision of a trial court must be heard by the intermediate appellate court. In the federal system, for example, when a district court declares an act of Congress unconstitutional, the appeal goes directly to the Supreme Court.

The word "jurisdiction" is also used in a sense other than as a criterion governing the activation of judicial activities. Jurisdiction, in this additional sense, refers to those matters which only a single court may hear as opposed to those matters which locate within the subject matter jurisdiction of more than one court. In this sense, then, jurisdiction is either exclusive or concurrent. Because of the dual court system that exists within the United States as a result of federalism, concurrent jurisdiction is a matter of some importance. This is especially true of civil cases between persons and corporations located in different states. Such "diversity of citizenship" cases may be heard either in a federal district court when the amount in controversy is $10,000 or more, or in the appropriate state court. Congress has sought to discourage the bringing of such cases into the federal district courts by increasing the amount in controversy because the resolution of such conflicts does not pertain to matters of distinctive federal concern. The reason that the Framers of the Constitution included diversity of citizenship within the subject matter jurisdiction of the federal courts is that they feared that state judges might be biased in favor of their own residents and against those from out of state.[12]

Standing

Its jurisdiction having been established, a court will require that a person who seeks judicial redress must have standing. Standing is definable as a court's determination of whether a person's dispute with another party is deserving of judicial resolution. As such, standing constitutes a limitation upon lawsuits, but unlike jurisdiction, a court has some discretion in applying the concept. However, because judges have discretion here, "generalizations about standing to sue are largely worthless as such."[13] Hence, it is more meaningful to focus upon the components of standing, each of which may properly be considered a discrete element. These are identified and discussed in the following paragraphs.

Case or controversy. In the federal courts and in the state courts except for state supreme courts, a litigant may gain access to the judiciary only if his dispute is a "case" or "controversy." For all practical purposes, the terms are synonymous: a case includes all suits, whereas a controversy includes only civil actions. As a limitation upon lawsuits, the case or controversy requirement stipulates that a real dispute must exist between two or more persons whose interests conflict. The source of this limitation, as far as the federal courts are concerned, is Article III of the Constitution, which restricts judicial power to "cases" and "controversies." Courts consequently will not decide hypothetical or feigned disputes. Hypothetical disputes take the form of advisory opinions. In some states, the governor, attorney general, or legislature may request the state supreme court to render an opinion about the constitutionality of proposed public policy.

Advisory opinions, however, are not given by the federal courts. This does not prevent a federal judge from privately consulting with the President or other governmental officials about legal or political matters. Former Justice Fortas, for example, advised President Johnson on a wide range of issues while he was a member of the Supreme Court. Though this practice raises ethical questions inasmuch as the judiciary is a separate branch of government, much more serious is a judge's consultation with private interests, and if he should do so for a fee this would constitute conflict of interest. Indeed, even the appearance of a breach of ethics is suspect. On the basis of a semblance of wrongdoing, former Attorney General John Mitchell (later a convicted felon) and President Nixon (spared Mitchell's fate by President Ford's pardon) brought pressure on Fortas to resign. This was the first time in history that such circumstances led to the resignation of a justice of the Supreme Court.

Feigned litigation takes the form of friendly suits. Most common are those between a stockholder and management over the expenditure of corporate assets. Another common type concerns the settlement of an estate, when a creditor sues the administrator or executor of the will or of the estate. It is obviously more difficult to ascertain whether a given case constitutes feigned litigation than whether an advisory opinion is requested.

Legal injury.   Simply because two or more persons have a conflict of interest does not automatically establish standing. The conflict must additionally pertain to a matter that is legally protected. A statutory or constitutional right must exist, or some personal or property interest must be affected. A legal injury may be either private or public. The difference between them is less than complete. A private injury is harmful to a person as an individual. A public injury, by contrast, adversely affects not only an individual but the community as a whole. A public injury, then, involves the commission of a crime, whereas a private injury may be described as a *tort*: the commission or omission of an unauthorized action whereby an injury is inflicted on a person, his property, or his reputation. A single act may produce both public and private injury, as when one person suffers bodily injury because of another's reckless operation of an automobile.

Examples of nonlegal injury include a business adversely affected by competition, an employee dismissed by an employer, a person jailed on conviction of a crime who is subsequently found innocent, or property whose value declines because of changes in zoning regulations. Historically, legal injury tended to be defined as economic injury. That definition has, however, been broadened to "reflect 'aesthetic, conservational, and recreational' as well as economic values. . . . A person or a family may have a spiritual stake in First Amendment values sufficient to give him standing to raise issues concerning the Establishment Clause and the Free Exercise Clause [of the First Amendment]."[14] Thus, parents and their children have

14

standing to challenge regulations requiring Bible reading at the beginning of each class day in their public school.[15]

The extension of legal injury to include the foregoing interests has been accompanied by a similar extension of what constitutes an economic interest. Thus, for example, a group of tenant farmers eligible for benefits under the Upland Cotton Program of the Food and Agriculture Act of 1965 challenged the validity of an amended regulation of the Secretary of Agriculture that enabled their landlords to demand that they assign them their benefits as a condition for obtaining a lease to work the land. As a result of the amended regulation, the tenants lacked a source of credit and were required to finance all their other needs—food, clothing, tools, and the like—through their landlords, at the high prices and interest rates established by them. Consequently, the tenants' crop profits were consumed each year in debt payments, and they were precluded from attaining a measure of economic independence from their landlords.[16]

Direct injury. In addition to the presence of a case or controversy involving a legally protected right, a person lacks standing if he himself is not directly injured. A person may not bring action solely on behalf of others who have indeed been injured. He may sue only to protect his own personal and property rights. Of course, if a person is a minor or otherwise legally incompetent, his next of kin or legal guardian may sue on his behalf. Or if a person asserts his own legally protected rights, he may couple to his own the rights of all other persons "similarly situated." Such class actions are commonplace in the area of civil rights, where the person instituting the action alleges a wrong that affects him directly as a member of a class or a group of which he is a member. The utility of the class action is twofold. First, the issue cannot be mooted once the case is initiated. For example, a class action brought by a parent to desegregate his child's school cannot be dismissed simply because the child has graduated by the time the case is finally heard. Second, it spares the courts the need to relitigate the same issue for every member of a class or group. Thus, a stockholder who secures judicial redress from wrongdoing by the officers of a corporation as the result of the case brought on his own and the other similarly situated stockholders' behalf precludes the necessity that each of the other stockholders bring his own individual case. Obviously, if one judicial decision can apply to each member of the class or group, it is a tremendous saving of judicial time and energy.

However, in bringing a class action, the individual or group that institutes the lawsuit must notify, bearing the costs out of their own pockets, all members of the class who can be identified.[17] The reason for such notice is to allow each member of the class to bring in his own attorney or to exclude himself from the case if he prefers not to be bound by the court's decision. Though the expense of notifying all members of a class may appear to inhibit future use of class actions, this is not invariably the result. Consumers who sue for monetary damages may find the going tougher, but civil rights advocates or environmentalists do not. Civil rights and environmental litigation most often involves a writ of injunction rather than a suit for damages. The plaintiffs act as "private attorneys general" to prevent or terminate allegedly illegal action by administrative agencies or other governmental bodies. The plaintiffs, moreover, are organizations such as a local chapter of the NAACP, the Sierra Club, or the Environmental Defense Fund, whose members are readily identifiable and can be notified of a pending class action via the organization's newsletter or bulletin.

A classic example of lack of direct injury concerned the question of the constitutionality of Connecticut's birth control law. In its initial decision, the Supreme Court held that the physician who brought the action suffered no personal loss of liberty or property.[18] Almost a generation later, another physician—this time jointly with several patients—sued to have the law declared unconstitutional. Again the Court refused, holding that no one had suffered injury because the law had not been enforced against any of the plaintiffs.[19] Finally, a doctor was convicted of violating the statute. Because prosecution had resulted, the Supreme Court found direct injury did exist. By a 7 to 2 vote, the Court held the law to be an unconstitutional invasion of the privacy of married persons.[20]

Another aspect of direct injury—the matter of taxpayer's suits—also requires mention. Most of the states allow a private person to challenge the purposes for which public money is spent. The only requirement is that some portion of the plaintiff's tax money be used for the expenditures to which he objects. The Supreme Court, however, held in 1923 that a federal taxpayer lacked standing to contest the constitutionality of the purposes for which federal funds were spent. The challenge was against the Maternity Act of 1921, which provided federal grants-in-aid for infant and maternity care. The Court's rationale was that a taxpayer's interest is shared with millions of others; it is minute and indeterminable; and its effect on future taxation is remote: hence, no direct injury.[21] The Court, however, limited the scope of this decision in 1968 when it ruled that a taxpayer had standing to challenge federal expenditures if the basis for his challenge was the establishment of religion clause of the First Amendment. This had been the basis of a taxpayer's challenge to the constitutionality of provisions in the Elementary and Secondary Education Act of 1965, which financed instruction in religiously operated schools through the purchase of textbooks and other instructional materials.[22]

Finality of action. When governmental action is challenged, an individual must exhaust his administrative remedies before a court will take jurisdiction of his case. If the matter is within the jurisdiction of the state courts, the individual must exhaust state judicial remedies before seeking redress in the federal courts. The matter must be "ripe for review." This means that if administrative remedies are provided, a person must seek such redress, and only when he has exhausted all such avenues does he gain standing to sue in the courts. Finality of action applies primarily to federal regulatory agencies—the Interstate Commerce Commission; the Securities and Exchange Commission; the Federal Communications, Power, and Trade Commissions; and the National Labor Relations Board —and to the Internal Revenue Service and the Selective Service System. Accordingly, one challenging the amount of income tax due must exhaust the remedies provided by the Internal Revenue Service and the Tax Court before seeking judicial relief. Similarly, one challenging his draft classification may not sue in court prior to completion of the internal review procedures of the Selective Service System. When a state law is challenged as unconstitutional, the state courts must be allowed an opportunity to resolve the question before a federal court intervenes. This is the *abstention doctrine*, whereby federal courts abstain from decision until authoritative state court interpretation of the matter has been obtained.

Given bureaucratic red tape, agency dilatoriness, and state court parochialism, administrative and state judicial remedies need not always be exhausted for finality of action to exist. When the agency's existence is attacked as unconstitutional; when it is acting *ultra vires* (beyond the scope of its authority); when irreparable harm may be done to the individual; when the agency or state court is being deliberately dilatory; or when the pursuit of agency or state court redress is obviously futile—these are instances where neither exhaustion of remedies nor the abstention doctrine need apply.

Illustrative of an exception to finality of action was the case of *Dombrowski* v. *Pfister*.[23] An organization active on behalf of Southern blacks' civil rights sought an injunction in a federal district court restraining state officials from enforcing state laws controlling subversive and Communist party activities against blacks because such enforcement threatened to deny them freedom of speech and association. The Supreme Court ruled that irreparable injury could result and that the abstention doctrine is inapplicable in cases that have a chilling effect on the exercise of First Amendment freedoms. More recently, however, the Court has limited exceptions to the abstention doctrine only to instances where irreparable injury to federally protected rights is clearly shown to be "both great and immediate" and where attempts by the state to enforce the challenged law are made in "bad faith."[24]

Finality of decision. This element of standing pertains to the finality of the court's decision as distinct from the finality of the action itself. In other words, the court's decision must be conclusive as between the parties to the case; it must not be susceptible to review by a nonjudicial body. Finality of decision, then, relates only to matters where the conclusive decision is made by persons other than judges. It does not recognize the fact that an appellate court may review the decision of a trial court. Nor does finality of decision anticipate the possibility that Congress or a state legislature may change the provisions of a statute subsequent to a judicial decision. What is crucial is that at the time of decision, the court's judgment was conclusive.

The classic example of this aspect of standing is an early Supreme Court decision in which the Court refused to decide a case involving a disabled veteran's eligibility for a Revolutionary War pension.[25] The pertinent statute authorized the Secretary of War to make the final determination of eligibility. The rationale for this decision, and for finality of action generally, is that courts are an independent branch of government whose autonomy would be destroyed if legislative or executive officials could override judicial decisions in specific cases. Veterans' pension benefits still remain a major area in which judicial decisions are not final. Conclusiveness, rather, is vested in the Veterans Administration.

However, when a veteran challenges the *constitutionality* of statutory provisions, the federal courts have finality of decision. Thus, the Supreme Court held that a conscientious objector who satisfactorily completed two years of alternative civilian service had standing to challenge the decision of the Veterans Administration to deny him educational benefits under the Veterans' Readjustment Benefits Act of 1966 on the basis that the decision denied him freedom of religion and the equal protection of the laws.[26]

Estoppel. A person who otherwise has standing will be "estopped," or precluded from suing, if he has previously alleged or denied facts or engaged in behavior that is inconsistent with anything he is now alleging or doing. Estoppel is simply the legal application of the axiom that one may not have his cake and eat it too. Hence, if a person has benefited from a provision of a statute, he may not subsequently challenge the constitutionality of the assessment or ordinance. Likewise, a person who recovers compensation for property taken for public use forfeits his right to challenge the taking of his property. Nor may a person who secures a license or permit then challenge the resultant costs or taxation. Estoppel, however, does not occur if no benefits are received or if benefits are obtained under duress.

Estoppel applies to governments as well as to private persons. In the field of civil, as well as criminal, law, once an issue of fact has been determined by a valid and final judgment, that issue cannot be litigated again between the same parties in any future lawsuit. Estoppel of this kind, called *collateral estoppel*, is part of the Fifth Amendment's guarantee against double jeopardy. Thus, when an individual has been acquitted of robbing one of a group of persons, he cannot subsequently be tried for robbing a second member of the group.[27]

Political questions. For standing to exist, the issue must be justiciable; it must be a matter that is proper for courts to resolve. The absence of any of the elements of standing makes a case nonjusticiable. Thus, when the parties seek an advisory opinion from a federal court, or when the question to be adjudicated has been mooted by subsequent developments, justiciability is lacking. Also falling within the realm of nonjusticiability are political questions. This label, like justiciability itself, is less than adequately descriptive.[28] All judicial decisions are political. They involve, as we have seen, policy making, and they clearly constitute the authoritative allocation of resources—which is what politics is all about. But from another standpoint, the label does indeed have utility. By terming nonjusticiable issues political questions, courts are better able to maintain the appearance of nonpolitical decision makers; their only task is merely to find or to declare what the law is, and their decision making, as a result, is completely nondiscretionary.

The simplest and most unequivocal definition of a political question is that a political question is whatever a court says it is. A matter will be considered such if the court believes it to be a matter more appropriate for resolution by either of the other branches of government, or one that the judges consider themselves incompetent to resolve because the character of the dispute is not amenable to resolution through judicial processes. Examples include: which of two state governments is the legal one;[29] a request that the Supreme Court enjoin the President from enforcing an act of Congress;[30] whether certain state constitutional amendments violated the republican form of government clause;[31] whether a constitutional amendment was properly ratified;[32] the rights of a part of a nation that asserts its independence;[33] the length of time the United States may rightfully occupy conquered territory;[34] the denial by the Civil Aeronautics Board of a citizen's application to engage in foreign air transportation;[35] the deportation of an enemy alien "deemed by the Attorney General to be dangerous to the public peace and safety of the United States."[36]

What was once a political question, but is so no longer, is legislative apportionment. Until 1962, how congressional and state legislative districts were apportioned, or even whether they were apportioned at all, was considered a nonjusticiable matter.[37] The Court ruled similarly with regard to Georgia's peculiar "county-unit" method of nominating its congressmen, senators, and governors.[38] But in *Baker* v. *Carr*, the Court held that federal courts do have jurisdiction over state legislative apportionment cases; such matters are justiciable; and private citizens have standing to sue.[39] In 1963, the Court voided Georgia's county-unit system;[40] in February 1964, a one person, one vote principle was applied to congressional elections;[41] and in June 1964, the one person, one vote principle was applied to both houses of the state legislatures.[42] Within a 27-month period, then, the historic rural domination of Congress and the state legislatures was destroyed. The Supreme Court has since extended the one person, one vote principle to local units of government, both political and administrative.[43]

These elements of standing serve several purposes. (1) They enable courts to avoid deciding officious and hypothetical matters. To invoke the authority of a court, the plaintiff must have a significant personal conflict. Access to the courts arguably should involve costs. It is quite reasonable that these costs should increase proportionately with the magnitude of the conflict, for the benefit received by the parties involved is a decision blessed with prestige and authority. (2) Standing also allows judges to avoid unnecessary conflicts with other political decision makers, especially legislators and administrators, and allows them to give themselves the assurance that if they decide a case they will not be overruled by officials outside the judicial system. (3) The rules governing standing allow judges a tactical flexibility—an ability to avoid conflict with other decision makers while maintaining the appearance of good legal form. No element of standing is so clear-cut that a judge has no discretion available to himself. That apportionment and districting were once political questions but now are matters of judicial decision substantiates the point. If a judge wishes to avoid making a decision, the rules of standing may provide him a convenient basis for doing so. On the other hand, if a judge wishes to decide a matter, he can just as easily disregard standing. After all, Marshall quite convincingly could have declared *Marbury* v. *Madison* to be a political question.

In short, the elements of standing, as a set of limitations upon lawsuits, enable courts to limit themselves to activities specified previously: administration of the laws, conflict resolution, and policy making. By avoiding hypothetical questions, limiting their decision making to personal and legally protected matters, and proceeding only when the matter is "ripe" for judicial scrutiny, judges restrict themselves to those roles which they are best able to perform.

Summary

In this chapter we have identified and explained the activities that American courts perform. Special attention has been given to judicial policy making and the reasons why American courts possess this power. The criteria that must be met before a court will accept a case (since courts cannot initiate action themselves) have also been defined and explained. The first criterion, jurisdiction, was treated in its subject matter, geographic, and hierarchical aspects. The second criterion, standing, was considered in its component parts: the case or controversy requirement, legal and direct injury, finality of action and decision, estoppel, and political questions.

Although these are technical subjects, they are basic to an understanding of the Supreme Court's decision-making processes. In Chapter 2 we continue in the same vein, discussing therein the criteria and constraints that limit and control the activities of courts and judges generally.

Notes to Chapter 1

1. Herbert Jacob, *Debtors in Court: The Consumption of Government Services* (Chicago: Rand McNally, 1969), pp. 16–17.
2. *Boddie* v. *Connecticut*, 40 U.S. 371 (1971).
3. See Kenneth M. Dolbeare, *Trial Courts in Urban Politics* (New York: Wiley, 1967), chaps. 7–8; and Martin A. Levin, "Urban Politics and Judicial Behavior," *Journal of Legal Studies* 1 (1972).
4. *Oregon* v. *Mitchell*, 400 U.S. 112 (1970).
5. As evidence of the Constitution as symbol, all federal officials either solemnly swear to "preserve, protect, and defend" or "support and defend" not the United States itself or the American people, but rather "the *Constitution* of the United States" (emphasis added).
6. *Ideas for the Ice Age* (New York: Viking, 1941), pp. 232–264.
7. 1 Cranch 137 (1803).
8. John A. Garraty, *Quarrels that Have Shaped the Constitution* (New York: Harper & Row, 1962), p. 13.
9. Marshall was confirmed as Chief Justice on January 27, 1801. Chief Justice Ellsworth had resigned because of ill health on September 30, 1800. Marshall, thus, was himself a lame duck appointee, although not one of the "midnight appointees" per se. The fact that Marshall took the oath of office as Chief Justice on February 4, 1801, and promptly began to preside over the session of the Court that began that same day without resigning his executive office as Secretary of State violated the spirit of separation of powers although not a specific constitutional provision. The dubiousness of his double jobholding was minimized by Jefferson's conciliatory request that Marshall stay on as Secretary of State until the new Administration became established. See *ibid.*, pp. 1–14; Charles Warren, *The Supreme Court in United States History* (Boston: Little, Brown, 1922), 1, 169–268.
10. A listing of the laws declared unconstitutional may be found in *The Supreme Court: Justice and the Law* (Washington, D.C.: Congressional Quarterly, 1973), pp. 113–118.
11. In support of this conclusion, see Howard James, *Crisis in the Courts*, rev. ed. (New York: McKay, 1971), pp. 20–35.
12. Exclusive jurisdiction is limited primarily to criminal cases. Crimes against the federal government are triable exclusively in federal courts, whereas those involving violation of a state law may be tried only in that state's courts.

13. *Association of Data Processing Service Organizations* v. *Camp*, 397 U.S. 150 (1970), at 151.

14. *Ibid.*, at 154. For a restrictive application of legal injury, see *Sierra Club* v. *Morton*, 405 U.S. 727 (1972).

15. *School District of Abington Township* v. *Schempp*, 374 U.S. 203 (1963).

16. *Barlow* v. *Collins*, 397 U.S. 159 (1970).

17. *Eisen* v. *Carlisle and Jacquelin*, 40 L Ed 2d 732 (1974). The decision was based on a provision of the Federal Rules of Civil Procedure and accordingly applies only to class actions brought in federal courts. "Notice" in this context means notification by first-class mail rather than by publication in a newspaper. In the Eisen case, the class consisted of some 2¼ million small investors who could be reached through mailing lists, who were allegedly defrauded by brokers who charged excessive fees. Postage costs alone paid by the investors initiating the action would consequently total $225,000.

18. *Tileston* v. *Ullman*, 318 U.S. 44 (1943).

19. *Poe* v. *Ullman*, 367 U.S. 497 (1961).

20. *Griswold* v. *Connecticut*, 381 U.S. 479 (1965). Cf. *O'Shea* v. *Littleton*, 38 L Ed 2d 674 (1974).

21. *Massachusetts* v. *Mellon*, 262 U.S. 447 (1923).

22. *Flast* v. *Cohen*, 392 U.S. 83 (1968).

23. 380 U.S. 479 (1965).

24. *Younger* v. *Harris*, 401 U.S. 37 (1971); *Samuels* v. *Mackell*, 401 U.S. 66 (1971); *Boyle* v. *Landry*, 401 U.S. 77 (1971); *Perez* v. *Ledesma*, 401 U.S. 82 (1971); *Dyson* v. *Stein*, 401 U.S. 200 (1971); and *Byrne* v. *Karalexis*, 401 U.S. 216 (1971). Cf. *Allee* v. *Medrano*, 40 L Ed 2d 566 (1974).

25. *Hayburn's Case*, 2 Dallas 409 (1792).

26. *Johnson* v. *Robinson*, 39 L Ed 2d 398 (1974). Also see *Hernandez* v. *Veterans' Administration*, 39 L Ed 2d 412 (1974).

27. See *Ashe* v. *Swenson*, 397 U.S. 436 (1970); *Turner* v. *Arkansas*, 407 U.S. 366 (1972); and *Wells* v. *Missouri*, 42 L Ed 2d 671 (1974).

28. In *Gilligan* v. *Morgan*, 37 L Ed 2d 407 (1973), at 415, the Court approvingly quoted *Flast* v. *Cohen*, 392 U.S. 83 (1968), and *Poe* v. *Ullman*, 367 U.S. 497 (1961), that "justiciability is itself a concept of uncertain meaning and scope. . . . it . . . 'is . . . not a legal concept with a fixed content or susceptible of scientific verification. Its utilization is the resultant of many subtle pressures. . . .' "

29. *Luther* v. *Borden*, 7 Howard 1 (1849).

30. *Mississippi* v. *Johnson*, 4 Wallace 475 (1867).

31. *Ohio ex rel. Davis* v. *Hildebrant*, 241 U.S. 565 (1916).

32. *Coleman* v. *Miller*, 307 U.S. 433 (1939).

33. *United States* v. *Palmer*, 3 Wheaton 610 (1818).

34. *Neely* v. *Henkel*, 180 U.S. 109 (1901).

35. *Chicago and Southern Airlines* v. *Watterman Steamship Corp.*, 333 U.S. 103 (1948).

36. *Ludecke* v. *Watkins*, 335 U.S. 160 (1948).

37. *Colegrove* v. *Green*, 328 U.S. 549 (1946); and *MacDougall* v. *Green*, 335 U.S. 281 (1948).

38. *Cook* v. *Fortson*, 329 U.S. 675 (1946); and *South* v. *Peters*, 339 U.S. 276 (1950).

39. 369 U.S. 186 (1962).

40. *Gray* v. *Sanders*, 372 U.S. 368 (1963).

41. *Wesberry* v. *Sanders*, 376 U.S. 1 (1964).

42. *Reynolds* v. *Sims*, 377 U.S. 533 (1964).

43. *Avery* v. *Midland County*, 390 U.S. 474 (1968); and *Hadley* v. *Kansas City Metropolitan Junior College District*, 397 U.S. 50 (1970). Cf. *Sailors* v. *Kent County Board of Education*, 387 U.S. 105 (1967); and *Abate* v. *Mundt*, 403 U.S. 182 (1971).

2 | *Norms, Values, and the Judicial Process*

In the conclusion of our discussion of standing in Chapter 1, reference was made to the opportunity those rules provide judges to manifest good legal form. Good legal form, of another sort, constitutes the essence of the judicial decision-making process. The "form" with which we are concerned here is comprised of two of the concepts that we mentioned at the beginning of the preceding chapter: norms and values.

Norms and the Judicial Process

Norms are of two types: those that operate in an environmental context—between the organization and the larger society of which it is a part —and those that are interaction maintaining. The latter type guides and controls activity within the organization itself.

In order to perform their activities successfully, judges should be guided by three norms of an environmental nature: impartiality, learning, and integrity. Possession of these attributes is difficult to demonstrate. What one person conceptualizes as an indicator of impartiality, another may perceive as bias. Learning may appear to be sophistry to one group and lack of common sense to another. One person's understanding of integrity may appear to be compromise to others. Consequently, recourse is had to devices that inculcate respect and reverence. This age-old tactic of mankind effects acceptance and belief with a minimum of inquiry or examination.

The essence of reverence and respect is a ritualized pattern of behavior. For judges, this has come to include the distinctive garb of a black robe, the occupancy of a seat elevated above the level occupied by others, the dispensation of justice surrounded by the ornaments of pomp and circumstance, and the use of oral and written discourse largely unintelligible to the layman. When he is off the bench, a judge is expected to be a faceless member of his community, not readily recognizable as a participant in any nonjudicial activity. Though judges constitute an integral part of the political process, they are expected to avoid participation in partisan politics. In both public and private life, the judge should epitomize the moral ideals of his community.

Informal guidelines of judicial conduct are contained in the Canons of Legal Ethics prepared for the American Bar Association in 1922 by a committee headed by then Chief Justice Taft, and in the Code of Judicial Conduct adopted by the House of Delegates of the American Bar Association in 1972. These guidelines, however, do not have the force of law and, in addition, are vague and imprecise. They combine Biblical injunctions, custom, and "Caesar's wife" admonitions to be above criticism or reproach. Thus, judges should not use the power or prestige of their office to persuade or coerce others to contribute to the success of private businesses or charitable organizations. They should not accept gifts from lawyers or litigants. They should not write a newspaper column nor appear on commercially sponsored broadcasts where legal advice is given. More generally, the official and private conduct of judges should be free from impropriety or the appearance thereof. Nor should judges accept inconsistent obligations of any sort that may interfere with, or give the impression of interfering with, their devotion to duty.

Of the three interaction-maintaining norms, only one, equitable division of labor, applies to the decision-making process. (The other two—adherence to precedent and legal reasoning—govern the form of the judicial decision and will be discussed subsequently.) Each member of a court is expected to perform his share of the work load. Given the crowded condition of most trial and appellate court dockets, especially those of trial courts in metropolitan areas, one unproductive judge who fails to decide his proportionate share of his courts' cases will adversely affect the overall productivity. At the appellate level, where a given case is normally decided by some or all of the court's judges, division of labor pertains to the writing of one's share of the court's opinions. What constitutes an equitable division of labor will vary, of course, from one court to another depending on the needs and perceptions of the incumbent judges.

A noteworthy aspect of sharing the judicial work load is the matter of judges disqualifying themselves from participation in certain sorts of cases. This practice, technically termed *recusal*, has recently been a matter of considerable controversy. Engendering the controversy was the participation of Justice Rehnquist in three decisions in which he had been involved as an Assistant Attorney General before his appointment to the Court. All three were emotionally charged decisions; all were decided favorably to the government; and in each case Rehnquist cast the deciding vote in the 5 to 4 decision.[1] In an apparently unprecedented action, Rehnquist was moved to justify his participation in these three cases when the antiwar activists petitioned (unsuccessfully) for a rehearing before the Supreme Court.[2] His fifteen-page memorandum opinion argued that all members of the Supreme Court have views on most matters that come to the Court for decision. The mere fact that they have publicly expressed those views before their appointment should not disqualify them from judging.

> Since most Justices come to this bench no earlier than their middle years, it would be unusual if they had not by that time formulated at least some tentative notions which would influence them in their interpretation of the sweeping clauses of the Constitution and their interaction with one another. It would be not merely unusual, but extraordinary, if they had not at least given opinions as to constitutional issues in their previous legal careers. Proof that a Justice's mind at the time he joined the Court was a complete tabula rasa in the area of constitutional adjudication would be evidence of lack of qualification, not lack of bias.[3]

In his opinion Rehnquist cited examples of other justices who participated in cases about which they had expressed themselves prior to appointment. Hugo Black, who had sponsored the Fair Labor Standards Act when he was a Senator from Alabama, participated in the decision that upheld the act's constitutionality[4] and in subsequent cases that construed its provisions. Felix Frankfurter, who had written extensively in the field of labor law and assisted in drafting the Norris-LaGuardia Act (which forbade the use of federal injunctions in labor disputes), wrote the Court's opinion in a leading decision of the act's scope.[5] Robert Jackson, as Attorney General, had decided an issue concerning the deportation of an alien, and then as Associate Justice wrote an opinion repudiating his earlier views.[6] Chief Justice Vinson participated in income tax cases even though he had drafted and prepared tax legislation when he was a member of the House of Representatives. Chief Justice Hughes had, before he assumed his position, written critically on aspects of the Court's economic policies. As Chief Justice, he participated in decisions that overturned these earlier policies.

Existing federal law provides that

> Any Justice or judge of the United States shall disqualify himself in any case in which he has a substantial interest, has been of counsel, is or has been a material witness, or is so related to or connected with any party or his attorney as to render it improper, in his opinion, for him to sit on the trial, or appeal, or other proceeding therein.[7]

This provision is not exactly a model of linguistic clarity. "Substantial interest" and "in his opinion" do not provide an unequivocal criterion by which to judge the precise sorts of conduct that should require recusal. A Senate bill, modeled upon the Code of Judicial Conduct that was adopted by the American Bar Association in 1972, attempts to eliminate the personal discretion contained in the existing law by requiring a judge to recuse himself "in any case in which his participation in the case will create an appearance of impropriety." The Senate bill also discards the old notion that a judge has a "duty to sit" in almost every case that he is called upon to decide. Numerous courts have ruled that a federal judge has a duty to participate in cases even though propriety suggests recusal. The bill also eliminates a judge's self-determination of whether his financial interest is "substantial." As much as one share of stock held by a judge meets the standards of "an interest" or "any stockholding."[8]

The ABA Code was substantially adopted by the United States Judicial Conference in 1973. The Judicial Conference, composed of twenty-five federal judges, is the governing body for the federal courts. Its chairman is the Chief Justice of the United States. Although the Judicial Conference's adoption of a stricter recusal rule will standardize nonparticipation at a more propitious level, the rule does not bind the justices of the Supreme Court. Nor is it clear that the Judicial Conference can sanction lower federal court judges who disregard the new rule. The conference, for example, has a rule that all federal judges must file a semiannual report of their outside earnings. Two dozen judges have refused to do so—some on the basis of conscience, others on the basis that the conference has no authority to impose such a rule.[9]

This discussion of recusal should not leave the reader with the impression that federal and state judges are morally obtuse or otherwise insensitive to the proprieties of nonparticipation. Many judges go out of their way to avoid any appearance of impropriety. Justice Douglas, for example, makes a practice of not participating in a case if someone with an interest in the result approaches him before the issue has been decided. Thus, he recused himself from the decision in the Kent State University case, in which the Court held that the parents of the killed students could sue a former Ohio governor and National Guardsmen for damages.[10] According to the Supreme Court's public information officer, a relative of one of the killed students visited Douglas and told him a "heart-rending story."[11]

The establishment, in recent years, of unified court systems has materially increased court productivity. In such a system, judges may be assigned from one court to another, wherever they are most needed. In the states, such assignments are commonly made under the superintendence of the state supreme court and usually involve the temporary transfer of county court judges from those districts or circuits with relatively little judicial business to those that are overloaded. The federal judicial system has been a unified court system since 1922. Both district court judges and those on the courts of appeals are subject to temporary assignments where needed.[12] Court productivity has been further increased because the presiding judge of a court usually has authority to specify the hours that his court is to be open for business. These administrative controls alleviate somewhat the problem of overcrowded dockets. This problem will only be solved by a substantial increase in the number of trial court judges, the streamlining of judicial procedures, and the addition of more supportive personnel—clerks, stenographers, prosecutors, bailiffs, probation officers, and record keepers.

Failure to adhere to norms may produce sanctions. The most severe sanction is loss of judicial office. Such loss may occur by impeachment, recall, or, if the judge is elected, failure to secure re-election. Several states provide additional means of removal: by address of the governor to both houses of the legislature, by joint resolution of the legislature, or by action of the state supreme court.[13] Under certain circumstances, judges may also be forced to resign. State and federal laws make criminal certain actions of judges. Conviction may result in a fine and/or imprisonment. At the federal level, only two statutes pertain to judicial behavior per se. One makes it a felony for a judge to peddle influence; the other makes it a misdemeanor for a judge to practice law. But even though a federal judge may be convicted of these or any other crimes (and, like all American residents, judges are also subject to the law), he does not as a result lose his office. Only by impeachment can this occur if the judge wishes to remain on the bench.[14]

Nine federal judges have been impeached by the House of Representatives. Eight others resigned before the House completed action. Four of the nine were successfully convicted by the Senate: an insane and alcoholic district court judge in 1804; a judge who supported secession in 1862; a judge of the short-lived Commerce Court who was removed in 1913 for "taking favors from litigants"; and, most recently, a judge who brought "his court into scandal and disrepute" in 1936. Four of the five acquittals also concerned federal district court judges; the fifth was Samuel Chase, a member of the Supreme Court, whom the Senate acquitted in 1805.[15]

Since 1789, only five federal judges have been indicted for criminal offenses. Two were district judges; two sat on the court of appeals, and one was a judge on the Customs Court. One was acquitted; charges against another were quashed; two were convicted; and the case of the fifth judge has not yet been tried. Martin Manton was convicted in 1939 for having sold his office to litigants in patent infringement cases. John Warren Davis was also indicted in 1939 for criminal conspiracy to obstruct justice and defraud the United States in connection with a bankruptcy action in his court. After juries twice disagreed, the indictment was quashed. Albert W. Johnson was found not guilty in 1945 of conspiracy charges involving corrupt administration. Otto Kerner, a former governor of Illinois and chairman of the National Advisory Commission on Civil Disorders, was indicted in December 1971, on charges of conspiracy, perjury, and income tax evasion—improprieties that he was alleged to have committed during 1960–1968 while he was governor. He was convicted in February 1973, for accepting a bribe from racetrack interests; he was sentenced to a three-year prison term and received a $5,000 fine. He resigned in July 1974, apparently because of warnings from congressmen that he would be impeached if he did not. The fifth judge, Paul P. Rao, Sr., of the United States Customs Court, was indicted on May 14, 1974, for lying to a special grand jury that was investigating corruption in New York State's judicial system.

Among the methods of removing judges from office, impeachment and recall are extremely difficult to employ. Defeat at the polls is somewhat commonplace, but more often than not failure of re-election has nothing to do with a judge's competence as a judge. More crucial is his political party affiliation if he is elected on a partisan ballot, a method employed by twelve states, or how well-known his opponent's name is if he runs on a nonpartisan ballot, a method used in eleven states. Also crucial to electoral success is the organized support of a large segment of the bar associations located within the geographical jurisdiction of a judge's court. Mitigating the effectiveness of re-election as a means of removing judges from office is the length of their terms of office—usually a minimum of six years—and the infrequency with which incumbents are challenged in localities where a nonpartisan ballot is employed.[16] The additional means of removal used by several states are apparently easier to implement. The states that vest their additional means of removal in the supreme court protect judicial independence by minimizing interference from the legislative or executive branches. Forced resignation of judges occurs primarily in response to removal proceedings and indictment for criminal offenses. By resigning his office, a judge may disarm those seeking to press formal charges. Abe Fortas, the only Supreme Court justice in history who was forced to resign, did so in response to the threat of congressional investigation of his financial involvement with a convicted financier. Several members of the Supreme Court were persuaded to resign by their fellow justices because of the physical or mental infirmities of old age.[17] But these instances were not a result of improper or illegal behavior on the part of the resigned justices.

Judges are also subject to sanctions less severe than removal from office. The most common is public criticism. Although media coverage of judicial activities is uneven, reports and editorials about judicial decisions and the off-the-bench behavior of judges are commonplace. More consistent coverage of judicial decisions, particularly those of state and federal supreme courts, is found in law journals. Law journal criticism focuses upon the opinions and decisions of judges, whereas that of the media extends to courtroom and off-the-bench behavior as well. Judges, of course, are expected to maintain decorum in their courtrooms and to preside with dignity, restraint, and dispassion. These same features should characterize a judge's decisions and opinions. His prose should manifest "craftsmanship"—that is, sound legal reasoning, adherence to precedent, deference to the decisions of higher courts, and respect for the opinions of other judges.

The most celebrated courtroom encounter in recent years was Judge Julius Hoffman's handling of the trial of the Chicago 7.[18] Of the criticisms vented on judges for their off-the-bench behavior, none surpasses that visited upon Supreme Court Justice William O. Douglas. His four marriages, three divorces, and numerous books and articles on subjects and in magazines considered less than respectable by many persons have garnered him not only media criticism but also several bills of impeachment. Most recently, in the spring of 1970, fifty-two House Republicans and an equal number of Democrats introduced an impeachment bill because of the appearance of portions of his book, *Points of Rebellion*,[19] immediately after a seven-page display of nude photos of oral-genital sex in an avant-garde magazine.[20] This effort failed when the subcommittee to which the resolution was referred concluded that no grounds for impeachment existed. In reality, however, the criticism to which Douglas has been subjected is basically political. For the past twenty years he has been the most consistently liberal of the justices. This, plus his free-wheeling life style, has made him a convenient target for conservatives.

Most of the criticism to which judges are subjected is the genteel sort found in the pages of legal journals. Public criticism usually attends only the most extreme instances of nonadherence to norms. The reverence that Americans accord their judges precludes the quantity and intensity of the criticism directed against other political decision makers. Further blunting public criticism is the ritualism of the judicial process. Ritualism, plus the public respect that emanates from it, enables judges to cloak their decision making in a veil of objectivity and impartiality. And, obviously, those who are viewed as objective and impartial cannot be faulted as often as those whose decisions are not similarly cloaked.

Values and the Judicial Process

Values are of the same two types as norms: environmental and interaction maintaining. Each type may be further divided into those that are transcendental or moral, and those that are pragmatic or that have functional outcomes.

Unlike the other branches of government, the judiciary has no coercive capability. Consequently, it must generate acceptance of its decision making by noncoercive means. We do not mean to imply that executive and legislative officials regularly utilize their coercive capabilities (police and military, and taxation) to secure compliance; rather that the judiciary has naught but noncoercive means. Thus, the judiciary must take special pains to justify its activities. None of the judiciary's three activities is so distinctive that it could not be performed by nonjudical decision makers. The reason that judges administer laws, resolve conflicts, and make policy is that certain values exist that justify the doing of these things by courts rather than by other organizations. At the environmental level, three moral or transcendental values operate to justify the judiciary's performance of its functions. The first of these is the consensual perception of the need for law and order. As applied, this means that the courts are viewed as the vehicle for the administration of the laws. The second value is the premium accorded individual liberty vis-à-vis governmental oppression. Although the belief that politicians and bureaucrats are destructive of the individual's rights may be more a mild case of mass paranoia than a likely probability, this concern—rooted in distrust of centralized government in general—is nonetheless basic to the judiciary's performance of its roles. The third major transcendental value is the perception of the Constitution as America's fundamental law. The guardian and expositor of this secular substitute for Holy Writ is the Supreme Court. Each of these values, then, is the basis of public support for the activities courts perform. Especially do they justify judicial policy making. And so long as American society believes that the Supreme Court alone is capable of authoritatively interpreting the fundamental law and of legitimizing the actions of the other participants in the governmental process, so long shall judicial policy making exist.

The pragmatic environmental values that support judicial decision making pertain particularly to administration of the laws and conflict resolution. Although moral values also cause society to delegate these functions to the courts, responsibility for sanctioning wrongdoers and resolving conflicts also hinges upon practical considerations. Performance of both these activities requires a high level of decision-making ability. The number of criminal and civil cases is voluminous. Those responsible for transforming input cases into output decisions must perforce be capable of rapid, efficient, and seemingly impartial decision making. More so than other political actors, judges possess these attributes. The structure, composition, and size of legislative bodies precludes their performing these tasks; the partisan coloration of executive decision making lacks impartiality; and administrative officials are highly bureaucratized, deficient in status, and bereft of symbols of authority. From a purely pragmatic perspective, then, judges constitute American society's professional decision makers. They have the training, the status, the authority symbols, and a nonspecialized orientation that enables them to produce decisions regardless of the specific character of the issues in any given case.

The rapidity and efficiency of judicial decision making have been sorely taxed for the past several years because of increases in the number of cases docketed, especially at the trial court level. Indeed, in many metropolitan areas, the courts are hopelessly swamped. Persons indicted who cannot afford bail frequently remain incarcerated for periods greater than that imposed by the sentencing judge. Detention facilities house two or more times the number of people they were built for. Hardened criminals and youthful offenders share the same cell. Rehabilitation is a mockery, and recidivism is the result. Though judges themselves are not to blame for this state of affairs, the intimate relationship between the courts and other officials of the criminal justice system prevents judges from escaping the resulting criticism unscathed. Nor is the picture brigher on the civil side of the ledger. Much time elapses after the docketing of a case before a judge is available to hear it. Not uncommonly, one, two, or even three years elapse. When there are appeals, delay becomes even more protracted.

If the courts are unable to reverse the trend toward ever more overloaded dockets and if the criminal justice system becomes ever more akin to a Byzantine maze, it is likely that judges may be forced to forfeit some part of the roles they now perform to nonjudicial decision makers. Support for proposals such as no-fault insurance and divorce laws can to some extent be traced to the fact of overburdened courts. And although most judges undoubtedly agree that the issues of property damage resulting from automobile accidents and the termination of marriages are better resolved without resort to the courts, it could happen that courts could be divested of significant portions of their subject matter jurisdiction if they continue to be unable to decide cases rapidly and efficiently.

Such a development appears rather remote at the moment because justification for judicial decision making is primarily supported by transcendental rather than by pragmatic values. Because the roles of judges are so supported, there is a tendency, aptly labeled "the cult of the robe," to imbue judges with characteristics they do not in reality possess. Hence the gap between professed norms and empirical behavior is bridged.

Transcendental and pragmatic values operate within the judiciary itself. The pragmatic values are those necessary to achieve effective small-group interaction: easy communication and smoothness of interaction among the judges sitting on a court, and personal satisfaction of each with the performance of his role. All three are mutually reinforcing; that is, the presence or absence of one or the other will materially affect the others. Effective verbal and written communication is especially important when decision making is a collective enterprise, as in the Supreme Court and appellate courts generally, because both a decision and (usually) an opinion must be reached by a majority. In the Supreme Court such communication is ensured by regular conferences at which the disposition of input cases is discussed and by frequent informal communications, both verbal and written, concerning the drafting of opinions and critiques thereof. Aiding communication is the readily available information about each case, which the justices' law clerks, the briefs filed by the litigants' attorneys, and the lower court records provide.

Smoothness of interaction usually results in a reasonably efficient productive process. Processing of input cases into output decisions must proceed without "hang-ups," a feature, previously noted, that rarely occurs in metropolitan trial courts. An equitable division of labor and reasonably effective task leadership[21] are also essential for smoothness of interaction. The existence of blocs within collegial courts (subgroups of judges who vote together a disproportionate share of the time) does not necessarily destroy smoothness of interaction for productive purposes. In such situations, each bloc will tend to have its own task leader—the person who is best able to articulate the bloc's position, argue it forcefully, and guide the group's discussion. During the 1950s for example, Justice Black functioned as task leader of the liberal bloc on the Supreme Court, while Justice Frankfurter functioned similarly for the conservatives. Softening conflict within collegial courts is the social leader—the judge who most effectively establishes and maintains group cohesion. He relieves tension and tends to be warm and friendly toward colleagues. Given that division is commonplace on such courts, differences of opinion on cases for decision do occasionally produce affective conflict. Supreme Court Justice McReynolds was excessively hostile to the original Jewish member of the Court, Justice Brandeis, and his hostility to Justice Clarke materially abetted the latter's decision to resign.

The personal satisfaction of the individual judge results from his perception of the importance of his role—that is, the knowledge that he is not an insignificant or unimportant decision maker. The status and prestige that accrues to occupants of judicial office is also rewarding. Even on collegial courts, each judge will cast between one-third and one-fifteenth of the votes, depending upon the court's size. Contrast this with the voting power of the average legislator. Moreover, even though a judge's views may be out of sympathy with the majority on his court, the role of dissenter provides him a forum from which to articulate and expound his position. The best evidence that a judge's lot is personally satisfying is that very few voluntarily leave the bench for extrajudicial employment. The vast majority die in harness, resign for reasons of health, or reach the compulsory retirement age. There were three twentieth-century exceptions on the Supreme Court. Charles Evans Hughes accepted the Republican nomination for President in 1916, but subsequently returned to the Court as Chief Justice in 1930. James Byrnes left at President Roosevelt's request in 1942, after but one term, to become director of economic stabilization—a wartime post, second in importance only to that of the President. Arthur Goldberg left in 1965, three years after he was appointed, to become

Ambassador to the United Nations. Lyndon Johnson, then President, apparently persuaded Goldberg to resign by appealing to his vanity. This opened the way for Johnson to appoint his close friend and confidant, Abe Fortas, to the "Jewish seat" on the Court.

Judges seldom leave the bench, but occasionally some do. The major reason now causing judges to depart voluntarily is inflation. Federal district court judges, for example, are paid a $40,000 annual salary; those on the courts of appeals receive $42,500. During the first half of 1974, five of the district court judges announced their resignation, all because of inadequate pay. The judges' salaries had not been increased since 1969, even though the cost of living in the United States had increased by more than 40 percent during this period. One of the departing judges left the Southern District of New York, which is one of the nation's most prestigious. The last previous departure from this district court had occurred in 1950.

Interaction-maintaining values of a transcendental nature are the rule of law, judicial justice, and an independent judiciary. In American politics, the rule of law is posited as the antithesis of the rule of men. Governmental activity is restricted to certain defined areas and, in addition, such action as government does take must accord with prespecified procedures. The courts, of course, determine what is licit and what is not. Judicial justice is distinguished from legislative and administrative justice. Judges charge that legislators and members of administrative agencies are incompetent to perform the functions of the judicial system because their decision making is uncertain, unequal, and capricious. In actuality, judges' decisions are equally unpredictable, but judges deny this accusation, alleging that: (1) their conduct is more principled and less partisan than that of legislators and administrators; (2) their decisions are based on public proceedings and are subject to review by appellate courts; (3) their training as lawyers allows them to resist popular pressures and passions more steadfastly than other decision makers.

These arguments and the values they support are important because they constitute the dogma that justifies the judiciary's performance of its activities. As such, judges never fail to pay them lip service whenever the opportunity presents itself. The rule of law, judicial justice, and an independent judiciary are not descriptive of empirical reality, however; indeed, they are not meant to be.

Norms and the Judicial Decision

The major norms governing the judicial decision are two interaction-maintaining norms: adherence to precedent and legal reasoning. These two norms not only guide and control behavior within the judiciary itself, but also operate environmentally, as cloaking devices whereby judicial decisions are given the appearance of stability, uniformity, and certainty. Precedents support "the desire for certainty in the law," whereas legal reasoning exists "in order to give the law some semblance of order and a quality of connectedness."[22] Hence, adherence to precedent and legal reasoning are useful supports of judicial policy making because they allow judges to appear faithful to fundamental law and principled—objective, impartial, and dispassionate—when they review the activities of the other branches of government.

Precedent

Precedent, or *stare decisis*, means that a court must abide by or adhere to previously decided cases. When a point of law has been settled by a court's decision, it becomes a precedent that should be followed in subsequent cases decided by that court and by courts whose jurisdiction is hierarchically below that of the court establishing the precedent. But because precedents are based upon previous decisions as well as the material facts that gave rise to those decisions, judges have a wide range of precedents from which to choose in arriving at their decision. The reason for this is that rarely, if ever, are the sets of facts in two different cases identical. Only the most commonplace cases limit a judge's discretion in any way. Even so, trial court judges rule on objections made by attorneys during the course of a trial; they have broad discretion in awarding damages in civil controversies; and in criminal cases the law provides the sentencing judge with a wide range of sanctions, monetary as well as penal.[23] Discretion is broader still at the appellate levels, where the issues are much less clearly defined. The wide range of precedents from which an appellate judge may choose enables him to justify almost any decision he makes. Nor are all precedents of equal weight. Those of ancient vintage, such as those established by Chief Justice Marshall, tend to carry greater weight and are accorded more sanctity than are more recent precedents.

Consequently, *stare decisis* is primarily a matter of form rather than substance. The norm does not require that all judges hearing a given case arrive at the same decision. Rather, the norm requires that each judge support his contrary judgment with a substantial line of precedents. On virtually all issues, the average judge can find sufficient precedents to support the contentions of either party to the case. Furthermore, if a judge should find his discretion limited more than he wishes by a restrictive line of precedents, several options are available whereby he may properly minimize these limitations. They are described in the following paragraphs.

Obiter dicta. The part of a previously decided case that constitutes the essence, the heart of a decision, is the *ratio decidendi*, or the principle of that case. It consists of the pertinent facts of the case, plus the court's decision as based upon those facts. *Obiter dicta* (or simply *dicta*), by contrast, are the portions of the court's decision that are not pertinent to the reasoning by which that court arrived at its decision. The determination of which portions of the previously rendered opinion constitute *dicta* is made by a subsequent court. Hence, if a court wishes to confine a precedent more narrowly than on its face it appears to be, the court simply declares portions of the reasoning upon which the previous decision was based to be *dicta*. A classic example occurred when the Supreme Court ruled that a previous decision holding that congressional legislation restricting the President's right to remove any executive appointee was unconstitutional applied only to purely executive officials, and not to those performing quasi-legislative or quasi-judicial functions.[24] *Dicta* are especially easy to establish when the earlier court sought to buttress its decision with as many arguments as possible, rather than reaching its decision by a single chain of reasoning. *Dicta* are also easy to establish when decision making is a group product, as in appellate courts. Although the decision has majority support, the coalition that is formed may result from compromise; that is, the members of the decision coalition agree as to how the Court should rule, but in order that a majority opinion may be reached in support of that decision, the pet reasons of individual members of the majority coalition may require inclusion, with the result that much of the reasoning may subsequently be declared *dicta*.

Distinguishing a precedent. A second means whereby judges avoid adherence to precedent is to hold that the situation presented in the case at hand is sufficiently dissimilar from that of the precedent. Hence, the properly understood principle of the earlier decision is inapplicable to the case at hand. Inasmuch as the facts of two cases are never identical, precedents may be distinguished at will. The only task is to detail the differences in situational context between the previously decided case and the one being decided. Examples abound. In 1951, the Supreme Court held that legislation prohibiting conspiracies to organize or to teach and advocate the forceable overthrow of the United States government was constitutional.[25] The conviction of eleven Communist Party leaders was thereby affirmed. Six years later, the Court distinguished "between advocacy of forceable overthrow as an abstract doctrine and advocacy of action to that end."[26] The latter type of advocacy had been the basis upon which Dennis and friends had been convicted. But by making the quoted distinction, the Court reversed the convictions of Yates *et al.* The Court came full circle four years later when it upheld the conviction of a former member of the Communist Party, notwithstanding the fact that he had publicly left the party in 1957, on the basis of the Dennis case.[27] But no sooner had the Court undistinguished the distinguished Dennis precedent when it reimposed the Yates distinction. While public attention focused on the Scales case, the Court decided a companion case to Scales, that brought by a little-known Communist Party county leader, John Noto. The Court reversed his conviction squarely on the basis of the Yates holding—that the government must establish advocacy of action rather than mere belief in the desirability of forceable overthrow of the government.[28] Similar circumlocutions occurred in a case that concerned a related aspect of internal security—congressional investigations. In 1957, the Court required congressional and state legislative investigations committees to meet certain standards before they could cite recalcitrant witnesses for contempt.[29] Two years later, however, the Court distinguished the Watkins precedent by authorizing investigating committees to "balance" the competing private and public interests at stake; that is, to balance the rights and liberties of individuals with the "security" of the state.[30] During the 1960s, however, the Court effectively returned to the Watkins position by tipping the balance in favor of individual freedom.[31]

Limiting a precedent in principle. When a precedent has been distinguished, it retains its full scope as far as cases other than the one for which it has been distinguished are concerned. But when a court limits a precedent in principle, the precedent loses its original scope for all other cases as well as the one to which it is being applied. The bringing of taxpayers' suits in the federal courts, discussed in connection with the direct injury aspect of standing, provides an apt example. In *Massachusetts* v. *Mellon*,[32] the Court flatly prohibited taxpayers' suits. *Flast* v. *Cohen*,[33] however, limited the Mellon precedent in principle by excluding from it cases that question the constitutionality of federal expenditures on establishment of religion grounds. A more recent example was the Court's decision in *Harris* v. *New York*,[34] which limited the rule of *Miranda* v. *Arizona*[35] that statements made to the police are inadmissible in a court of law unless the accused has been notified of his rights. Such statements still may not be used as evidence of guilt; the Harris decision said, however, that such statements could be used to impeach the credibility of the accused.

Ignoring a precedent. Less common than the preceding methods of limiting *stare decisis* is the tactic of simply ignoring a relevant precedent. This tactic is relatively rare because it suggests that the judge or court in question have ignored the relevant precedent out of ignorance—because they failed to do their homework. If the court's decisions are important enough to warrant law journal scrutiny, the fact that a precedent was ignored will be noted and commented upon adversely. Hence, unlike the other devices used to limit *stare decisis*, ignoring a precedent entails a cost —that the judge who wrote the opinion is deficient in legal scholarship.

Ignoring a precedent also smacks of intellectual dishonesty when there is evidence that the omission was deliberate rather than an oversight. Ignoring a precedent can also occasion a lack of congruence between the decision making of trial courts and that of the supreme court to which they are subject. Thus, for example, the Supreme Court in 1928 had ruled that the power of the states to fix prices was narrowly limited by the due process of law clause of the Fourteenth Amendment.[36] Subsequently, the Court removed this restriction.[37] But although the Court ignored the Ribnik precedent, the lower courts continued to consider Ribnik as controlling authority in price fixing cases. Finally, in 1941, the Court recognized the lack of congruence between its policy making and that of many of the states and expressly overruled the Ribnik decision.[38]

Overruling precedent. Although the previously described methods of avoiding *stare decisis* give judges a wide range of discretion, they also allow the additional option of formally overruling precedents. Because of the availability of the other methods of avoiding precedent, overruling does not occur very frequently. During its history, the Supreme Court has directly overruled precedent perhaps one hundred times. What is interesting about these overrulings is that the Court has been able to justify doing so because a precedent other than the one overruled existed, which supported the decision arrived at. In other words, a court can overrule a decision while purporting to adhere to *stare decisis*! This is possible because, as noted previously, on almost any given issue there exists a variety of precedents, incompatible with one another, that offer judges alternative decision- and policy-making avenues. Thus, when the Supreme Court in *Mapp* v. *Ohio*[39] overruled its previous decision that states may admit as evidence the fruits of an illegal search or seizure,[40] it did so because of the incompatibility of the Wolf decision with the Court's later precedent that no person can be convicted on the basis of an involuntary confession.[41]

Mapp v. *Ohio* also illustrates a second point in addition to the presence of precedents that allow another precedent to be overruled; namely, that when a court does overrule precedent, such a result does not normally occur simply because of changes in the court's personnel—that is, because a heretofore conservative court is now staffed with liberals, or vice versa. To be sure, there have been such instances. Perhaps the classic example was the Legal Tender cases. In 1870, by a 4 to 3 vote, the Court declared unconstitutional an act of Congress, passed for the purpose of financing the Civil War, whereby paper money was made legal tender for the payment of debts between private persons.[42] The effect of this decision would have been the ruination of many borrowers if they had had to pay their debts in hard money. One year previously, in 1869, Congress had increased the size of the Court to nine members. Neither of these vacancies had been filled at the time the Hepburn case was decided. Grant, President at the time, strongly supported the constitutionality of the legal tender law. He promptly nominated two persons to the Court's vacancies whose views on the matter were compatible with his own. After their confirmation, the government moved that the Hepburn decision be reconsidered. The petition was granted, and one year later the new appointees joined with the three dissenters in overruling the Hepburn precedent.[43] Although changes in personnel are by no means irrelevant in overruling precedent, their influence is able to be minimized and made covert for three reasons: (1) the previously mentioned existence of a variety of precedents; (2) changed circumstances or conditions; and (3) the benefit of additional knowledge or experience. The last two bases for overruling precedent are closely related. Both received exemplification in the famous School Desegregation cases,[44] in which the Court cited changes in the character of public education since 1896 when the "separate but equal" doctrine was enunciated,[45] and also the knowledge that had been gained concerning the psychological effects on children subjected to legally required segregation.

Furthermore, the Supreme Court on numerous occasions has stated that precedent does not preclude the Court's overruling itself, especially with regard to constitutional interpretation. A recent statement of this position is found in an opinion of Justice Powell:

> To be sure, stare decisis promotes the important considerations of consistency and predictability in judicial decisions and represents a wise and appropriate policy in most instances. But that doctrine has never been thought to stand as an absolute bar to reconsideration of a prior decision, especially with respect to matters of constitutional interpretation. Where the Court errs in its construction of a statute, correction may always be accomplished by legislative action. Revision of a constitutional interpretation, on the other hand, is often impossible as a practical matter, for it requires the cumbersome route of constitutional amendment. It is thus not only our prerogative but also our duty to re-examine a precedent where its reasoning or understanding of the Constitution is fairly called into question. And if the precedent or its rationale is of doubtful validity, then it should not stand. As Chief Justice Taney commented more than a century ago, a constitutional decision of this Court should be "always open to discussion when it is supposed to have been founded in error, [so] that [our] judicial authority should hereafter depend altogether on the force of the reasoning by which it is supported." The Passenger cases, 7 How 283, 470, 12 L Ed 702 (1849).[46]

Legal Reasoning

The other interaction-maintaining norm that governs judicial decision making is the requirement that judges utilize legal reasoning and legal terminology in arriving at their decisions. The technique is basically that of analogy—reasoning by example. Purely logical or empirical processes are not employed; hence, there is no "science" of law. Law develops inductively—from the specific to the general; science develops deductively—from the formulation of theories and hypotheses to the specific testing thereof. Science, then, is concerned with formulating a set of interrelated concepts, constructs, and propositions that presents a systematic view of phenomena by specifying relationships among variables with the purpose of explaining and predicting the phenomena being investigated.[47] Law, by comparison, is not concerned with explanation and prediction, but rather with the specification of the rules of action prescribed by the governing power of the community, which rules of action regulate, limit, control, and protect the behavior of the members of the community.

When a case or controversy is brought to a court for resolution, the judicial task is to ascertain the degree of congruence between the facts of the present controversy and those of related controversies. The weakness of such a procedure is that, as previously noted, rarely are the facts of two cases identical. This lack of factual identity between different cases gives law a flexibility in that judges must analogize between cases that are dissimilar. It also gives judges discretion to decide cases compatibly with their personal attitudes and values. The reason, of course, is that in reasoning by analogy, what one judge perceives as an analogous case will not necessarily be so perceived by another. Hence, "reasoning by example is a low grade of rational behavior." It is "quite suitable for poetry because of the aesthetic advantages of ambiguity and a blurring of imagery." But when precision and inter-judge agreement on the appropriate examples are desired, "it doesn't work as well."[48]

Legal reasoning is employed whether the issue is one of constitutional interpretation or the interpretation of the provisions of a statute. Most judicial decisions at all levels involve statutory construction. Offsetting the frequency of statutory construction is the landmark character of many of the decisions involving constitutional interpretation, the heart of judicial review. Depending upon whether the issue is constitutional or statutory, different types of analogy are employed. They are described in the following paragraphs.

Constitutional Interpretation

Modes of constitutional interpretation are four in number. We discuss each in turn. The reader should note that only occasionally does each exist in pure form. More commonly, a given opinion will combine more than a single mode.

The intention of the Framers of the Constitution. The reasoning entailed here seeks to equate the judges' decision with what the Framers intended when they drafted the constitutional provision being litigated.

The Framers are defined as those among the fifty-five delegates to the Constitutional Convention who participated most frequently in the proceedings. Excluded from consideration are the delegates to the various state conventions who voted to ratify the Constitution, as well as those who selected the state ratifying convention delegates in the first place. Furthermore, evidence of what transpired at the Constitutional Convention is almost entirely limited to the incomplete notes taken by James Madison. Beyond the fact that intentions are highly subjective and decidedly personal, and that decisions made one day were changed or rescinded the next, is the evidence that many of the Constitution's most litigated provisions are the result of compromise. On the question of the division of powers between the national government and the states, for example, advocates of both centralization and decentralization argue that the Framers' intention exclusively supports their particular position. Nor is the intention of the Framers any clearer when constitutional amendments are considered. What the Framers of the Fourteenth Amendment meant by the phrase, "due process of law," has generated heated controversy that began during the lifetime of many of the participant congressmen and continues to the present time.[49]

The meaning of the words. Whereas the intention of the Framers places a premium upon reasoning that is historically grounded, the meaning of the words focuses upon lexicographic skill. The "meaning" mode attempts to define the words of the Constitution according to what they meant at the time the document or its amendment was written. Some authorities argue that this and the preceding mode are essentially backward-looking; that they make American society the prisoner of its past; and that they assume a fixed meaning that can be changed only by constitutional amendment. This conclusion, however, is false. Most of the creative and pre-cedent-shattering decisions of the later years of the Warren Court were based upon either or both of these types of reasoning. For example, Justice Black, in his opinion of the Court in *Wesberry* v. *Sanders*,[50] used both modes to rule that the one person, one vote principle was dictated by the provision of Article I of the Constitution, which states that "the House of Representatives shall be composed of members chosen every second year by the people of the several states." By this one stroke, the historic rural domination of Congress was broken and the path cleared for a series of subsequent rulings, four months later, that the one person, one vote principle also applied to both houses of the state legislatures. An earlier example of the innovative effects of these approaches concerns access to the federal courts. Article III of the Constitution extends the jurisdiction of the federal courts to "citizens of different States." On the basis of the eighteenth-century meaning of the words, corporations would not be allowed to bring suits in federal courts on the basis of diversity of state citizenship (residence) since only individual persons could be counted as "citizens." On the other hand, if we were to ignore the existence of a corporation and look instead at the residency of the stockholders, and if the stockholders were all residents of a single state, then diversity would be complete if the other party to the case resided in a state different from that of the stockholders. This was Chief Justice Marshall's ruling in an 1810 decision.[51] But with the growth of national corporations having stockholders in a number of states, Marshall's decision quickly became a millstone around the neck of American business. Denial of access to the federal courts was effectively precluding corporate enterprises from securing redress of their grievances through judicial means. In 1845, the Supreme Court rode to business' rescue.[52] Noting that Marshall himself regretted his 1810 decision, the Court coupled the phrase "citizens of different states" with that giving Congress power to establish the jurisdiction of the lower federal courts and held that "Congress may give the courts jurisdiction between citizens in many other forms than that in which it has been conferred."[53] Hence, a corporation was deemed to be a "citizen" of the state in which it was incorporated for jurisdictional purposes. In the words of one authority,

> In the next two decades the Court polished the . . . theory, trimmed its appearance, and finished with the most remarkable fiction in American law. A conclusive and unrebuttable presumption was established that all stockholders of a corporation were citizens of the state in which the corporation was chartered. . . . By operation of this fiction, every one of the shareholders of the General Motors Corporation is a citizen of Delaware despite the fact that there are more shareholders than there are Delawareans.[54]

Logical analysis. This mode is based upon the syllogism, which consists, quite simply, of a major premise, a minor premise, and a conclusion. The major premise sets forth a proposition: "a law repugnant to the Constitution is void." The minor premise contains an assertion related to the major premise: "law X is repugnant to the Constitution." From the major and minor premise the conclusion logically follows: "law X is unconstitutional." The foregoing example is the essence of Chief Justice Marshall's reasoning in *Marbury* v. *Madison*,[55] which, in addition to formally establishing the Court's policy-making function, is perhaps the classic example of the use of logical analysis in American constitutional law. Marshall began his opinion by noting that the United States has a limited system of government and that it is the Constitution, the fundamental law, that sets these limits. He then asserted: "It is a proposition too plain to be contested, that the Constitution controls any legislative act repugnant to it"; otherwise, "the legislature may alter the Constitution by an ordinary act." From this Marshall concluded that "all those who have framed written constitutions contemplate them as forming the fundamental and paramount law of the nation, and, consequently, the theory of every such government must be, that an act of the legislature, repugnant to the Constitution, is void." This argument, logically unassailable, assumes that Congress would enact a law it thought unconstitutional. Such an assumption is obviously demeaning to Congress. Marshall, however, indirectly addressed himself to it: "It is emphatically the province and duty of the judicial department to say what the law is. . . . If two laws conflict with each other, the courts must decide . . . So if a law be in opposition to the Constitution . . . so that the court must either decide that case conformably to the law, disregarding the Constitution; or conformably to the Constitution, disregarding the law; the court must determine which . . . governs the case. This is of the very essence of judicial duty." Again the argument is plausible, but nonetheless specious. For it omits from consideration the possibility that Congress is as capable as the Court to determine the constitutionality of its own actions. But again, Marshall anticipated the objection: "Why does a judge swear to discharge his duties agreeably to the Constitution of the United States, if that Constitution forms no rule for his government?" A note of indignation is added: "How immoral to impose it on them [the judges], if they were to be used as the instruments, and the knowing instruments, for violating what they swear to support!" The argument reduces to sheer dissimulation: each member of Congress, plus the President, effectively takes the same oath as the justices of the Supreme Court. Why assume that congressmen are more likely to violate their oath than the justices of the Supreme Court?

The point of the foregoing is that logical analysis exists independently of factual or empirical analysis. Almost any conclusion can be given logical form. There is no necessary correlation between logic and a reasonable decision. Logical reasoning may be unjust or even absurd, but so long as the argument conforms to the requirements of proper inference, a court's decision may not be impugned as illogical. Hence, logical analysis enables judges to make decisions compatibly with their personal policy preferences and at the same time causing their opinions and decisions to exhibit a semblance of order and a quality of connectedness. Justice Holmes stated the matter well:

> The life of the law has not been logic: it has been experience. The felt
> necessities of the time, the prevalent moral and political theories,
> intuitions of public policy, avowed or unconscious, even the prejudices
> which judges share with their fellow-men, have had a good deal more to
> do than the syllogism in determining the rules by which men should be
> governed.[56]

The adaptive mode. This mode of constitutional interpretation is based upon changing conditions and the lessons of experience. Chief Justice Marshall expressed it well in *McCulloch* v. *Maryland*,[57] a decision at least equally as important as *Marbury* v. *Madison*.[58] In his McCulloch opinion, he gave broad interpretation to the powers of the federal government at the expense of the states: "we must never forget that it is a Constitution we are expounding," a Constitution that is "intended to endure for ages to come, and, consequently, to be adapted to the various crises of human affairs." At the heart of the adaptive mode is the recognition that though the Framers built exceedingly well, neither they nor anyone else was able to foresee the needs of a dynamic, rapidly changing society very far into the future. Hence the Court's inclusion of corporations within the compass of federal court diversity jurisdiction, mentioned previously. So also its extension of the admiralty jurisdiction of the federal courts from waters that "ebbed and flowed"[59] to those of navigable streams and lakes as well.[60] Apart from jurisdictional questions, the School Desegregation cases[61] illustrate well the effect of changing conditions and the lessons of experience. In comparison with the other modes of analysis, the adaptive argument is risky. The reason, of course, is that the adaptive mode does not preserve the outward appearance of fixity and stability that a fundamental law ought to have. Hence, opposition to the Court's decision making may be provoked by those supportive of the status quo and those who require political certainty and governmental absolutes. Consequently, adaptive arguments are seldom used and even then only in conjunction with one or more of the other modes.

Statutory Construction

In addition to the four modes of constitutional interpretation, there exist two modes of interpretation that apply to the construction of statutes. Whereas the presence of the previously discussed approaches in an opinion indicates that the case turns on a constitutional issue, those discussed in the following paragraphs indicate that the issue concerns the interpretation and application of either an act of Congress, a rule or regulation of a federal regulatory agency, the action of any one of the units or officials of the executive branch, or the procedural rules prescribed by the Supreme Court to govern the activities and operations of the lower federal courts.

The plain-meaning rule. This mode of statutory construction is equivalent to the meaning of the words mode of constitutional interpretation. The focus is upon the literal text of the statute, rule, or regulation, and the objective is simply to construe what the provision says. The difficulty with the plain-meaning rule is that the English language is ambiguous. The typical word has a multiplicity of meanings. It is difficult enough for an individual to express himself precisely, absent the use of mathematical symbols. When decision making is a collective enterprise, as it is in a legislature or governmental bureaucracy, ambiguity increases prodigiously.

Furthermore, most legislative enactments are a result of compromise, which means that clarity and precision are further obfuscated. Nor is it unknown for Congress to be under such pressure to do something that it enacts a law in order to pass the buck to the courts. The Submerged Lands Act of 1953 is an illustration. This act transferred offshore mineral rights from the federal government to the states within the three-mile limit. But several states claimed that their boundaries extended three leagues, not three miles, from their coastlines—a difference of some seven miles. The act as passed contained the three-mile limit, but also the proviso that "nothing in this section is to be construed as questioning or in any manner prejudicing the existence of any State's seaward boundary beyond three geographical miles if it was so provided by its constitution or laws prior to or at the time such state became a member of the Union, or if it has been heretofore approved by Congress."[62] The result has been a stream of cases fixing the boundaries of the coastal states.[63]

Among relatively clearly worded congressional legislation is the Mann Act, passed in 1910, the major provision of which reads as follows:

> That any person who shall knowingly transport or cause to be trans-
> ported, or aid or assist in obtaining transportation for, or in transporting,
> in interstate or foreign commerce, or in any territory or in the District
> of Columbia, any woman or girl for the purpose of prostitution or
> debauchery, or for any other immoral purpose, or with the intent and
> purpose to induce, entice, or compel such woman or girl to become
> a prostitute or to give herself up to debauchery, or to engage in any
> other immoral practice . . . shall be deemed guilty of a felony. . . .[64]

The Mann Act, then, is one of many efforts of American officialdom to regulate sexual behavior. Its constitutionality, as a proper effort to regulate interstate commerce, was upheld three years after its enactment.[65] What is interesting, however, is not that the act was found constitutional, but rather the efforts of the Supreme Court to interpret the provision just quoted. The first of these concerned the transportation of one's mistress across a state line. Over the objections of three justices, including both of the Court's Roman Catholics, Chief Justice White and Justice McKenna, the Court affirmed the convictions on the basis that the words of the statute applied to voluntary, as well as involuntary, debauchery, even though the venture was nonremunerative.[66] A second effort occurred in a case where a madam and her husband took two of their employees on a vacation to Yellowstone National Park. The girls did not work while on vacation, but did resume their profession after returning. The majority held, four justices dissenting, that the sole purpose of the journey "was to provide innocent recreation and a holiday" for the two girls. Hence, no immoral purpose existed.[67] Lastly, members of a Mormon sect practicing polygamy were convicted for transporting their several wives across state lines. The Court, through Justice Douglas, upheld the convictions on the ground that "the establishment or maintenance of polygamous households is a notorious example of promiscuity." The three dissenters argued that "etymologically, the words 'polygyny' and 'polygamy' are quite distinct from 'prostitution,' 'debauchery' and words of that ilk."[68] Apparently, the crucial distinction for Justice Douglas, who has been married four times, is that four wives are permissible only so long as a man has them consecutively, rather than concurrently.

Legislative history. In contrast to the plain-meaning rule, this mode of interpreting statutes looks behind the face of the statute to ascertain the spirit of the law, to determine what the legislators really meant, as distinct from what the law, rule, or regulation says. Hence, this approach is equivalent to the intention of the Framers mode of constitutional interpretation. But unlike those using constitutional interpretation, those using legislative history have much more information to analyze and evaluate: the debates that attended the passage of the legislation; majority and minority committee reports; the statements and views of the sponsors of the legislation; the testimony and comments given by legislators, government officials, and interested private persons at hearings when the legislation was proposed; and previous court decisions interpreting the statute. Although all Supreme Court justices have resorted to this approach, among recent members of the Court, Justice Frankfurter was most closely associated with it. The legislative history mode appears on its face to be superior to the plain-meaning rule, but it is not. As guides to legislative intent, both suffer from the same deficiencies. Many legislative committees are notably biased and self-serving; much of the content of the *Congressional Record* was never uttered on the floor of either the House or the Senate. The adequacy of the legislative history approach has been well described by one authority as "the psychoanalysis of Congress":

> The assumption that congressmen behave like judges are supposed to behave just isn't supported by the available research findings, notwithstanding the fact that the highest title that one can bestow upon a member of the national legislature is to call him—even if he was only a justice of the peace once forty years earlier—not "Senator" but "Judge." Such admiration is reciprocated by the majority of Supreme Court justices who have had no congressional experience and who exhibit the greatest confidence in their capacity for the divination of legislative intent through the study of legislative history.[69]

Judicial Restraint

A criterion governing the judicial decision to which some judges and legal scholars verbally subscribe is judicial restraint. As articulated, the criterion stipulates that judges, at least those serving lifetime appointments, are remote from popular desires and sentiments and that their decision-making

46

competencies are limited. Hence, they should defer to those decision makers who are publicly accountable. Deference should also be accorded state governmental officials because of the federal character of the governmental system. Not all wisdom emanates from Washington, and such that does is not concentrated in the justices' Marble Palace. Furthermore, many issues, especially those of an economic nature, are highly technical and exceedingly complex. Resolution of these matters should be left to the experts. Accordingly, the Court should not declare congressional or executive acts unconstitutional; state decision making should be upheld, and the rules and regulations of the various federal regulatory commissions should receive judicial support. Consequently, judicial restraint encompasses both constitutional interpretation and statutory construction. Cases concerning state legislation pose constitutional questions, as do many acts of Congress and much executive action. On the other hand, those pertaining to the regulatory commissions usually require only statutory interpretation.

Judicial restraint gained currency in the later decades of the nineteenth century, when a majority of justices supported the principles of laissez-faire economics. State and federal legislation regulatory of business was struck down rather systematically as violative of the due process clauses of the Fifth and Fourteenth Amendments; as state encroachments on the power of Congress to regulate interstate commerce; or, if the legislation were federal, as being beyond the scope of the commerce power. The Interstate Commerce Commission, the first of the federal regulatory commissions, was similarly emasculated.[70] What the Court voided was anti-business laws and regulations. Where labor was concerned, the pattern was reversed: prolabor actions were overturned; antilabor decisions were affirmed. The economic reforms of the early New Deal received especially harsh treatment, or so large segments of American society believed. Judicial restraint became the slogan of those who would save the New Deal. When the looming constitutional crisis was averted by the "switch in time that saved nine" (in reference to President Roosevelt's Court-packing proposal), judicial restraint became the standard of "liberal" judicial decision making.[71]

Unlike the other modes of constitutional interpretation and statutory construction, judicial restraint is amenable to empirical analysis. If it is a type of legal reasoning, it ought to be applied in a relatively even-handed fashion; that is, across the board. We may consequently hypothesize that if a justice subscribes to judicial restraint, it should be manifest not only in his opinion, but also in his voting behavior. Analysis of business regulation and labor union cases in the Warren Court in the 1953–1959 terms indicates that judicial restraint was not applied across the board by those justices who professed to follow it.[72] Judicial restraint, then, serves only to cloak the discretionary character of judicial decision making and to help preserve the view that judges merely find, and do not make, law.

Strict Construction

A final criterion governing the judicial decision that, like judicial restraint, is applicable to statutory construction as well as to constitutional interpretation, is strict construction. President Nixon gave this concept lip service in his speeches about the judiciary and in his nominations of justices to the Supreme Court. But what Nixon meant by his use of strict construction differs markedly from its true legalistic meanings. First, strict construction refers to a literal adherence to the provisions of the Constitution. In this sense, it may be considered analogous to the meaning of the words approach to constitutional interpretation. Thus, for example, when the First Amendment says "no law" shall be made "abridging the freedom of speech, or of the press; or the right of the people peaceably to assemble," this means, according to such justices as Black and Douglas, *no* law— none, period. Freedom of speech and press, they maintain, cannot be restricted merely because Congress or a state may be concerned about subversive activities, the threat of public disturbance, or the spread of obscene movies or books. The other meaning of strict construction pertains to the construction and application of criminal laws. If there is any ambiguity or lack of clarity in the provisions of such a law (and, as we have seen, there invariably is), such ambiguity or lack of clarity as does exist is to be resolved in the defendant's favor. The reasons are twofold. First, when an action is defined as criminal, those subject to the law ought to be clearly informed of what constitutes the illicit activity. Second, because of the severity of criminal penalties and the stigma attached to a person convicted of a crime, the definition of crime should be the responsibility of lawmakers, rather than judges.[73]

Given President Nixon's criticisms of the Warren Court for lack of "strict construction," it is pertinent to ascertain whether his indictment is supportable. With regard to the first of the meanings of strict construction that were discussed, reference may be made to the decisions handed down by the Warren Court in its last eleven terms (1958–1968) that concern the First Amendment. In 26 of 28 such decisions (93 percent), government action was deemed violative of the provisions thereof. During the same period, 36 of 47 obscenity decisions (77 percent) favored the accused. With regard to the second meaning of strict construction, the set of 32 cases decided during the last eleven terms of the Warren Court that involved the construction of federal criminal statutes is pertinent. In all but 9 (72 percent), the Court resolved doubt or ambiguity in the defendants' favor.

Clearly, in view of the foregoing, President Nixon's indictment of the Warren Court's decision making is not supportable. He must, then, have meant something other than the traditional legalistic understanding of the phrase, "strict construction." His concern with rising crime rates and the law-and-order posture taken by Vice President Agnew and Attorney

General Mitchell, as well as the Nixon Administration's espousal of a "Southern strategy," suggests that what was meant was a lessening of Supreme Court support for individual freedom and human equality—a willingness to allow the states to make their own policies in such issue areas as race relations, and a willingness to allow federal and state law enforcement officials a freer hand. It would, of course, be impolitic for a President to admit this in so many words. Americans like to think that their courts and judges are dispassionate, objective, and unconcerned with policy making. Hence the need for politicians to transfer bland, dispassionate legal phrases to the political arena to cloak their own personal policy preferences.

As an illustration, reference may be made to *United States* v. *Bass*.[74] The defendant was convicted of possessing firearms in violation of the Omnibus Crime Control and Safe Streets Act of 1968. The act makes it a felony for "any person who . . . has been convicted . . . of a felony . . . and who receives, possesses, or transports in interstate commerce . . . any firearm."[75] The critical question was whether the term "interstate commerce" applied only to "transports," or to "receives" and "possesses" as well. The government contended that the former interpretation was correct and presented no proof of any interstate transaction. The five holdover justices from the Warren Court held that the wording of the provision lacked clarity and that the intent of Congress was also unclear. Hence, the statute was to be strictly construed: The phrase "in interstate commerce" modifies all three verbs, not merely "transports." The two participating Nixon appointees—Chief Justice Burger and Justice Blackmun—dissented, arguing that the provision was clear enough and that the government's reading of the statute was correct.

Summary

In this chapter we focused upon the criteria that govern the judicial process. We initially identified the norms and values that judges are expected to observe. Special attention was paid to recusal—self-disqualification by a judge from participating in a case—and to the sanctions to which judges are subject for failure to abide by the norms that should guide their conduct.

We also discussed the two norms that govern the judicial decision: adherence to precedent and legal reasoning. The various limitations upon precedent were identified, as were the specific forms of legal reasoning employed in constitutional interpretation and in construing the meaning of statutory provisions. Two other norms that many authorities maintain ought to govern a judge's decision were also examined: judicial restraint and strict construction. On the basis of an empirical analysis of selected justices of the Supreme Court, we found that judicial restraint does not, in fact, motivate the justices' voting behavior. The criterion of strict construction was considered in the context of President Nixon's use of the concept to guide him in his selection of nominees to fill federal judicial vacancies. It became clear that like judicial restraint, strict construction is often utilized to justify and rationalize personal policy preferences rather than as an even-handed guide to judicial decision making.

Notes to Chapter 2

1. *Laird* v. *Tatum*, 408 U.S. 1 (1972), which held that the Army's intelligence system of surveillance of civilian antiwar activists did not constitute a justiciable controversy. Rehnquist had testified before a Senate subcommittee that the protestors had no right to stop the surveillance. *Gravel* v. *United States*, 408 U.S. 606 (1972), which held that congressional immunity did not prevent a grand jury from asking Senator Gravel (Dem., Alaska) or his aides how he had obtained copies of the Pentagon Papers. Rehnquist had been the Justice Department official who prepared the government's unsuccessful suit to block publication of the Pentagon Papers. *Branzburg* v. *Hayes*, 408 U.S. 665 (1972), which held that the First Amendment does not give journalists the right to refuse to disclose to grand juries the sources of confidential information they have received. Rehnquist had argued the government's case in a public meeting and helped prepare the government's press subpoena guidelines.

Rehnquist did disqualify himself from participating in *United States* v. *District Court*, 407 U.S. 297 (1972), which held that warrantless wiretapping by government officials in domestic security cases violated the Fourth Amendment; and in *Kastigar* v. *United States*, 406 U.S. 441 (1972); and in *Zicarelli* v. *New Jersey Investigating Commission*, 406 U.S. 472 (1972), which held that witnesses can be compelled to testify even though they may later be convicted on the basis of other evidence they are forced to discuss. Rehnquist had been scheduled to argue the government's case in *Kastigar* and *Zicarelli*. He had made public statements supportive of warrantless wiretapping. In none of these cases would his participation have determined the outcome, however.

2. *Laird* v. *Tatum*, 409 U.S. 824 (1972). Rehnquist also denied the request that he recuse himself from the rehearing (also denied) in *Gravel* v. *United States*, 409 U.S. 902 (1972).

3. *Laird* v. *Tatum*, 409 U.S. 824 (1972), at 835.

4. *United States* v. *Darby*, 312 U.S. 100 (1941).

5. *United States* v. *Hutcheson*, 312 U.S. 219 (1941).

6. *McGrath* v. *Kristensen*, 340 U.S. 162 (1950), at 176–178.

7. 28 USC 455.

8. The bill passed Congress on November 21, 1974, and is now the Judicial Disqualification Act. See *Congressional Quarterly Weekly Report*, November 30, 1974, p. 3226.

9. *Ibid.* Also see John P. MacKenzie, "Judges: To Sit or Not to Sit," *Washington Post*, June 2, 1974, p. C3.

10. *Scheuer* v. *Rhodes*, 40 L Ed 2d 90 (1974).

11. *New York Times*, April 18, 1974, pp. 1, 30.

12. James Willard Hurst, *The Growth of American Law* (Boston: Little, Brown, 1950), p. 114; Richard J. Richardson and Kenneth N. Vines, *The Politics of Federal Courts* (Boston: Little, Brown, 1970), pp. 109–112.

13. Henry J. Abraham, *The Judicial Process*, 2d ed. (New York: Oxford University Press, 1968), p. 46. Also see "Section III: The Judiciary" of the biennially published *Book of the States* (Lexington, Ky.: Council of State Governments).

14. The Judicial Council of the United States or that of one of the federal courts of appeals may discipline a judge by stripping him of his duties, but not of his title or salary. See *Chandler* v. *Judicial Council of the Tenth Circuit*, 382 U.S. 1003 (1966), and 398 U.S. 74 (1970).

15. Abraham, *op. cit.*, fn. 13 *supra*, pp. 43–45.

16. Susan B. Hannah, *An Evaluation of Judicial Elections in Michigan, 1948–1968* (unpublished Ph.D. Dissertation, Michigan State University, 1972).

17. For details, see Charles Fairman, "The Retirement of Federal Judges," *Harvard Law Review* 51 (1938): 397–443; reprinted in Robert Scigliano, *The Courts* (Boston: Little, Brown, 1962), pp. 104–119.

18. Accounts critical of Judge Hoffman are: Mark L. Levine *et al.*, eds., *The Tales of Hoffman* (New York: Bantam Books, 1970); and *Contempt* (Chicago: Swallow, 1970). A balanced treatment of the trial is J. Anthony Lukas, *The Barnyard Epithet and Other Obscenities* (New York: Harper & Row, 1970). The defendants' convictions for conspiracy to cross state lines with the intent to incite a riot were reversed by a federal court of appeals. New trials were ordered on the contempt citations. Upon retrial, in December 1973, contempt charges against two of the defendants were dropped; two other defendants and the attorney of one of them were acquitted; and the remainder, plus two attorneys, were found guilty of a handful of contempt charges and sentenced to a period equal to the time they had already spent in jail.

19. (New York: Random House, 1970).

20. *Evergreen Review* 14 (1970): 41–43.

21. See David J. Danelski, "The Influence of the Chief Justice in the Decisional Process of the Supreme Court," in Thomas P. Jahnige and Sheldon Goldman, *The Federal Judicial System* (New York: Holt, Rinehart and Winston, 1968), pp. 151–156.

22. Jay A. Sigler, *An Introduction to the Legal System* (Homewood, Ill.: Dorsey, 1968), p. 24.

23. See, for example, Wayne Morse and Ronald H. Beattie, "Study of the Variances in Sentences Imposed by Circuit Judges," in James R. Klonoski and Robert I. Mendelson, eds., *The Politics of Local Justice* (Boston: Little, Brown, 1970), pp. 175–186; Hans Zeisel, "Methodological Problems in Studies of Sentencing," *Law and Society Review* 3 (May 1969): 621–631; and Daniel H. Swett, "Cultural Bias in the American Legal System," *Law and Society Review* 4 (August 1969): 79–110.

24. *Myers* v. *United States*, 272 U.S. 52 (1926); *Humphrey's Executor* v. *United States*, 295 U.S. 602 (1935).

25. *Dennis* v. *United States*, 341 U.S. 494 (1951).

26. *Yates* v. *United States*, 354 U.S. 298 (1957), at 320.

27. *Scales* v. *United States*, 367 U.S. 203 (1961).

28. *Noto* v. *United States*, 367 U.S. 290 (1961).

29. *Watkins* v. *United States*, 354 U.S. 178 (1957); and *Sweezy* v. *New Hampshire*, 354 U.S. 234 (1957).

30. *Barenblatt* v. *United States*, 360 U.S. 109 (1959); and *Uphaus* v. *Wyman*, 360 U.S. 72 (1959).

31. *Slagle* v. *Ohio*, 366 U.S. 259 (1961); *Deutsch* v. *United States*, 367 U.S. 456 (1961); *Russell* v. *United States*, 369 U.S. 749 (1962); *Silber* v. *United States*, 370 U.S. 717 (1962); *Yellin* v. *United States*, 374 U.S. 109 (1963); *DeGregory* v. *New Hampshire*, 383 U.S. 825 (1966); *Gojack* v. *United States*, 384 U.S. 702 (1966); *Dombrowski* v. *Eastland*, 387 U.S. 82 (1967).

32. 262 U.S. 447 (1923).

33. 392 U.S. 83 (1968).

34. 28 L Ed 2d 1 (1971). Also see *Michigan* v. *Tucker*, 41 L Ed 2d 182 (1974); and *Oregon* v. *Hass*, 43 L Ed 2d 570 (1975).

35. 384 U.S. 436 (1966).

36. *Ribnik* v. *McBride*, 277 U.S. 350 (1928).

37. E.g., *Nebbia* v. *New York*, 281 U.S. 502 (1934); and *West Coast Hotel Co.* v. *Parrish*, 300 U.S. 379 (1937).

38. *Olsen* v. *Nebraska*, 313 U.S. 237 (1941).

39. 367 U.S. 643 (1961).

40. *Wolf* v. *Colorado*, 338 U.S. 25 (1949).

41. *Rogers* v. *Richmond*, 375 U.S. 534 (1961).

42. *Hepburn* v. *Griswold*, 8 Wallace 703 (1870).

43. *Knox* v. *Lee*, 12 Wallace 457 (1871); and *Parker* v. *Davis*, 12 Wallace 461 (1871).

44. *Brown* v. *Board of Education*, 347 U.S. 483 (1954).

45. *Plessy* v. *Ferguson*, 163 U.S. 537 (1896).

46. *Mitchell* v. *W. T. Grant Co.*, 40 L Ed 2d 406 (1974), at 425. The Court has even held that *stare decisis* need not always apply to questions of statutory interpretation. As an example, see *Boys Markets* v. *Retail Clerk's Union*, 398 U.S. 235 (1970).

47. Fred N. Kerlinger, *Foundations of Behavioral Research* (New York: Holt, Rinehart and Winston, 1964), p. 11.

48. Sigler, *op. cit.*, fn. 22 *supra*, p. 26.

49. See the opinions of Justices Frankfurter and Black in *Adamson* v. *California*, 332 U.S. 46 (1947), at 59 and 68. Also see Charles Fairman, "Does the Fourteenth Amendment Incorporate the Bill of Rights? The Original Understanding," *Stanford Law Review* 2 (1940): 5–139. On the intention of the Framers generally, see William Anderson, "The Intention of the Framers: A Note on Constitutional Interpretation," *American Political Science Review* 49 (1955): 340–352.

50. 376 U.S. 1 (1964).

51. *Bank of the United States* v. *Deveaux*, 5 Cranch 84 (1810).

52. *Louisville, Cincinnati, & Charleston Railroad Co.* v. *Letson*, 2 Howard 497 (1845).

53. *Id.* at 554.

54. John P. Frank, *Justice Daniel Dissenting* (Cambridge, Mass.: Harvard University Press, 1964), pp. 218–219.

55. 1 Cranch 137 (1803), at 176–178, 180.

56. Quoted in Max Lerner, ed., *The Mind and Faith of Justice Holmes* (New York: Modern Library, 1943), pp. 51–52.

57. 4 Wheaton 316 (1819), at 407, 415.

58. 1 Cranch 137 (1803).

59. *The Steamboat Thomas Jefferson*, 10 Wheaton 428 (1825).

60. *Genessee Chief* v. *Fitzhugh*, 12 Howard 443 (1851).

61. *Brown* v. *Board of Education*, 347 U.S. 483 (1954).

62. 67 Stat 29, 43 USC §§ 1301–1315, section 4.

63. *United States* v. *Louisiana*, 363 U.S. 1 (1960); *United States* v. *Florida*, 363 U.S. 121 (1960); *United States* v. *California*, 381 U.S. 139 (1965); *United States* v. *Louisiana*, 389 U.S. 155 (1967); *United States* v. *Louisiana*, 394 U.S. 1 (1969); *United States* v. *Louisiana*, 394 U.S. 11 (1969); *United States* v. *Maine*, 43 L Ed 2d 363 (1975).

64. 36 Stat 825, 18 USCA §398, section 2.

65. *Hoke* v. *United States*, 227 U.S. 308 (1913).

66. *Caminetti* v. *United States*, 242 U.S. 470 (1917).

67. *Mortensen* v. *United States*, 322 U.S. 369 (1944).

68. *Cleveland* v. *United States*, 329 U.S. 14 (1946). Excerpts from these three Mann Act decisions may be found in Walter F. Murphy and C. Herman Pritchett, *Courts, Judges, and Politics*, 2d ed. (New York: Random House, 1974), pp. 421–429.

69. Glendon A. Schubert, *Constitutional Politics* (New York: Holt, Rinehart and Winston, 1960), p. 243.

70. Sidney Fine, *Laissez Faire and the General-Welfare State* (Ann Arbor: University of Michigan Press, 1956); and Benjamin R. Twiss, *Lawyers and the Constitution: How Laissez-Faire Came to the Supreme Court* (Princeton, N.J.: Princeton University Press, 1942).

71. Alpheus T. Mason, *The Supreme Court from Taft to Warren* (New York: Norton, 1964).

72. See Harold J. Spaeth, "The Judicial Restraint of Mr. Justice Frankfurter— Myth or Reality?," *Midwest Journal of Political Science* 8 (February 1964): 22–38.

73. See *Huddleston* v. *United States*, 39 L Ed 2d 782 (1974), at 794, for a fuller statement of both reasons.

74. 404 U.S. 336 (1971).

75. 18 USC App Sec. 1202(a).

3 | *The Framework of Supreme Court Decision Making*

The purpose of this chapter is to provide an outline of the decision-making process in the Supreme Court and some information on the structure and operation of the Court. The treatment will be deliberately sketchy; much of the detail will be left for the chapters on the separate stages of decision making. Nor will we attempt to provide at this point any *explanation* of decision making; that, too, will be left for appropriate later chapters. In this chapter we want only to present an overview—a context within which to view the importance of each stage of decision making.

The Structure of the Federal Courts

Article III, section 1 of the Constitution provides that "the judicial power of the United States, shall be vested in one supreme Court, and in such inferior Courts as the Congress may from time to time ordain and establish." Thus, the Supreme Court is the only federal court specifically provided for in the Constitution.

In one of the first acts of the new federal government, Congress passed the Judiciary Act of 1789. Among other things, this law created the structure of the federal court system. It provided for (1) a Supreme Court of six members, (2) federal district courts, and (3) circuit courts, which were staffed with a combination of Supreme Court justices and district court judges.[1] In the century following, the structure of the federal judicial system underwent a number of significant changes,[2] until in 1891 the circuit courts were abolished and a set of intermediate appellate tribunals (called federal Courts of Appeals) were created. This tripartite structure has endured to the present day.[3]

Table 3.1
*Distribution of Federal District
Courts, 1974*

NO. OF DISTRICTS IN STATE	NO. OF STATES
4	3
3	9
2	12
1	26

Jurisdiction of the Federal Courts

Article III, section 2 of the Constitution provides for federal court jurisdiction over cases on two bases: the subject matter of the dispute in a case and the nature of the parties. With regard to the subject matter of the dispute, the federal courts may hear cases arising under the Constitution, a federal law, a federal treaty, or admiralty or maritime laws. With regard to the nature of the parties, the federal courts may hear cases involving (1) the United States as a party, (2) one of the states as a party,[4] (3) a dispute between citizens of different states, (4) ambassadors or other appointed representatives of a foreign nation recognized by the United States, or (5) a dispute between citizens of the same state claiming lands under grants from different states.

It should be noted that simply granting jurisdiction to the federal courts does not necessarily mean that it will be exercised. Jurisdiction, once granted, may be of two types: *exclusive* or *concurrent*. Exclusive jurisdiction means that only the particular court or courts in question may exercise the jurisdiction; concurrent jurisdiction is jurisdiction that is shared with other courts. A substantial amount of the jurisdiction granted to the federal courts by the Constitution has been concurrently granted, by Congress, to state courts.[5] In addition, as we noted in the preceding chapter, a court may have *original* jurisdiction, *appellate* jurisdiction, or both.

Federal District Courts

There are 94 federal district courts, staffed by an authorized total of 400 judges.[6] Among these are one district court in the District of Columbia, 4 in the territories and at least one in every state. With one exception, the geographic jurisdiction of the district courts does not cross state lines,[7] although in the more populous states there are a number of district courts, each having jurisdiction over a section of the state. The number of district courts per state varies from 1 to 4. Table 3.1 shows the distribution of district courts among the states.[8]

Table 3.2
United States Courts of Appeals, 1974

CIRCUIT*	NO. OF JUDGES	NO. OF STATES IN CIRCUIT	NO. OF DISTRICTS IN CIRCUIT
Dist. of Columbia	9	D.C. only	1
First	3	4†	5
Second	9	3	6
Third	9	3†	6
Fourth	7	5	9
Fifth	15	6†	19
Sixth	9	4	9
Seventh	8	3	7
Eighth	8	7	10
Ninth	13	9†	14
Tenth	7	6	8

*States and Territories in Each Circuit:
First: ME, MA, NH, RI, Puerto Rico; *Second:* CN, NY, VT; *Third:* DE, NJ, PA, Virgin Islands; *Fourth:* MD, NC, SC, VA, WV; *Fifth:* AL, FL, GA, LA, MS, TX, Canal Zone; *Sixth:* KY, MI, OH, TN; *Seventh:* IL, IN, WI; *Eighth:* AR, IA, MN, MO, NE, ND, SD; *Ninth:* AK, AZ, CA, HI, ID, MT, NV, OR, WA, Guam; *Tenth:* CO, KS, NM, OK, UT, WY.

†Plus one territory.

The district courts have original jurisdiction only. That jurisdiction extends to all types of cases arising under the federal jurisdiction just outlined except cases involving a suit between two or more states.[9]

United States Courts of Appeals

The United States and its territories are divided into 11 judicial districts (called circuits), and each of these circuits contains a United States Court of Appeals. One of the circuits is called the District of Columbia Judicial Circuit, and includes only the district. All of the other circuits are numbered, and contain from 3 to 9 states and from 5 to 18 district courts. Each state or territory is wholly contained within a single circuit. In 1973, the Courts of Appeals were staffed by a total of 97 judges, and the number of judges in each circuit varied between a low of 3 and high of 14. Table 3.2 lists the circuits and the number of judges, states, and districts in each, and identifies the states and territories that comprise each circuit. With regard to the states that are contained in each circuit, it can be seen that most of the groupings are regional. This fact is due to more than historical accident, and periodic proposals for revision of the boundaries of the circuits always meet with the objection that their regional character must be preserved.[10]

The jurisdiction of the Courts of Appeals is appellate only, and extends to cases appealed from (1) United States district courts, (2) United States territorial courts, the United States Tax Court, and some courts in the District of Columbia, (3) independent regulatory commissions, and (4) some federal administrative agencies and departments.[11]

The Structure of Supreme Court Decision Making

Membership and Selection

Although the Constitution provides for the existence of a Supreme Court, it says nothing about the size and membership of the Court except for prescribing the method of selection and stating that there shall be a Chief Justice. The size of the Court was fixed by an act of Congress. The Judiciary Act of 1789 set the initial size of the Court at five associate justices in addition to the Chief Justice. Between that time and 1869, when the number of associate justices was fixed at eight (the present number), the number of associate justices varied between four and nine.[12]

When a vacancy occurs on the Court, the President nominates a candidate to fill the vacancy and sends the name of that nominee to the Senate. The Senate considers the nomination and, if a majority of senators voting support the nominee, he is confirmed and takes his place on the Court.[13]

Jurisdiction

Unlike the other major federal constitutional courts, the Supreme Court has both original and appellate jurisdiction. The Constitution specifies the original jurisdiction of the Court. Such jurisdiction is granted "in all cases affecting Ambassadors, other Public Ministers and Consuls, and those in which a State shall be Party."[14]

The same article extends appellate jurisdiction to the Court in all other matters within the jurisdiction of the federal courts, but "with such exceptions, and under such regulations as the Congress shall make." Thus, Congress is granted control over the Supreme Court's appellate jurisdiction. This is, as we shall see, an important potential "weapon" for Congress in a struggle over policy with the Court. Congress has given the Court appellate jurisdiction in all matters covered by the federal courts' jurisdiction previously discussed, and has provided that the Court may take cases coming from (1) federal district courts, (2) United States Courts of Appeals, (3) the United States Court of Claims and the United States

Table 3.3
Number of Cases Brought to the
Supreme Court, 1966–1972 Terms

TERM	NO. OF CASES
1966	3356
1967	3586
1968	3918
1969	4150
1970	4212
1971	4533
1972	4640

Court of Customs and Patent Appeals, (4) territorial courts, and (5) the highest court in a state, if a "substantial federal question" is involved in a case.[15]

Bringing Cases to the Court

One of the most striking things about the Supreme Court is the sheer size of its work load, and how that work load continues to increase over time. Table 3.3 lists the number of cases brought to the Court for review in the 1966–1972 terms.[16] By the 1972 term, the number of requests for decision had exceeded 4600, an increase of 38.3 percent in only seven years.[17]

The Supreme Court's annual term normally runs from the first or second week in October of a given year through the end of June of the following year. It should be obvious that the Court cannot give full consideration to more than 4600 cases in a mere nine months. Some means must be employed to whittle down the requests for decision to a manageable number. In any given term the Court spends most of the first month or so deciding which cases (in addition to those held over from the preceding term) it will decide during that term. Then, through April, the Court spends most of its time considering the cases it has agreed to decide. May and June are taken up with the writing of opinions and the announcing of decisions.[18]

There are generally three ways a case may come to the Court for decision: (1) by a request for decision under the Court's original jurisdiction, (2) by a *writ of appeal* (the party requesting review of such a case has a statutorily granted right to consideration of his claim by the Court), and (3) by a *writ of certiorari* (consideration of such cases by the Court is, by law, purely discretionary).[98] In order to handle these requests administratively, the Court has established three "dockets," and each request for decision is assigned to one of these. The *Original Docket* contains all

Table 3.4
Final Disposition of Cases, 1972 Term

DOCKET	NO. OF CASES	CASES DISPOSED OF ON MERITS	PERCENT OF CASES DISPOSED OF ON MERITS
Original	8	2	25.0
Appellate	1771	374	21.1
Miscellaneous	1969	67	3.4
Total	3748	443	11.8

requests for decision under the Court's original jurisdiction—ten to twenty during any given term. Petitions for certiorari come in two forms and are divided between the two remaining dockets. Listed on the *Miscellaneous Docket* are petitions filed *in forma pauperis* (in the manner of pauper), which are usually requests for review by indigent prison inmates.[20] They are often a single typed or handwritten sheet prepared without any professional aid. Other petitions for certiorari that are filed by lawyers in accord with the strict format requirements the Court has laid down are listed on the *Appellate Docket*. In addition, the Appellate Docket contains all applications for a writ of appeal.

During a given term, the justices meet periodically in conference to discuss, among other things, these requests for decision.[21] The justices discuss the requests and then vote on whether they should be granted. If any four justices vote to grant a petition, it is accepted. If only seven justices participate in the discussion, three votes are enough. The data in Table 3.4 on the disposition of cases in the 1972 term demonstrate that the overwhelming majority of cases fall by the wayside at this stage.[22] In only about one case in ten of the 3748 cases disposed of was the Court willing to meet the legal issue presented.

Nor does the willingness of the Court to consider the merits of a case necessarily mean that it is given full-scale consideration. Some cases are so clear-cut that the Court decides to dispose of them *summarily*, that is, on the basis of only the information submitted with the request for decision. Other, more complex, cases are accepted for full review and set down for oral argument. (In 1972, 133 or 8.7 percent of the cases on the Appellate Docket were accepted for argument, as were 21 or 1.0 percent of the cases on the Miscellaneous Docket.[23])

Oral Argument

Once a case is accepted for argument, but before the argument takes place, the lawyers for the parties submit *briefs*, containing the legal arguments and precedents for the position the attorneys plan to argue. The party bringing the case to the Court has 45 days to submit 40 copies of its brief, and the brief of the other party in reply must be filed within 30 days thereafter. In addition, the Court may permit other persons or groups who are not parties to the case but who can establish an interest in its outcome to participate. Such a person or group (termed *amicus curiae*, a "friend of the court") may submit written briefs and occasionally participate in oral argument.

When oral argument occurs, the lawyers for the parties appear before the justices in the courtroom of the Supreme Court building, which is directly across the street from the United States Capitol. The justices are seated behind a raised bench, with the Chief Justice in the center, the associate justice most senior in length of service on his right, the second most senior associate justice on his left, and the remaining associate justices alternating by seniority out to both ends of the bench. Below the bench is a lectern at which each lawyer stands when it is his turn to present argument.

Time for argument is strictly limited. Usually, each side is allotted one hour, and sometimes only one-half hour. In order to apprise the arguing counsel of the time he has consumed, two lights are attached to the lectern. A white light flashes when only five minutes remain; a red light flashes when all time has expired, and the lawyer must immediately cease.

Rule 44 of the Court states:

> Oral argument should undertake to emphasize and clarify the written argument appearing in the briefs theretofore filed. The court looks with disfavor on any oral argument that is read from a prepared text.[24]

To illuminate the issues involved in a case, the justices may frequently interrrupt the lawyer presenting argument with questions. Many legal scholars, Court observers, and even justices have said that oral argument can determine the outcome of a case. The late Justice John Marshall Harlan once said that oral argument "may in many cases make the difference between winning and losing, no matter how good the briefs are."[25]

If the United States government is involved in the case, the lawyer who appears for it will be the Solicitor General of the United States or a member of his staff. No case to which the federal government is a party may be appealed to the Supreme Court without the approval of the Solicitor General, and, in addition to presenting the government's case before the Supreme Court, he is charged with overseeing all other federal appeals in the lower courts.[26] The Solicitor General's job is of great importance within the federal government, and the post is usually filled by a lawyer of great ability and reputation. For example, President Kennedy's first Solicitor General was Archibald Cox, then a Harvard law professor and later the first Watergate special prosecutor. One of Lyndon Johnson's

Solicitors General was Thurgood Marshall, whom Johnson later nominated as the first black member of the Supreme Court.

The Vote on the Merits

On Fridays the justices meet in the Supreme Court building for their weekly conference. In addition to discussing what cases the Court will accept for decision, the justices discuss and vote on the cases that were argued during that week.[27]

Since 1972, the justices when in conference sit at a table shaped like an inverted U.[28] In the center of the base of the U sits Chief Justice Burger, flanked by Justice Stewart at his right and Justice White at his left. Along the right side of the table, in order of increasing distance from the base, sit Justices Marshall, Brennan, and Douglas; along the left side sit Justices Blackmun, Rehnquist, and Powell.

During the conference, when a case is called up for discussion, the Chief Justice speaks first. He discusses the facts of the case and outlines his view of how it should be decided. This gives the "Chief" a special opportunity to influence the decisions of his colleagues, by establishing the issues for discussion. When the Chief Justice has finished, the senior associate justice has the next opportunity to speak. Thereafter each justice can state his views in order of decreasing seniority. After every justice has had his opportunity to speak, a vote is taken, this time in reverse order of seniority with the Chief Justice voting last.[29] The vote in each appellate decision will be on whether to *affirm* the ruling of the lower court (i.e., to say the ruling was correct), or to *reverse* that ruling (i.e., to say the ruling was incorrect). The reasons for the ruling remain to be stated in the Opinion of the Court.[30]

Opinion Assignment

Once a majority of justices have agreed on the outcome of a case, two alternative courses are possible. If the case is deemed to be simple and little legal reasoning is necessary to justify the result, the decision may be announced in a *per curiam* ("for the court") opinion. Such an opinion is unsigned and is usually quite short. Most often it speaks for a unanimous Court.

In most cases, however, one of the justices in the majority must be selected to write a signed, often lengthy, Opinion of the Court. Such a "majority opinion"[31] sets out the legal reasoning on which the decision is based and the policy made by the Court, which is (in theory, at least) binding on lower courts in similar cases.

If the Chief Justice is in the majority, the right to assign the majority opinion is his. He may keep it for himself or assign it to one of the other majority members, which he does by circulating a list of assignments after the conference. If the "Chief" is not in the majority, the task of opinion assignment falls to the most senior associate justice in the majority.[32]

Building a Majority

The justice who is assigned a majority opinion begins by writing a draft. The draft is then circulated to the other members of the Court. At this time, the other justices may either commit themselves to the opinion, indicate their disagreement and intent to write their own opinion, or request changes. The opinion writer will usually try to accommodate such requests for changes (at least until a majority of the justices have agreed to the opinion[33]), especially if they are not major. Thus, the opinion may go through a number of drafts[34] until the writer is satisfied with the size of the majority he has garnered, or until he is convinced that he cannot get one.[35]

When this process is complete, the result is announced in open court. Until April 11, 1965, the announcement of decisions was restricted to three Mondays a month. Although this procedure is still usually followed, decisions are sometimes announced on other days.[36] The decisions are announced orally and the opinion writer may read his opinion verbatim or just summarize it. In addition, any justice who has *dissented* (disagreed with the result the Court has reached), or *concurred* (agreed with the result but not necessarily with the reasons for it[37]) and has written an opinion will announce his views at this time.

The Court's Support Personnel

Before this section is concluded, some mention must be made of the other personnel who work for the Supreme Court. Operating the highest court in the land is no small matter. For example, in fiscal 1974 the Congress appropriated $6.217 million for the Court.[38]

Aside from the salaries of the justices (which are currently $60,000 for the associate justices and $62,500 for the Chief Justice), much of the money goes to pay for the salaries of the people who perform various support services for the justices. The most important of these are the three law clerks each of the justices is authorized to employ.[39] The clerks are selected by the justices they will serve. They are selected mostly from among the top graduates of the most prestigious law schools[40] and are paid an annual salary of $17,500. In the 1973 term, all twenty-eight were white. Three have been black; one each was employed by the late Justices Frankfurter and Warren, and Thurgood Marshall employed one for the 1974 term. Four clerks have been women.[41]

The clerks perform whatever tasks their justices assign to them. It appears that the lion's share of time of most of the clerks is spent wading through and writing memoranda on the myriad certiorari petitions pressed on the Court. They also are required to research precedents and background material for opinions the justices intend to write. There is, however, no evidence available to support the often-heard charge that the clerks are responsible for or influence the policy decisions made by the justices. As Henry Abraham has said,

> The clerks are important tools for the justices in the judicial process, perhaps indispensable ones, yet they are hardly classifiable as powers behind the throne. Essentially, they are law *clerks*—able, intelligent, and undoubtedly often, if not always, of considerable procedural aid to their justices. But they are not members of the Court in any sense of the term.[42]

In the basement of the Court is a print shop, where printed copies of the Court's opinions are prepared. For security purposes, to prevent premature leaks of the Court's decisions, tourists are not permitted to view the print shop, and opinions are kept under lock and key until they are announced in open court.

In addition to the law clerks, print shop workers, and various clerical employees, many other types of personnel serve the Court.

> Inside—functioning much like the citizenry of a miniature city—are cooks, laundry workers, a barber, a half-dozen carpenters and electricians, 50 police officers, a nurse and a retired medical corpsman, . . . and a curator. . . .[43]

Sources and Limits of the Supreme Court's Power

We conclude this chapter with a discussion of the resources the Court has at its disposal in the exercise of its decision-making power and the potential limits on its use of that power.

Sources of the Court's Power

Surely the most important source of the Supreme Court's power is its ability to exercise *judicial review;* that is, the Court can examine a federal or state law in relation to the federal Constitution to determine whether the law is consistent with the Constitution. In exercising judicial review, the Court draws on its power of *constitutional interpretation*—the right to state what the legal meaning of a constitutional provision is. If the Court determines that the provisions of a law in question are inconsistent with its interpretation of the Constitution, it declares that the law is *unconstitutional*—void and without legal force.

The right to exercise judicial review of state laws was bestowed on the Court by the Congress in the Judiciary Act of 1789. The right to exercise judicial review of federal laws was claimed by the Court in *Marbury* v. *Madison* (1803), which was discussed in Chapter 1.

The vague language employed in some of the most important provisions of the Constitution (e.g., "necessary and proper," "equal protection," "due process") affords the justices a substantial range of options in making their decisions. Thus, as we shall see, the choices of the justices in any given case is dependent less on the words themselves than on the policy views, in regard to those words, of the particular nine men who sit on the Court at any point in time.

In addition to the power of constitutional interpretation, the Court also has the power of *statutory construction;* that is, as the court at the top of the federal pyramid, it makes the final judicial determination of the meaning of federal statutes. In such matters as economic regulation, this power can be as important in policy making as is constitutional interpretation in fields like civil liberties.

The Constitution affords the justices substantial protection from outside influences in the exercise of these powers. The fact that they serve "during good behavior" (i.e., for life) and may be removed only by impeachment removes from them much of the popular pressure that affects other makers of political decisions. The Constitution also provides that the salaries of the justices may not be reduced during their tenure, which allows them financial protection.[44]

The major protection afforded the Court in the exercise of its power is the almost mystical place it occupies in the mind of the general public. Indeed, the Court has gone to some lengths to nurture and maintain the public's view of it. The general strategy of the justices has been to maintain that its decisions are basically automatic and based purely on legal criteria, and then to shroud the Court's activity in secrecy and mystery. This picture of the Court's operation received probably its most extreme exposition in an opinion by Justice Owen Roberts declaring the Agricultural Adjustment Act of 1933 unconstitutional:

> When an act of Congress is appropriately challenged in the Courts as not conforming to the constitutional mandate the judicial branch of Government has only one duty—to lay the article of the Constitution which is invoked beside the statute which is challenged and to decide whether the latter squares with the former.[45]

Although the remainder of this book will have as one of its major points that this is an inaccurate picture of Supreme Court decision making, it is clear that this is a desirable public face for the Court to present. If the public can be made to believe that the Constitution, not the justices, is responsible for the voiding of a popular law, the potential for damage to the Court is greatly diminished.

Although public reaction to the Supreme Court's decisions was quite negative in the later years of the Warren Court, recently sentiment seems to be shifting slightly in the Court's favor, and at a time when the public's rating of other branches of the government is declining.[46] Perhaps more important, public opinion surveys indicate that the Court receives a highly positive rating from that large segment of the public that is not able to articulate any specific likes or dislikes about the Court. In a 1966 survey, people were asked whether there was anything specific that the Court had done that they liked or disliked. Respondents were also asked how well they thought the Court was doing its job. Of those respondents who were unable to state either a specific like or dislike, and who had an opinion of the Court's job, 81.7 percent said the Court was doing its job very well. This compares favorably with the 92.5 percent who said "very well" among those who articulated only likes about the Court. Indeed, even among those who stated only dislikes, a not-insubstantial 37.0 percent responded "very well."[47] This base of public support is an important resource for the Court in its decision making.

Limits on the Court's Power

It should be made clear that despite the substantial resources possessed by the Court, it also faces important potential checks on the exercise of its power. In the first place, the Court is a passive institution. The justices cannot go out and seek controversies, but must wait for someone to bring a case to them. Technical requirements such as standing, discussed in Chapter 1, are important in this regard.

The Court is also influenced by other institutions and actors. The major such influence on the Court is the joint power of the President and the Senate to fill vacancies on the Court. The impact of the views of President Nixon's appointees on the Court, which is discussed in Chapter 5, demonstrates how a trend in the Court's decisions can be altered by the appointment of new justices.

In addition, the Court depends upon the executive branch for enforcement of its decisions. Depending upon his reaction to a particular decision, the President may instruct his subordinates to enforce the policy vigorously, reluctantly, or not at all. Congress may refuse to appropriate funds for the enforcement of a decision it does not like. Given its constitutionally granted control over the Court's appellate jurisdiction, Congress may remove issues from the Court's jurisdiction if it does not like the way the justices have been deciding a given issue.

If the Court has employed constitutional interpretation in deciding a case, and Congress disagrees with the decision, Congress can pass a constitutional amendment to reverse the Court. If, on the other hand, a decision was based on statutory construction, Congress can simply pass a new law stating that the statute does not mean what the Court said it did.

As we have seen, the Supreme Court can accept only a limited number of cases each year. Thus, it must depend on lower courts to apply the policy it makes in similar cases. It is quite possible for lower-court judges to resist doing this (as did Southern judges in racial discrimination cases, substantially mitigating the influence of the Court in a policy area), especially since the Court's opinions, because they contain bargained results, often provide less than a clear mandate to the lower courts.

Finally, there is public opinion. Just as positive support for the Court is an important resource, negative reaction to a decision or set of decisions provides a potential check. Certainly widespread public disapproval of a particular policy made by the Court must give the justices pause before they push further in that direction. More importantly, such negative re-actions will provide an important resource for other political actors should they choose to move against the Court in a particular area.

Summary

In this chapter we have outlined the framework of Supreme Court decision making. We first provided some information on the lower federal courts. We then briefly discussed the four major stages of the Court's decision making: the decision whether to take a case, the vote on the merits, the assignment of the majority opinion, and the building of a majority opinion coalition. A full chapter will subsequently be devoted to each of these stages. In addition, we provided some information on the other personnel employed by the Court. Finally, we discussed the major sources of the Court's power and some potential checks on the exercise of that power. These checks will be considered in detail in later chapters.

Before turning to these detailed discussions, we present in the next chapter the theory of Supreme Court decision making we employ to explain the Court's behavior.

Notes to Chapter 3

1. See Richard J. Richardson and Kenneth N. Vines, *The Politics of Federal Courts* (Boston: Little, Brown, 1970), pp. 18–23.

2. For details of these changes see *ibid.*, pp. 23–29.

3. These three types of federal courts comprise the major federal *constitutional* courts (courts whose basis for existence is Article III of the Constitution). In addition, there are federal *legislative* courts (courts whose basis for existence is the legislative powers granted to the Congress in Article I of the Constitution). Today there are only two types of legislative courts: the United States Court of Military Appeals (which is the highest court in the military justice system) and the courts of the United States territories. Finally, there are the "special" con-

stitutional courts (courts that were originally set up by Congress as legislative courts, but that have since been converted by Congress to constitutional status). There are three such courts: the Court of Claims, the Customs Court, and the Court of Customs and Patent Appeals. For a discussion of these legislative and "special" courts, see Henry J. Abraham, *The Judicial Process*, 2d ed. (New York: Oxford University Press, 1968), pp. 146–155.

4. The Eleventh Amendment to the Constitution excluded from this jurisdiction a suit against a state by either an individual or a foreign country.

5. Congress denied the full range of federal jurisdiction to the lower federal courts until 1875 (see Richardson and Vines, *op. cit.*, fn. 1 *supra*, p. 29). Indeed, even today the state courts are granted *exclusive* jurisdiction over cases involving disputes between citizens of two or more states unless the amount of money involved is $10,000 or more.

6. *Annual Report of the Director of the Administrative Office of the United States Courts 1973* (Washington, D.C.: Government Printing Office, 1974), p. 90.

7. "The one exception occurs where the state of Wyoming and those portions of Yellowstone National Park situated in Montana and Idaho constitute one judicial district." Richardson and Vines, *op. cit.*, fn. 1 *supra*, p. 38, fn. 2.

8. The source of these data, and of the data in Table 3.2, is the *Annual Report of the Director of the Administrative Office of the United States Courts 1973*, *op. cit.*, fn. 6 *supra*, pp. 89–100.

9. In addition, the district courts may have jurisdiction over only some cases of a certain type (e.g., they have jurisdiction over only some cases in which a state is a party).

10. See Richardson and Vines, *op. cit.*, fn. 1 *supra*, pp. 41–42. Boundary revision is, however, presently under consideration. In 1972, Congress passed a law creating a Commission on Revision of the Federal Court Appellate System of the United States, which was charged with, among other things, studying and proposing revisions in the geographic boundaries of the circuits. See *Congressional Quarterly Almanac* 28, 1972 (Washington, D.C.: Congressional Quarterly, 1973): 608.

11. Abraham, *op. cit.*, fn. 3 *supra*, p. 160.

12. As we will see in Chapter 5, various political considerations have been involved in the alteration of the size of the Court.

13. For the details of this process, see Chapter 5.

14. Article III, section 2, clause 2. Congress has provided, however, that such jurisdiction is *exclusive* only when a case involves a dispute between two or more states. In *Marbury* v. *Madison*, 1 Cranch 137 (1803), the case that first established the Court's power of judicial review, the Court ruled that Congress cannot, by statute, expand this original jurisdiction.

15. Abraham, *op. cit.*, fn. 3 *supra*, p. 174.

16. The sources for these statistics are: for 1966–1968, *Congressional Quarterly Almanac*, 25, 1969 (Washington, D.C.: Congressional Quarterly, 1970), 128; for 1969–1972, *Harvard Law Review* 87 (1973), 310.

17. This continuing increase in case load has led some legal experts to propose a new court, to stand between the courts of appeals and the Supreme Court, in order to reduce the pressure on the Court. This proposal is discussed in Chapter 6.

18. These tasks, of course, overlap during the periods described.

19. A fourth, and seldom used, way is by a *writ of certification*, a request by a lower court for instructions by the Supreme Court on a matter of law.

20. When a petition for certiorari filed *in forma pauperis* is accepted for review, the Supreme Court appoints a lawyer to handle the case. Such appointments are considered a high honor, and the attorneys receiving them are often well known and more qualified than the average lawyer who appears before the Court. The appointed lawyer receives no fee; the only reimbursement he receives is for first-class round trip transportation between his home and Washington. The Court assumes the cost of printing briefs.

For a fascinating account of such a case see Anthony Lewis, *Gideon's Trumpet* (New York: Vintage, 1964). The case was *Gideon* v. *Wainwright*, 372 U.S. 335 (1963), which guaranteed appointed counsel to indigent defendants in all felony cases. The lawyer appointed to represent the petitioner was (later to be Associate Supreme Court Justice) Abe Fortas.

The funds for travel and brief printing come from the $25 fee the Court charges for admission to its bar. Abraham, *op. cit.*, fn. 3 *supra*, p. 195.

21. For a detailed analysis of this stage of the Court's decision making, see Chapter 6.

22. The source of these data is *Harvard Law Review* 87 (1973): 306. The 892 cases that were held on the dockets for the next term are excluded.

23. *Ibid.*

24. Robert L. Stern and Eugene Gressman, *Supreme Court Practice*, 3d ed. (Washington, D.C.: Bureau of National Affairs, 1962), p. 564.

25. Quoted in Lewis, *op. cit.*, fn. 23 *supra*, p. 162.

26. Abraham, *op. cit.*, fn. 3 *supra*, p. 195.

27. Sometimes this vote is a tentative one. The justices may bring up a case again at a later conference and discuss it more fully, at which time previous votes may be changed.

28. Before 1972, the justices sat at a rectangular table.

29. The Supreme Court correspondent for the *New York Times* has reported that the Court recently changed this procedure, and that the justices vote in the same order in which they discuss the case: the Chief Justice first, and then the associate justices in declining order of seniority. See Warren Weaver, Jr., "The Supreme Court at Work: A Look at the Inner Sanctum," *New York Times*, February 6, 1975, p. 65. In a conversation with Harold Spaeth on May 2, 1975, Professors Beverly Blair Cook of the University of Wisconsin at Milwaukee and Sidney Ulmer of the University of Kentucky stated that their separate sources within the Court report that Weaver is in error and that the order in which the justices vote has not been altered.

30. If, for any reason, all of the nine justices do not participate in the case (at least six must, to create a quorum), and the number participating is six or eight, the possibility of a tie vote is present. If there is a tie, the effect is to affirm the ruling of the lower court.

31. We use the term "majority opinion" generically. In fact, an opinion really cannot be termed a majority opinion until and unless a majority of the justices agree to it.

32. For a recent exception, see the discussion in Chapter 8.

33. See Chapter 8.

34. This can often be a lengthy and laborious process. After the death of Justice Brandeis, among his papers was found the thirty-fourth draft of an opinion! Linda Mathews, "Supreme Court—a Miniature World Governed by Tradition," *Los Angeles Times*, Feb. 2, 1974, pp. 1, 21,

35. In the 1972 term, for example, there was no majority opinion in 9 of the 140 cases decided by full opinion. *Harvard Law Review* 87 (1973): 303. In such situations, the opinion is not termed a majority opinion, but an opinion announcing the "Judgment of the Court."

36. Abraham, *op. cit.*, fn. 3 *supra*, p. 219 n.

37. Concurrences may be of two types. On the one hand, a justice may agree with the result but not with the justification or policy views of the dominant faction of the majority. The justice is then said to *concur in the result,* and any opinion he writes is termed a *separate concurring opinion.* On the other hand, a justice may agree with the views of the majority and assent to the majority opinion, but he may also write a concurring opinion that enunciates his reasons for joining the majority and delineates his understanding of the policy made in the opinion of the Court, or that replies to an argument made in a dissenting opinion.

38. *Congressional Quarterly Weekly Report*, Nov. 17, 1973, p. 3042.

39. The Chief Justice is entitled to one additional clerk.

40. In the 1965 term, for example, twelve of the nineteen clerks came from the Harvard, Yale, and University of Pennsylvania law schools. Abraham, *op. cit.*, fn. 3 *supra*, p. 242.

41. James A. Kidney, "Anonymous Law Clerks Serve Justices, Gain Experience," *Washington Post*, June 16, 1973, p. L6.

42. *Op. cit.*, fn. 3 *supra*, p. 243.

43. Mathews, *op. cit.*, fn. 34 *supra*, p. 1.

44. This, of course, does not mean that Congress must increase their salaries. In 1964, to demonstrate its displeasure with the trend of Court decisions, Congress granted the justices only a "$4,500 raise, $3,000 less than that given all other federal judges." Abraham, *op. cit.*, fn. 3 *supra*, p. 171 n.

45. *United States* v. *Butler*, 297 U.S. 1 (1936), at 79.

46. In a 1969 Gallup national survey, only 38 percent of those expressing an opinion rated the Court's performance as good or excellent. By 1973, this group had increased to 42 percent. *The Gallup Opinion Index*, August 1973, p. 9.

47. Walter F. Murphy and Joseph Tanenhaus, *The Study of Public Law* (New York: Random House, 1972), p. 43, Table 2.3.

4 | *The Theory of Supreme Court Decision Making*

In this chapter, we present a theory of Supreme Court decision making. The theory focuses on the decisions of the justices—what cases they agree to take, how they vote, what coalitions they join—rather than the policies enunciated in the Court's opinions. In other words, our theory attempts to predict what the justices will do, rather than what they will say.

Assumptions

Our theory postulates that political decisions in general, and those of the Supreme Court in particular, are the consequence of three factors: goals, rules, and situations. First, we assume that actors in political situations are goal oriented; that is, they have certain goals they wish to accomplish in those situations. Furthermore, the choices of such actors when making decisions are instrumental; when they choose among a number of alternatives, they pick the alternative that they perceive will yield them the greatest net benefit in terms of their goals.

Second, we assume that, in addition to his goals, an actor's choices will depend on the "rules of the game." These rules of the game, or rule structures, are the various formal and informal rules and norms within the framework of which decisions are made. As such, they specify which types of actions are permissible and which are impermissible, the circumstances and conditions under which choice may be exercised, and the manner of choosing.

An example of formal rule structures are the rules of Congress, which include the formal rules of the House and Senate, the provisions of the Constitution that pertain to Congress, various election laws, and the

70

criminal statutes governing congressional behavior. Informal rule structures include such practices as the custom of senatorial courtesy, aspects of the seniority and committee systems, and the expectations of certain actors about what types of behavior are "proper."

Rule structures, in and of themselves, are not neutral with regard to the outcomes of decisions; they may significantly affect outcomes. A certain set of rules, for example, may make one goal relatively easy to achieve, while making the achievement of another difficult, if not impossible. Thus, the bicameral character of Congress makes the passage of legislation considerably more difficult than if Congress were unicameral. Consequently, those whose goals are wedded to the status quo find their goals considerably easier to achieve in Congress than do those whose goals require change and reform. Other rules, beyond the requirement that a bill pass both Houses of Congress with identical language, advantage those whose goals depend for their success on retention of the status quo (e.g., the Senate's unlimited debate rule that permits filibusters[1]).

Indeed, the same individual may choose differently under different rule structures. For example, consider two alternative election systems. In the first system, only two candidates are permitted. If a group of voters prefers candidate *A* to candidate *B*, it is always in the best interests of each voter to vote for his first choice. In the second system, however, three candidates are permitted, and the candidate with the most votes wins (i.e., a plurality election system). Thus, in addition to candidates *A* and *B*, a third candidate, *C*, is eligible. Our hypothetical group of voters still prefers candidate *A* to candidate *B*, but they also prefer both candidates to candidate *C*. Assume that the electorate is divided as follows:

> Group I (15 percent of the voters): First choice is candidate *A* (but second choice is candidate *B*).
>
> Group II (40 percent of the voters): First choice is candidate *B*.
>
> Group III (45 percent of the voters): First choice is candidate *C*.

If everyone votes for his first choice, candidate *C* will win with 45 percent of the vote. If, however, the voters in Group I dislike candidate *C* enough, it might pay them to vote for candidate *B* instead of their first choice. Then candidate *B* will win with 55 percent of the vote. Thus, different rules may lead to different choices and hence produce different outcomes.[2]

This example can also serve to illustrate our third, and probably most obvious, assumption: that decisions are also dependent on particular situations. An alternative that may be best for the success of a person's goals in one set of circumstances may not be best in a different set of circumstances. Returning to our example of the plurality election system, assume that the division of the electorate is instead as follows: Group I (15 percent), Group II (30 percent), and Group III (55 percent). Then no matter how much the voters in Group I dislike candidate *C*, it will not profit them to vote for candidate *B*, since candidate *C* is sure to win. All they can do is make the best of a bad situation and vote for their first choice (or, perhaps, stay home).

Thus all three factors—goals, rules, and situations—may affect decisions and outcomes. We now consider our assumptions as they specifically apply to the Supreme Court.

First, we assume that the primary goals of Supreme Court justices in the decision-making process are *policy goals*. Each member of the Court has preferences concerning the policy questions faced by the Court, and when the justices make decisions they want the outcomes to approximate as nearly as possible those policy preferences.

Second, the plausibility of our assumption about the goals of the justices is enhanced by a consideration of the Court's rules. The Supreme Court's rule structure permits the justices greater freedom than other political decision makers to base their decisions solely upon personal policy preferences for a number of reasons: (1) the lack of electoral accountability, (2) the lack of ambition for higher office, and (3) the fact that the Supreme Court is the court of last resort. We discuss each reason in turn.

The Supreme Court is virtually unique among decision-making bodies in the American governmental system because the justices are not accountable to the electorate. This lack of accountability is heightened by the absence of an effective removal power. A justice, once appointed, serves until he retires, resigns, or dies. There is, of course, the power of impeachment, which is vested in Congress. The importance of this power is negligible, however. Only once has a Supreme Court justice been impeached: Samuel Chase in 1804. But this effort came to naught when the Senate acquitted him. The lack of an effective removal power differentiates justices from such officials as Cabinet officers who, like the justices, are not elected but serve only at the pleasure of the President, and from members of the federal regulatory agencies (e.g., Interstate Commerce Commission, National Labor Relations Board, Federal Trade Commission, Federal Communications Commission), who are appointed and may not be removed from office, except for cause, but who must be reappointed at the end of their term if they are to remain in office.

The lack of electoral accountability is crucial to the free play of personal policy preferences. The requirement that elected public officeholders must face the voters every two, four, or six years is clearly an important constraint on their decision-making ability. The desire of such persons to be re-elected to their offices is a concern totally absent from the context of Supreme Court decision making.

The lack of ambition for higher office also means that personal policy preferences are more freely expressed. Most officeholders arguably desire an office more prestigious than the one they are occupying,[3] and such desire will obviously affect their behavior. Accordingly, an individual may make decisions on the basis of how they will affect the probability of his attaining that office. For at least a century, such ambition appears to have been possessed by only one or two of the justices who have sat on the Supreme Court. In other words, service on the Supreme Court has been viewed as the pinnacle of a political career, rather than as a way station to other offices. The only office in the American political system that may be higher in prestige is the Presidency, and some individuals might not even agree with this assessment. Charles Evans Hughes did resign as associate justice in 1916 to accept the Republican nomination for President. However, he returned to the Court as Chief Justice fourteen years later even though it meant ending the career of his son as Solicitor General.[4] Salmon P. Chase, Lincoln's rival for the Presidency, states that the only office he "heartedly desired" was that of Chief Justice, a goal he attained in 1864. William Howard Taft, when asked "in March 1910 whether he liked being President, replied, 'On the whole, yes. I would rather be Chief Justice of the United States.'"[5]

Other than Hughes, only two twentieth-century justices resigned to accept other offices. James Byrnes, after barely one year on the Court, resigned in 1942 at the request of President Roosevelt to accept the position of "Assistant President," as Director of Economic Stabilization. This move was dictated by the exigencies of World War II. Arthur Goldberg resigned in 1965 after three years' service to become United States Ambassador to the United Nations. This appointment, however, can hardly be considered a promotion.

Apart from ambition for higher office, another type of ambition is the desire for increased power within a given institution. A member of the House of Representatives, for example, may be completely satisfied to remain in that office for the rest of his life, but he may wish to increase his influence over outcomes in the House by securing a particular committee assignment or a party leadership position. The achievement of either of these goals depends on the decisions of other members of the House. Hence, his decisions on matters of interest to these other members will be affected to some extent by their preferences.

The reason why this type of ambition is not conspicuous among the justices is not completely clear. However, it is certainly less prevalent among them than among members of the state and federal legislatures. A marked difference between the Court and other governmental institutions is that there is little division of labor within the Court. Except for an occasional instance of self-disqualification, all the justices participate in each decision. The result is that, except for the Chief Justice, all the justices are equal. It is, therefore, possible that some associate justices may covet the Chief Justiceship. A case in point, perhaps the only one, was Justice Jackson. When Jackson thought that Justice Black and others had intervened to block his promotion after the death of Chief Justice Stone in 1946 while he was serving abroad as Chief Prosecutor at the Nuremberg Trials, Jackson "precipitated one of the ugliest feuds in judicial history."[6] But given the infrequency of a vacant Chief Justiceship,[7] plus the lack of evidence that such a promotion is a general desire of the sitting associate justices, it seems safe to assume that such a motivation does not affect the justices' personal preferences.[8]

The third and final reason for the free play of personal policy preferences as the motivating factor in Supreme Court decisions is the Court's position as the court of last resort. It cannot be overruled by any other court. In matters of statutory interpretation, Congress can indeed overrule the Court. But Congress, of course, is not a court. Moreover, Congress rarely attempts to overrule the Court and even when it does, most such attempts prove unsuccessful. This differentiates the Supreme Court from other federal and state courts. Even though lower-court judges may be disinclined to follow precedent when making decisions, they must nonetheless take into account the fact that higher courts can reverse them. The Court is especially supreme in matters of constitutional interpretation. Constitutional interpretation can be reversed only if the justices overrule themselves or if a constitutional amendment is passed. The latter check is a negligible one, for only four such amendments have been passed: the Eleventh Amendment in 1798 reversed the decision in *Chisholm* v. *Georgia*, 2 Dall. 419 (1793), which permitted an individual to sue a state in the federal courts; the Fourteenth Amendment in 1868 reversed the decision in *Dred Scott* v. *Sanford*, 19 How. 393 (1857), which held blacks not to be citizens of the United States; the Sixteenth Amendment in 1913 reversed the decision in *Pollock* v. *Farmer's Loan and Trust Co.*, 157 U.S. 429 (1895), which prohibited a federal income tax; and the Twenty-sixth Amendment in 1971 reversed part of *Oregon* v. *Mitchell*, 400 U.S. 112 (1970), which denied 18- to 20-year-olds the right to vote in state elections.

Finally, we assume (as we did generally) that situations affect the justices' decisions. Situational factors are specific in nature, and detailed consideration of this matter will be left to the chapters on the various stages of decision making in the court. As we shall see, situational circumstances affect such decisions as to whom the majority opinion is assigned (see Chapter 8) and whether a justice joins in the opinion of the Court (see Chapter 9).

We now turn to a consideration of the means we will employ to identify the justices' personal policy preferences. However, before we can identify those preferences, we must define and then operationalize the constructs of "belief," "attitude," and "value," which are the psychological components of personal policy preferences.

The Definition of Belief, Attitude, and Value

In referring to belief, attitude, and value as constructs, we do so consciously. Any construct, as distinct from a concept, is an invention, an artificial creation, of a scientist that is used for analytic and explanatory purposes. A *concept* is an abstraction formed by generalizing about a set of particulars; for example, weight, aggression, intelligence, or sexuality. A *construct* is like a concept in that it also is an abstraction formed by generalizing about a set of particulars. In addition, a construct is an internal and unobservable process, usually psychological, that is used to explain behavior.

The point of this discussion is simply to emphasize that we are not dealing with entities whose existence out there in the "real" world can be demonstrated. Beliefs, attitudes, and values cannot be seen, smelled, tasted, heard, or felt. But as constructs, they form an integral part of systematic explanation.[9]

In our effort to define the psychological determinants of behavior we should first note that, in the jargon of social science, our "independent variable" is personal policy preferences; our "dependent variable" is decision making—the decisions of the justices.

Our definition of the three components of personal policy preferences—beliefs, attitudes, and values—begins with attitudes. Even though there are virtually as many definitions of "attitude" as there are attitude theorists, it is the construct most commonly employed as an explanation of behavior. To avoid any increase in the number of definitions of attitude, we have adapted an existing one that adequately suits our needs:

> An attitude is a (1) relatively enduring, (2) organization of interrelated beliefs that describe, evaluate, and advocate action with respect to an object or situation, (3) with each belief having cognitive, affective, and behavioral components. (4) Each one of these beliefs is a predisposition that, when suitably activated, results in some preferential response for the attitude object or situation, or toward the maintenance or preservation of the attitude itself. (5) Since an attitude object must always be encountered within some situation about which we also have an attitude, a minimum condition for social behavior is the activation of at least two interacting attitudes, one concerning the attitude object and the other concerning the situation.[10]

Because the construct of attitude is fundamental to our theory of Supreme Court decision making, we provide the following explanation of each of the elements of the foregoing definition.

(1) The view that attitudes are "relatively enduring" is generally accepted by attitude theorists,[11] especially with reference to adults who have assumed a specific role in society. But be this as it may, research to date reveals little evidence of any shifts in the attitudes of Supreme Court justices.[12] Although it is not possible to differentiate precisely between

enduring and temporary predispositions, our effort to operationalize the construct of attitude (in the next section of this chapter) clearly supports their enduring character. Note that we are not concerned with the source of attitudes—that is, whether they are hereditary and/or learned. Determination of source is of great interest to the fields of genetics and education, but it is peripheral to the explanation and prediction of Supreme Court decision making. Consequently, we consider the definition of attitude to be altogether independent of its source.[13]

(2) Attitude theorists also agree that an attitude is not a basic, irreducible element within the personality.[14] Rather, the basic element is considered to be beliefs. Here, we again use an existing definition of belief instead of formulating one of our own.

> A *belief* is any simple proposition, conscious or unconscious, inferred from what a person says or does, capable of being preceded by the phrase "I believe that. . . . " The content of a belief may describe the object of belief as true or false, correct or incorrect; evaluate it as good or bad; or advocate a certain course of action or a certain state of existence as desirable or undesirable.[15]

For reasons specified in connection with element (3) of our definition of attitude, the only distinction we make between beliefs and attitudes is their level of generality. In this respect, and stated most simply, *an attitude is nothing more than a set of interrelated beliefs about at least one object and the situation in which it is encountered.*

(3) Beliefs, and therefore attitudes, are conceived to have cognitive, affective, and behavioral components. *Cognition* refers to the image or perceptual map of reality held by an individual. Thus, for example, a person's attitude toward law enforcement may encompass attitudes toward police, attitudes toward the importance attached to individual freedom, and attitudes about specific laws that make certain actions criminal. *Affect,* by comparison, refers to the feelings or emotions a person has about one or the other of his beliefs or attitudes. Questionnaire items that seek to determine how strongly the respondent feels about such matters as capital punishment, gay liberation, or abortion reform typify efforts to measure affect. But because our focus is Supreme Court decision making (the votes of the justices), our concern with the cognitive and affective components of the justices' attitudes is peripheral at best.

Although many theorists argue that beliefs have only a cognitive component, persuasive arguments have been presented for conceptualizing beliefs and attitudes as structurally analogous.[16] A basic advantage of these arguments is that such a conceptualization is parsimonious. When beliefs are considered to be the basic, irreducible element within the personality and an attitude is viewed as the sum total of the interrelated beliefs about an object and the situation in which it is encountered, a hierarchical relationship results. The only difference is in level of generality. Most specific are beliefs, followed by attitudes. And if we define *value*, again quite simply, as merely *an interrelated set of attitudes*, we have a concise structure encompassing all three of the psychological determinants of behavior.

(4) The preferential responses with which we are concerned here are the votes of the justices in the cases they decide. In Chapters 8 and 9, we consider other aspects of decision making (the assignment and writing of opinions); but at this point in the presentation of the theory, we analyze justices' opinions only so that we may classify cases into legal and semantic categories and explain discrepancies in the voting of individual justices. Note that in no way do we consider verbal activity to be beyond our scope of concern; but knowledge about what the justices do, rather than what they say, is of paramount importance to the formulation of our theory. Hence our focus upon attitude to explain the Court's decision making. Furthermore, all attitudes, in Rokeach's phrase, are assumed to be "agendas for action."[17] In other words, every attitude disposes its holder to act in some preferential fashion.

(5) Given our definition of attitude as an organization of beliefs, more than a single predisposition to respond is required to activate an attitude. Activation of an attitude involves attitude toward object (AO) as well as attitude toward situation (AS). The major deficiency in efforts to measure public opinion is that researchers have tended to focus upon attitudes toward objects (persons, institutions, places, and things) rather than the situations in which objects are encountered. In order to predict and explain behavior, it is simply not sufficient to know a person's attitude toward such "objects" as criminal defendants, business, labor unions, blacks, students, or indigents. We must also know the situation, that is, the setting, in which the attitude object is encountered. A white person may well respond to a black sitting next to him at a lunch counter in an entirely different manner than he does to a black who moves in next door to him, or a black who is employed as his job supervisor. Insofar as Supreme Court voting is concerned, the major AO's are conceptualized as the legal or human persons involved in the legal process; for example, criminal defendants, blacks, labor unions, businesses, injured persons, and indigents. The major AS's are conceptualized as the dominant legal issue in the case: search and seizure, right to counsel, double jeopardy, federal antitrust regulation, liability, mootness, and so on. In short, behavior is a function of the interaction of AO and AS.

The importance of distinguishing between AO and AS, which has been forcefully argued by Rokeach,[18] has been empirically demonstrated. One study, of a set of fifty-eight Supreme Court cases decided between 1958 and 1966, in which "business" was the AO for five distinct AS's, showed that the justices' behavior is indeed a function of the interaction between

AO and *AS*; the five attitude situations explained at least two-thirds of the justices' votes, and attitude toward business explained the remaining one-third.[19] Similar results were obtained in another study of the Supreme Court that covered the period from 1958 to 1969: justices do not reach decisions on the basis that a litigant is a labor union, that he is a person exercising freedom of communication, or that he is black or nonblack. In such instances, then, attitude toward situation is a much better predictor of decision than are these attitude objects. The reverse was found to be true, however, when the attitude object was a "security risk" or an injured person.[20]

Operationalization of Attitude and Value

We have stated and explained the assumptions underlying our theory and the constructs of belief, attitude, and value. But as the proof of the pudding is in the eating, so the utility of a theory is in its explanatory and predictive power. Hence, we need to apply and test the ideas that have been developed thus far in this chapter. Application of a theory requires that the essential elements in the theory be operationalized. For us the crucial construct is attitude. The definition of attitude just formulated is a conceptual one—a set of interrelated beliefs that a person has toward some object and the situation within which it is encountered. To operationalize this definition, a single methodological technique is employed: cumulative scale analysis (or, as it is sometimes called, Guttman scale analysis).

Attitudes

Although the literature on cumulative scaling is substantial, it is not complex and does not require mathematical expertise. Cumulative scaling was begun during World War II as an effort to devise a solution to the problem of consistency in attitude and public opinion research.[21] Consider, for example, a questionnaire or a test attempting to determine people's attitudes toward alcoholism or drug abuse, or to measure scholastic achievement. How can those preparing the questions know that each question really pertains to the matter being studied? A person's attitudes about alcoholism, for example, may be the result of his attitudes toward drunken drivers. A test intended to evaluate academic achievement may really measure a person's aptitude for learning rather than his knowledge about a specific subject. Another aspect of the problem of consistency is the requirement that each question have the same meaning for every respondent—that the questions should not be ambiguous.

Resolution of the problem of consistency is therefore basic to much of social science research, such as that concerning aptitude and achievement testing, neurotic behavior, social status, and public opinion. Cumulative scaling postulates that one way to solve the problem of consistency is to rank order respondents on the basis of their favorableness/unfavorableness to the matter being investigated. As a pertinent illustration, consider a series of questions dealing with a public policy issue such as freedom of speech or involuntary confessions; each respondent is instructed either to support or to oppose the specific action described in each question. Cumulative scaling simply assumes that "if a person endorses a more extreme statement, he should endorse all less extreme statements if the statements are to be considered a scale."[22] This merely means that if 75 percent of the respondents agree with one statement, and 65 percent agree with another, those who agree with the latter statement (which is "more extreme" because a smaller group supports it) must also be among the 75 percent who agree with the first statement.

It is in this sense that cumulative scaling solves the problem of consistency. The idea of cumulative scaling is not that any given respondent must answer each question with the same response; rather it is that once a respondent changes his response from favorable to unfavorable, he must continue to respond negatively to all statements that contain a proportion of favorable votes smaller than the proportion contained in the most extreme statement that he did support.

Consider the following example. A group of people is asked to answer yes or no to five questions in order to gauge their attitudes toward First Amendment freedoms: (1) 90 percent agree that a newsman may comment unfavorably on a judge's decision; (2) 75 percent agree that a newspaper may publish documents that the Defense Department has classified as secret; (3) 65 percent agree that a student may not be expelled for ridiculing the college president in the campus newspaper; (4) 40 percent agree that a shopping center may not forbid pamphleteering on its premises; and (5) 25 percent agree that civil service employees should be allowed to participate in partisan political activities.

Note, initially, that the foregoing questions are not pre-ordered on the basis of their extremeness. The ordering of the questions is solely and simply a function of the decreasing percentage of the respondents who answered yes. Thus, the second question is more extreme than the first only because fewer respondents agreed with it, not because in some ideal world it ought to be more extreme, or because the researcher thinks for some reason that it should be so.

After the questions have been ordered, the crucial step is to determine if the respondents have answered the questions in a consistent fashion. As already mentioned, for a set of questions to constitute a scale, it is necessary that each respondent respond consistently. This means that the 25 percent who responded positively to question 5 must be among those who answered yes to the other questions. Conversely, those who said in response to question 1 that a newsman should not comment unfavorably on a judge's decision should also have said "no" to questions 2 through 5. Similarly, a person who answered yes to question 3 and no to question 4 should have responded favorably to questions 1 and 2, and unfavorably to 5. If such consistency prevails for all the respondents, then a valid cumulative scale exists, and we may properly infer that the questions asked do indeed measure, albeit roughly, the respondents' attitudes toward First Amendment freedoms.

Now let us apply cumulative scaling to the Supreme Court. Assume that the ten cases in Figure 4.1 all concern the right to counsel. Assume further that a + vote indicates that the right to counsel was denied; a − vote indicates that the right was not abridged. Observe that all the justices supported the least extreme case—the one decided by a 9 to 0 vote. Justice *I,* however, voted that the right to counsel was not denied in Case 2. But Justice *I* remained consistent by voting against denial in all the other, more extreme cases. A similar pattern prevails for all the other justices: Once a justice votes against denial he does so in each of the more extremely decided cases. Conversely, once a justice begins to support the right to counsel, he does so in all less extremely decided cases.

The pattern of votes displayed in Figure 4.1 is not one that is likely to occur by chance. In a nine-member body such as the Supreme Court, in which a simple majority of the justices determines the outcome of a case decided on the merits, the justices may combine in 256 different voting alignments as follows. A unaminous vote that requires agreement by all the justices can occur in only one way; each of the 9 justices can dissent alone to produce an 8 to 1 decision; 36 different pairs of justices may dissent to produce a 7 to 2 decision; 84 different combinations of 3 justices may dissent to produce a 6 to 3 decision; and 4 justices may combine in 126 different ways to produce a 5 to 4 decision. The sum of these combinations equals 256. In constructing a cumulative scale, however, this sum must be doubled, because in constructing a scale, "directionality" is assigned. This means that each of the decisions in Figure 4.1 is classified as being either pro or con the right to counsel. Consequently, each of the 9 justices may be the sole dissenter in an 8 to 1 decision *upholding* the right to counsel, and each correspondingly may be the sole dissenter in a 1 to 8 decision *denying* the right to counsel. Thus, the number of possible combinations that the 9 justices may form for cumulative scale purposes is 512. Given the perfectly consistent pattern of voting combinations in Figure 4.1, we may reliably infer that the justices voted as they did in these cases because of their attitudes toward the right to counsel.

Note that Figure 4.1 is labeled "perfect cumulative scale." This means that the justices voted in a perfectly consistent fashion. Perfection is, however, seldom encountered in real-world data. Rather, a few votes will normally deviate from a pattern of perfectly consistent responses. Assume, for example, that Justice *A* in Figure 4.1 had cast a negative vote in Case 3,

| | JUSTICES | | | | | | | | | |
CASE	*A*	*B*	*C*	*D*	*E*	*F*	*G*	*H*	*I*	VOTE
1	+	+	+	+	+	+	+	+	+	9–0
2	+	+	+	+	+	+	+	+	–	8–1
3	+	+	+	+	+	+	+	–	–	7–2
4	+	+	+	+	+	+	–	–	–	6–3
5	+	+	+	+	+	+	–	–	–	6–3
6	+	+	+	+	+	–	–	–	–	5–4
7	+	+	+	+	–	–	–	–	–	4–5
8	+	+	+	+	–	–	–	–	–	4–5
9	+	+	–	–	–	–	–	–	–	2–7
10	+	–	–	–	–	–	–	–	–	1–8

Figure 4.1
Perfect cumulative scale.

or that Justice *E* had voted positively in Case 9. Each of these two votes would be an "inconsistency" or nonscale response. Too many such non-scale responses would destroy the consistent pattern of voting that, as noted, is crucial to scale construction.

How many nonscale responses are "too many"? The answer is de-termined by the formula for the coefficient of reproducibility (*R*), which is easily calculated and which, as applied to Supreme Court decision making, is:

$$R = 1 - \frac{NSR}{V}.$$

In this formula, NSR = the total number of nonscale responses in cases in which there is more than one dissenting vote, and V = the total number of votes cast in cases in which there is more than one dissenting vote. Unani-mously decided cases, as well as those in which there is a sole dissent, are excluded from calculation because their inclusion would unduly inflate the coefficient of reproducibility. (The higher the coefficient, the better the scale. A perfect scale's $R = 1.00$.) Such inflation of *R* results because non-scale responses can only occur in decisions in which there are dissenting votes. The more dissents per case, the more numerous the possible combina-tions of justices, and thus the greater likelihood of inconsistent votes.

For the calculation of *R*, we use Figure 4.1 and the two nonscale votes just mentioned. Cases 1, 2, and 10 are excluded from calculation because they are either unanimous or sole dissent decisions. Thus, $R = 1 - 2/63 = .968$. The denominator, 63, is obtained by counting the seven cases 3 through 9, each of which contains at least two dissenting votes. In each case, 9 justices voted: $7 \times 9 = 63$. According to Louis Guttman, the creator of cumulative scaling, if R is less than .90 not enough consistency of response is present to consider the cases a scale.[23]

Two additional points about cumulative scaling need be made before we conclude our discussion of the operationalization of attitude. First, a set of cases that forms a scale of the justices' votes during a given period may not form an acceptable scale for another group of justices or for the same group during another period. This may be because different justices have differing attitudes. Or two sets of justices may have different perceptions and, as a result, a given set of cases may tap different attitudes. Thus, for example, decisions of the Warren and Burger Courts that require the states to abide by the provisions of the Bill of Rights are largely explained by the justices' attitudes toward civil liberties and the rights of persons accused of crime. It is possible that at earlier periods in American history, these same sorts of decisions were explained by the justices' attitudes toward federalism rather than civil liberties. It is also possible that changing circumstances and conditions may cause a justice, over time, to decide cases on the basis of attitudes different from those that formerly motivated his votes. There is, for example, considerable evidence that many cases involving regulation of business that were decided by the Warren Court on the basis of the justices' attitudes toward business are now being decided on the basis of the justices' attitudes toward the degree of autonomy that the federal regulatory agencies should possess.

Second, cumulative scaling is not a means whereby the scope or content of a scale may be ascertained. Cumulative scaling presumes that the cases pertaining to a given issue area have been identified before a scale is constructed. In this sense, then, cumulative scaling is a heuristic device, one that allows a researcher to test such hypotheses as: the justices' votes in double jeopardy cases are determined by their attitudes toward double jeopardy; or state regulation of obscenity is a function of the justices' attitudes about the First Amendment. In other words, "sheer scalability is not sufficient; an item may happen to scale with an area, and yet may not have the content defining the area. . . ."[24] Clearly, then, to determine whether the votes of the justices are explained by their attitudes toward the issue before them requires that the cases themselves have a common content.

Given this discussion of cumulative scaling, we can operationally define our basic construct, attitude, as a set of cumulatively scalable cases that are as finely drawn as the character and quality of the data permit.

What is meant by "as finely drawn as the character and quality of the data permit"? Inasmuch as explanation is a function of precise measurement, it is important that apples not be mixed with oranges. The deck must not be stacked to favor either overly simplistic or unduly complex explanation. Concern that the deck not be stacked is warranted because, on the one hand, legal scholars and traditionally oriented political scientists argue that each case is unique;[25] on the other hand, judicial behavioralists have maintained that Supreme Court decision making may be explained by the operation of a few attitudes. For example, behavioralists have concluded that "civil liberty decisions may be explained by . . . attitude toward claimed civil liberty deprivations";[26] that "their votes . . . are motivated by each justice's attitude toward civil liberty";[27] and that the "core value of general liberalism" is "political equality" and that it accounts for nearly all votes in race, reapportionment, and citizenship cases.[28]

If, in operationalizing the construct of attitude, we employ a methodology that portends complexity of Supreme Court decision making, each case tends to become unique unto itself. As a consequence, theory and the explanations flowing therefrom become nonexistent. On the other hand, if we make attitude operational in a manner that precludes complexity, precise explanation is lost because that which is distinctive or discrete becomes merged into a mixed bag.

The latter danger is the more serious. Because the Court is small, its stable membership, the frequency with which the justices interact, their practice of rationalizing their votes through written opinions, and their capacity to communicate and to generalize, all combine to produce highly uniform behavior on the part of the justices. As a result, exceedingly gross cumulative scales, encompassing as much as 40 percent of the nonunanimous decisions of a term of the Court, have been constructed with a coefficient of reproducibility (R) at or above the conventional minimum of .90.[29] Hence the importance of Guttman's caveat: "Sheer scalability is not sufficient; an item may happen to scale with an area, and yet not have the content defining the area. . . ."[30] Accordingly, we must devise a research strategy that allows complexity, if it is present, to be revealed. Conversely, if simplicity exists, the strategy must as readily permit its manifestation.

To return to the operational definition of attitude, in forming cumulative scales, we categorize cases on the basis of their legal and semantic content. As with the conceptual definition of attitude, each cumulative scale must contain a designated attitude object (AO) and a designated attitude situation (AS).

In order to construct scales as refined as the data permit and to ensure consistency with the conceptual definition of attitude, it is necessary to employ a longitudinal perspective, that is, the decisions being analyzed must extend over a period of several years. Such a perspective is mandatory. The alternative course, of considering decisions only on a term-by-term, or cross-sectional, basis, precludes construction of refined scale categories, because more often than not the Court will decide no more than two or three cases pertaining to a single category in any given term.[31] So limited a number of cases in a scale severely limits a scale's reliability and validity. This difficulty is overcome, however, if an analysis of several successive terms is undertaken.

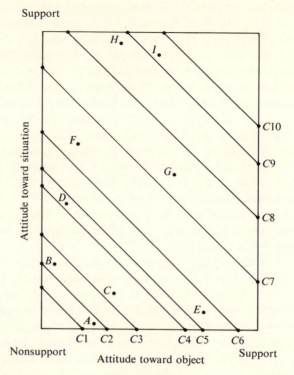

Figure 4.2
Geometric representation of a cumulative pattern of decision making generated by two attitudes.

In this procedure, initial efforts at scale construction are nothing more than an impressionistic content analysis of the individual cases. These cases are formed, via trial and error, into a series of cumulative scales. The objective of the procedure is fourfold:

1. To categorize as large a proportion of the universe of cases as possible. Ability to explain past decisions and to predict the outcome of future cases depends upon how completely previous decisions have been validly and reliably categorized.

2. To formulate category scales that are as specific in content as possible. Precision is an integral component of explanation and prediction.

3. To form each category on the basis of a major *AO* and *AS*. This, as mentioned, is to ensure compatibility with the definition of attitude.

4. To approximate perfect reproducibility ($R = 1.00$) in each category scale. The smaller the proportion of nonscale responses, the greater the validity and reliability of the scales.

At this point, it may appear that the third of these objectives is incompatible with the theory underlying cumulative scaling. This theory

		JUDGES									
		A	*B*	*C*	*D*	*E*	*F*	*G*	*H*	*I*	
	C1	+	+	+	+	+	+	+	+	+	9–0
	C2	−	+	+	+	+	+	+	+	+	8–1
	C3	−	−	+	+	+	+	+	+	+	7–2
C	C4	−	−	−	+	+	+	+	+	+	6–3
A	C5	−	−	−	−	+	+	+	+	+	5–4
S	C6	−	−	−	−	−	+	+	+	+	4–5
E	C7	−	−	−	−	−	−	+	+	+	3–6
S	C8	−	−	−	−	−	−	−	+	+	2–7
	C9	−	−	−	−	−	−	−	−	+	1–8
	C10	−	−	−	−	−	−	−	−	−	0–9

Figure 4.3

Cumulative pattern of decision generated by the two attitudes in Figure 4.2.

assumes that if a set of questions or cases is scalable it is because a single underlying attitude motivates the respondents' behavior. On the other hand, we are assuming, on the basis of our conceptual definition of attitude, that behavior is a function of both attitude toward object and attitude toward situation. This inconsistency is more apparent than real, however.[32]

Consider Figure 4.2, which presents an alternative to the assumption that if a cumulative scale is formed, only a single underlying attitude motivates the respondents' behavior. $C1$ through $C10$ represent the range of a set of cases in terms of their extremeness. The letters A through I represent the judges. The horizontal axis represents some attitude toward object, say, criminal defendants; the vertical axis represents the attitude toward situation within which the AO is encountered—double jeopardy or right to counsel, for example. Assume that a judge votes favorably to the criminal defendant in all cases where his location in Figure 4.2 is to the right of the line segments between the vertical and horizontal axes that represent the location of the cases on the scale. If his location is to the left of the line segments of certain of the cases, he votes against the criminal defendant. Thus, Judge A votes in favor of the criminal defendant only in case 1, Judge E votes in favor of the defendants in cases 1 through 5, and Judge I votes in their favor in all but case 10. The result is the cumulative pattern of behavior presented in Figure 4.3. The pattern, of course, produces a perfect scale, because the coefficient of reproducibility (R) equals 1.00.

We cannot, however, infer that the pattern of behavior shown in Figure 4.3 was produced solely by the judges' attitudes toward the criminal defendants. If that were true, then the rank order of the judges, from least to most favorable, would be the left-to-right progression along the horizontal axis: *B, D, F, A, C, H, I, G, E*. Nor, on the other hand, is the pattern of behavior simply a result of the judges' attitudes toward the situations in which the criminal defendants were encountered. If that were true, then the ranking of the judges would be the bottom-to-top progression along the vertical axis: *A, E, C, B, D, G, F, I, H*. Clearly, then, the only conclusion is that the judges' votes are a function of the interaction *between AO* and *AS*, and that cumulative scaling is consistent with such an explanation.

Given the four objectives of cumulative scale construction, the ideal result is one in which each case locates in a category scale; the content of each category scale is highly refined; and the reproducibility (*R*) of each scale is 1.00. Practically, however, the following constraints on category refinement exist:

1. The number of nonunanimous cases decided by the Court during a given period. In order to construct reliable category scales, it is necessary that a large portion of the Court's decisions be nonunanimous. To the extent that unanimity characterizes the Court's decisions, the justices cannot be rank ordered because they are in agreement with one another. Thus, from the standpoint of scale construction, the more disagreement among the justices the better.

2. Equality of marginal differences over cases and across category scales. It is desirable that each category scale contain at least one case of each marginal combination between 8 to 1 and 1 to 8. If such a pattern obtains on a given scale, then it should be possible to rank each of the justices distinctively so that no justice is tied with another.

3. Length of individual judicial membership on the Court during a given period. Ideally, the Court should have a common membership during the entire period being analyzed. This ensures that each justice, except for occasional instances of self-disqualification, will participate in all the cases decided.

The construction of refined category scales depends directly upon these three considerations. Maintenance of a longitudinal perspective is especially important. A cross-sectional (term-by-term) analysis simply does not provide enough cases to form refined scales. The Court might decide an average of only two or three transportation regulation or antitrust cases per term, which is too few for constructing a reliable scale. An analysis of several successive terms is much more likely to provide enough cases for construction of refined category scales.

In operationalizing the construct of attitude, the major *AO* and *AS* of each category scale are determined by the particular content of each set of decisions. As mentioned, this is a trial-and-error process in which the major *AO* and *AS* of each category scale are described in terms of the legal and semantic content of the scale. Because accurate estimation of the major *AO* and *AS* of a scale depends upon the content of the cases therein, a given scale's level of generality will vary from the highly specific to the broadly general. Thus, major *AO*'s may be as broad as "criminal defendants" and "taxpayers," or as specific as "aliens" and "debtors." Major *AS*'s range from "federal regulation" to "deportation" (see Appendix to Chapter 7 for a complete listing). It should be emphasized that their content depends directly upon the issues decided by the Court.

A careful reading of the *AO*'s and *AS*'s listed in the Appendix to Chapter 7 reveals that the *AS*'s tend to be more specific than *AO*'s. Consequently, the major *AS*'s load on the specific end of a continuum; major *AO*'s load on the generic end. When the *AO* and *AS* of a given category scale are viewed in conjunction with each other, specificity of content tends to obtain. But even so, the character of the major *AO* and *AS* that our typical category scale generates is not as refined as is ideally desirable. In our scales, there appear to be subsidiary *AO*'s and *AS*'s that cannot readily be tapped. Thus, for example, the "self-incrimination" scale appears to contain four subsets: cases concerning the granting of immunity from prosecution to persons compelled to testify; cases involving incriminating actions that constitute harmless error on the part of police or prosecutors; cases in which there has been disbarment or loss of government employment for refusal to testify; and cases involving the requirement that arresting officers inform those in their custody of their constitutional rights—the so-called Miranda warning cases. Similarly, it would be desirable, in constructing the "rights of unions vis-à-vis business" and the "rights of business vis-à-vis unions" scales, to construct a separate scale for each of the specific rights involved—for example, the right to strike, the right to picket peacefully; the right to representation elections, and the right to discharge or lay off employees. This, however, is not possible either because the cases are too few in number or because there is a lack of rank-order discrimination among the justices. The School Desegregation cases are an example of the latter. Of the nineteen Warren Court school cases in the "desegregation" scale, all but two of those pertaining to schools were unanimously decided.

Our inability to thoroughly refine the content of our scales is unfortunate. It is the price that must be paid by an analyst to analyze data that he cannot generate himself. On the other hand, our data comprise the actual decisions of real decision makers.

We may now summarize our discussion of the operationalization of the construct of attitude. The attitudes explaining the voting of the justices may successfully be tapped to the extent that valid cumulative scales, which are based on the legal and semantic categories into which the Court's decision making may be divided, are formed. Neither the fact that the categories are initially established by means of an intuitive content analysis and then refined by repeated trials to maximize the four objectives of cumulative scale construction just listed, nor the fact that the resulting category scales are less than ideally refined, gainsays the validity of the theory. Validity, for our purposes, is a result of explanatory and predictive power. To repeat, an attitude is operationally defined as a set of cumulatively scaled cases, which are based upon a major *AO* and *AS* as finely drawn as the character and quality of the data permit.

Values

Having operationalized attitude, we now proceed to operationalize value. We previously defined "value" simply as a set of interrelated attitudes. Given this definition, values are structurally and functionally analogous to attitudes, differing from attitudes only in that they (values) are more general.[33] In making values operational, we maintain our emphasis upon the previous definition. Hence, what is needed is a measure of interrelatedness among attitudes.

Such a measure is readily obtained from the rank order of the justices on each scale. Thus, in Figure 4.2, Judge *I*'s votes make him most supportive, and Judge *A* is ranked ninth. The other judges, *B* through *H*, are ranked second through eighth, respectively. What we need is a measure of the similarity of the justices' rank order on a given scale with their rank order on each of the other scales. Several such measures of association have been formulated, all equally precise. For technical reasons, we shall use Kendall's rank correlation coefficient, tau *b*.[34] This coefficient has a range of $+1.00$ to -1.00. If the rank of the justices on one scale were identical to their rank on another, tau *b* would equal $+1.00$. If the rank on one scale were the opposite of the rank on the other, tau *b* would equal -1.00.[35]

The measure of interrelatedness between a pair of category scales is set, albeit somewhat arbitrarily, at tau *b* equal to at least $+.6$. We choose this level because a situation where two ranks of nine justices produce a tau *b* greater than or equal to $+.6$ is likely to occur by chance approximately once in a hundred situations.[36] Conventionally, a relationship that is statistically significant at this level (.01) is more than marginally rigorous. Even so, this operational definition of value is not wholly adequate. As noted, tau *b* measures the relationship between the rank order of the justices on only a *pair* of category scales. And we would certainly hope that the major values motivating Supreme Court decision making would comprise more than two attitudes each. Consequently, we shall be forced to resort to multidimensional techniques of analysis—those that measure the interrelationship among the justices' rank orders on all of our category scales simultaneously, not just between two at a time.

However, it is not uncommon to find that a category scale will, on the one hand, associate with most of the other scales that constitute a value at a level well in excess of $+.6$, while, on the other hand, also associating with some of the scales that constitute the value at a level considerably *below* $+.6$. Thus, we may find ourselves faced with a situation similar to that

Table 4.1

Tau b *Correlations between Hypothetical Pairs of Category Scales*

	A	B	C	D	E
A	—	.40	.90	.85	.70
B	—	—	.45	.95	.90
C	—	—	—	.50	.85
D	—	—	—	—	.55
E	—	—	—	—	—

Note: Average correlation = .71.

shown in Table 4.1. The five scales intercorrelate highly, at +.71. But each scale correlates with at least one of the others at a level below +.6: scale *A* with *B*, *B* with *C*, *C* with *D*, and *D* with *E*. If we discarded each scale that had a correlation of less than +.6, we would have no value whatsoever because each of the scales constituting the value has a correlation with one or two of the other scales that is less than +.6.

Accordingly, it becomes necessary to relax the measure of interrelatedness that must prevail between a pair of scales for that pair to constitute a portion of a value. Instead of focusing upon the interrelatedness between a *pair* of scales, we measure the interrelatedness among *all* the scales constituting a value. If the sum total of all the correlation coefficients between all the pairs of scales that the multidimensional analyses identify as constituting a cluster or dimension averages at least +.6, then a value exists. In Table 4.1 the sum total of the coefficients produces an average correlation of +.71. Hence, those five scales constitute a value.

It is also desirable that each scale that appears to be part of a value show an average and median correlation with the other scales constituting a value of at least +.6. Each of the hypothetical scales in Table 4.1 meets this criterion: scale *E* produces an average correlation of .75 (.70 + .90 + .85 + .55 ÷ 4); scales *A* and *D* produce .71; and scales *B* and *C* produce .68. We impose this additional constraint on the operational definition of value in order to avoid including in a value a scale that correlates only marginally with the other scales that form the value.

Our operational definition of value, then, is a set of category scales (attitudes) in which (1) the sum total of all the correlation coefficients between all the pairs of scales averages (and produces a median of) at least +.6, and in which (2) each category scale has an average and median correlation with the other associated category scales of at least +.6.

Operationally, then, values are dependent upon attitudes. Because they are a combination of several attitudes, values are not necessarily related to any specific attitude object or situation. The differences among the attitudes that constitute the value are *AO* and *AS* differences. Thus, several attitudes that interassociate to form a value may differ as to *AO*, *AS*, or *AO* and *AS*; a value is therefore cognitively more complex than an attitude. For this reason, we assume values to be less subject to change than attitudes.

As previously indicated, both attitudes and values are considered to be relatively enduring. An additional reason for considering the justices' attitudes and values to be stable is the public nature of their decision making. When an individual makes a public choice, he perforce commits himself to consistency to a greater extent than he does when his choice and decisions are private. The decisions of the justices are public in two respects: (1) Their votes are a matter of public record, published by the Government Printing Office and by two private publishers. The communications media, law reviews, and casebooks also disseminate their votes and opinions widely. (2) As noted in Chapter 2, one of the major norms governing judicial decisions is the expectation that the justices will behave consonantly with what has previously been decided—that they will adhere to precedent.

Value Systems

This concludes our discussion of the operationalization of the constructs of attitude and value. The decisions that we will analyze are those made during most of the years of the Warren Court, plus those made by the Burger Court. We expect these decisions to form several dozen cumulative scales, each of which will represent an attitude. These attitudes, in turn, should interrelate or intercorrelate to form a substantially smaller number of values. Each scale will contain the rank order of the justices with regard to the attitude that motivated the justices' votes in the cases constituting the scale. These rank orders can be transformed into scale scores, as we shall explain in Chapter 7. The scale scores, ranging from $+1.00$ to -1.00, are a rough indicator of the extent to which each of the justices supports or opposes the attitude that motivated the justices' votes in the cases constituting that scale. A justice's scale scores become useful when a number of scales intercorrelate to form a value. By averaging a justice's scale scores on each of the scales that constitute a value, we obtain a rough indication of the extent to which each of the justices supports or opposes the value in question.

Rather than describing each justice's support of or opposition to each of the values that explains his behavior, it will be convenient to create a construct that allows us to describe in a word or two a justice's response to *all* the relevant values that explain his decision making. For this purpose, we use the construct *value system*. We define it simply as *the particular configuration, or pattern, of a justice's values.* Consider, for example, a decision maker whose votes are explainable by his response to three values.

Assume that these values are dichotomous—that the decision maker either supports or opposes each of them. His value system, then, must consist of one of eight response patterns: He either supports or opposes all three of the values; he supports two and opposes one; or he supports one and opposes two. The eight possible combinations are mathematically described as 2^3: two choices (support or nonsupport) of each of three separate values $(2 \times 2 \times 2)$. Similarly, if four dichotomous values explain a decision maker's behavior, his value system is one of 2^4, or sixteen, combinations $(2 \times 2 \times 2 \times 2)$. Conceptually, then, a value system is the combination of support or nonsupport of the relevant values that explain a decision maker's votes.

Operationalization of value system follows directly from the conceptual definition. The data to be analyzed are indeed dichotomous. A justice must vote either for or against the party whose case is being reviewed. The scale scores that measure the degree to which a justice supports or opposes a given issue range from $+1.00$ to -1.00. Accordingly, the operational definition of value system is a justice's combination of support (between $+1.00$ and $.00$) or nonsupport (between -1.00 and $.00$) of the values that explain his voting behavior.

Methodology

Because our basic construct is attitude, and because cumulative scale analysis is a useful way to determine the attitudes that explain the justices' votes, we use cumulative scaling as our basic methodological instrument. In order to refine the Court's decisions as much as possible, we employ cumulative scaling in a more rigorous fashion than is customary among researchers.

First, we disregard Guttman's "probably desirable" minimum of "at least ten items [cases]" in each scale.[37] We asserted previously that it is improper to stack the deck in favor of either a large number or a small number of cumulative scales. If a set of cases pertaining to an attitude object and attitude situation produces a sufficient variety of voting alignments so that the justices may be distinctively rank ordered, we do not care that the total number of cases is less than the "probably desirable" minimum of ten. There is nothing sacred about this or any other number. It is quite possible to put together a couple of dozen civil liberties cases, half of which were decided 9 to 0 in favor of the civil liberties claimant, and half of which were decided favorably by a vote in which the same two justices invariably dissented. Our scale would produce only two distinctive rankings, one in which seven justices were tied for first place and the other two justices trailed behind together.

Second, the cases in each scale are themselves ordered unvaryingly from 9 to 0 to 0 to 9. We need not explain either the technique or the rationale for doing this. Interested readers may consult the reference cited.[38]

Third, although an acceptable cumulative scale is conventionally described as one in which the coefficient of reproducibility (R) is at least .90, we use a minimum of .95. Because the voting patterns of the justices in a given scale may be unusually extreme, it is possible that R at worst could be no lower than .85 or .90. To ensure that, in our cumulative scales, R is substantially above the empirically lowest possible point, we use a measure devised for this purpose—the minimal marginal reproducibility (*MMR*). It is described and explained in the reference cited.[39] Suffice it to say that R should be ten or more points higher than the *MMR* of each scale.

Fourth, the inconsistent or nonscale votes in each scale are randomly spread among the justices and cases contained therein. If a case contains more than two nonscale votes, it is likely that such a case belongs in some other scale. Or if as many as one-third of the inconsistent votes are cast by only one justice, it is likely that that justice is responding to an attitude different from that of the other justices.

We are able to refine our cumulative scales to the extent required by these four criteria for a number of interrelated reasons: (1) The Court is small and its membership is stable. Since the end of World War II, the average length of service of the seventeen justices who died, resigned, or retired has been thirteen years. (2) Interaction among the justices is frequent and takes the form of regularly scheduled face-to-face confrontations as well as informal face-to-face and written interactions. (3) The justices possess a superior capacity to generalize and to communicate, evidenced by decisions that are accompanied by extended opinions that are closely reasoned and carefully articulated.

Once category scales that are as refined as possible have been constructed, the rank order of the justices on each scale is correlated with the justices' rank order on every other scale using the tau *b* rank-order correlation described previously. A computer program is available for calculating these correlation coefficients.[40] The coefficients for each and every pair of category scales constitute the input for the multidimensional analyses. These analyses collapse the scales (which represent attitudes) into a small number of factors or clusters (which represent values). To minimize the risk of misinterpretation, we use three separate multidimensional or data reduction techniques of analysis: cluster analysis, metric multidimensional scaling, and factor analysis. These three analytical techniques are employed to determine the values that explain the Court's decision making. Because cluster analysis, metric multidimensional scaling, and factor analysis require a more technical explanation than is of interest to the general reader, such explanation is provided in the Appendix to this chapter.

Summary

In this chapter we presented a detailed explanation of a theory whereby the decisions of the Supreme Court may be explained. The assumptions underlying the theory were specified and the constructs based upon these assumptions were defined and operationalized. Special attention was paid to the constructs of attitude and value, which are basic to the theory. Our basic analytical technique, cumulative scale analysis, was also explained in a detailed, but nontechnical, manner and applied both to the decision making of the Court and to the constructs of attitude and value. The theory presented in this chapter is applied to the various stages of the Court's decision-making process that are the subject of the remaining chapters of this book.

Appendix to Chapter 4

This Appendix presents a short description, as nontechnical as possible, of each of the three multidimensional techniques of analysis used to identify the values that explain the Court's decision making. All three techniques are computer dependent.

Cluster Analysis

According to the theory of Supreme Court decision making as described, beliefs, attitudes, and values are the constructs that are used to explain the votes of the justices. Each of these constructs differs from the other two only in level of generality. Though there are many types of cluster analysis that an analyst may use, we utilize one that is hierarchical in nature in order to ensure compatibility with our definition of belief, attitude, and value.

This clustering method is LAWS and is based on a criterion of *L*argest *A*verage *W*ithin-cluster *S*imilarity.[41] In other words, the existence of a cluster is determined by the average measure of interrelationship possessed by each pair of elements in the cluster. Our "elements" are the rank-order correlation coefficients for each pair of category scales. For an illustration, refer again to Table 4.1. Scales *A*, *C*, and *E* cluster together with an average within-cluster similarity of .817 (.90 + .70 + .85 ÷ 3). If Scale *D* were added, similarity would decline to .725.

The major objectives of LAWS are "to construct sets of successively more inclusive clusters" and "to form these clusters in such a manner that the elements within each cluster are as similar to one another as possible and as dissimilar from all other elements as possible."[42] To achieve these objectives requires: (1) that the data determine the form of the resulting hierarchical clusters; (2) that the interrelationships among pairs of elements not be misrepresented; (3) that arbitrary classification decisions be avoided;

and (4) that the hierarchical structure realistically display the nature of the structure of the interrelationships among the pairs of elements. The LAWS method achieves these objectives by focusing upon within-cluster characteristics as determined by the calculation of average within-cluster similarity. This similarity is measured by the original tau *b* correlation coefficients throughout an analysis.

Nonetheless, no hierarchical clustering method is completely satisfactory. The major weakness of LAWS is that in forming clusters, each element is not considered in relation to all the other elements. Hence, an element may appear in more than one cluster. In short, "the objective of obtaining a realistic mapping of element interrelationships is not entirely compatible with the objective of displaying only the predominant structure of relationships by keeping the number of clusters relatively low," nor is "the objective of keeping within-cluster similarity as high as possible . . . necessarily compatible with keeping within-cluster differentiations as large as possible, given the constraints imposed by the objective of constructing a hierarchy."[43]

Metric Multidimensional Scaling

Supplementing cluster analysis is metric multidimensional scaling, the purpose of which is to fit a set of points, representing data, into the number of dimensions required to reveal the relationships existing among the data points. Metric multidimensional scaling is a data reduction technique that disentangles the complex multiple relationships that cannot be perceived by visually observing a correlation matrix.

The technique we employ operates as follows.[44] Given a symmetric matrix of dissimilarities, (s_{ij}), between objects, find a configuration of points in Euclidean space whose interpoint distances, (d_{ij}), are such that $d_{ij} = s_{ij}$. The "objects" are the correlation coefficients of all the possible pairs of category scales. These coefficients are transformed into a matrix of dissimilarities by means of the formula $d_{ij} = \sqrt{2(1 - r_{ij})}$, where $r_{ij} =$ the correlation coefficient between the rank orders of two category scales. Any given s_{ij} then ranges from .00 (no dissimilarity) to 2.00 (complete dissimilarity). An initial configuration is then generated,[45] after which each point in the configuration is moved successively until one or more of nine goodness-of-fit criteria are met. We do not expect real data to fit perfectly into a space of any dimensionality. Only if real data correspond exactly to a geometric shape, such as a rectangle, cube, or circle, will perfect fit result.

Factor Analysis

There are many types of factor analysis. The one we use, principal axes with varimax rotation, is one of the most popular.[46] The purpose of factor analysis is to reduce the relationships among the variables in a correlation matrix to a small number of categories or "factors." The output of principal axes factor analysis is a set of Euclidean coordinates that represent those variables in the correlation matrix that correspond to each such coordinate or factor. The first coordinate corresponds to the axis that accounts for the largest proportion of the interrelationships. The second coordinate corresponds to the axis accounting for the next-largest proportion of the interrelationships that are orthogonal, or independent, of the first, and so on. The principal axes are then rotated so that each variable in the correlation matrix loads highly (i.e., approaches $+1.00$ or -1.00) on only one axis (factor) and has a loading of approximately .00 on all the other factors. With real data, however, such "simple structure" rarely results. What usually happens is that a variable's highest single loading over several factors is no higher than .50 or .60. The square of this loading specifies the proportion of variance accounted for. In the typical case, only 25 or 36 percent of the variance is explained. A variable will load lower, but rarely .00, on the other factors—typically between .2 and .4. If enough factors are generated, each variable may achieve a highest loading approaching $+1.00$ or -1.00 on one factor and may approximate .00 on all the other factors. But if the number of factors required to achieve this result virtually equals the number of variables in the correlation matrix, the analyst has not reduced his data to proportions that are much more manageable than those of the correlation matrix with which he started.

Notes to Chapter 4

1. For a detailed discussion of the rule structure of Congress and its impact on outcomes, see Lewis A. Froman, Jr., *The Congressional Process: Strategies, Rules, and Procedures* (Boston: Little, Brown, 1967).

2. For a more extensive consideration of this point, see William H. Riker and Peter C. Ordeshook, *An Introduction to Positive Political Theory* (Englewood Cliffs, N.J.: Prentice-Hall, 1973), pp. 97–100, plus the references cited therein.

3. For a general treatment of this point, see Joseph A. Schlesinger, *Ambition and Politics* (Chicago: Rand McNally, 1966).

4. Alpheus T. Mason, "The Chief Justice of the United States: Primus Inter Pares," *Journal of Public Law* 17 (1968): 25.

5. *Ibid.*, p. 24.

6. *Ibid.*, p. 25.

7. During the first 181 years of the Supreme Court's history—that is, until 1969—14 persons were appointed Chief Justice, an average of 1 every 13 years. The first Chief Justice, John Jay, was appointed simultaneously with the original associate justices on September 24, 1789. Jay's successor, John Rutledge, was a recess appointee who presided over only two cases before being rejected by the Senate. If these two are excluded from consideration, the length of service of the average Chief Justice has been 15 years. On the Rutledge appointment, see Charles

Warren, *The Supreme Court in United States History* (Boston: Little, Brown, 1922), 1, 124–139.

8. Noah Swayne, who had been appointed to the Court in 1862, "was extremely desirous of promotion" to the Chief Justiceship upon Taney's death in 1864. *Ibid.*, 3, 123. Harlan Fiske Stone did admit his "candidacy" for the position in 1930 upon the resignation of Chief Justice Taft. Alpheus T. Mason, *Harlan Fiske Stone: Pillar of the Law* (New York: Viking, 1956), pp. 274–282. No evidence has been discovered, however, that either justice altered his personal policy preferences because of ambition for the Chief Justiceship.

9. For a more complete discussion of concepts and constructs, see Fred N. Kerlinger, *Foundations of Behavioral Research* (New York: Holt, Rinehart and Winston, 1965), pp. 4–49.

10. Adapted from Milton Rokeach, "The Nature of Attitudes," in *International Encyclopedia of the Social Sciences*, 1968 ed., 1, 449–457.

11. Marvin E. Shaw and Jack M. Wright, *Scales for the Measurement of Attitudes* (New York: McGraw-Hill, 1967), p. 3.

12. Glendon Schubert, *The Judicial Mind* (Evanston, Ill.: Northwestern University Press, 1965), pp. 228–233; Harold J. Spaeth and David J. Peterson, "The Analysis and Interpretation of Dimensionality: The Case of Civil Liberties Decision Making," *American Journal of Political Science* 15 (Aug. 1971): 415–441.

13. Milton Rokeach, *Beliefs, Attitudes and Values* (San Francisco: Jossey-Bass, 1968), p. 112.

14. Shaw and Wright, *op. cit.*, fn. 11 *supra*, p. 4; and Milton Rokeach, *The Open and Closed Mind* (New York: Basic Books, 1960), pp. 31–53.

15. Rokeach, *op. cit.*, fn. 13 *supra*, p. 113. Italics added.

16. Rokeach, *op. cit.*, fn. 10 *supra*, pp. 450–451.

17. *Ibid.*, p. 453.

18. *Ibid.*, pp. 452–453; Rokeach, *op. cit.*, fn. 13 *supra*, pp. 126–129.

19. Harold J. Spaeth and Douglas R. Parker, "Effects of Attitude toward Situation upon Attitude toward Object," *Journal of Psychology* 73 (1969): 173–182. Also see Milton Rokeach and Peter Kliejunas, "Behavior as a Function of Attitude-toward-Object and Attitude-toward-Situation," *Journal of Personality and Social Psychology* 22 (1972): 194–201.

20. Harold J. Spaeth *et al.*, "Is Justice Blind: An Empirical Investigation of a Normative Ideal," *Law & Society Review* 7 (Fall 1972): 119–137.

21. Louis Guttman, "The Basis for Scalogram Analysis," in S. A. Stouffer *et al.*, eds., *Measurement and Prediction* (Princeton, N.J.: Princeton University Press, 1950), pp. 60–90.

22. *Ibid.*, p. 62.

23. *Ibid.*, p. 77.

24. *Ibid.*, p. 85.

25. Wallace Mendelson, "The Neo-Behavioral Approach to the Judicial Process: A Critique," *American Political Science Review* 57 (1963): 593–603.

26. S. Sidney Ulmer, "The Analysis of Behavior Patterns on the United States Supreme Court," *Journal of Politics* 22 (1960): 648; and "Quantitative Analysis of Judicial Processes: Some Practical and Theoretical Applications," *Law and Contemporary Problems* 28 (1963): 170.

27. Harold J. Spaeth, *The Warren Court* (San Francisco: Chandler, 1966), pp. 18–19.

28. Schubert, *op. cit.*, fn. 12 *supra*, pp. 177–178, 280.

29. *Ibid.*; Harold J. Spaeth, "Unidimensionality and Item Invariance in Judicial Scaling," *Behavioral Science* 10 (1965): 290–304.

30. Guttman, *op. cit.*, fn. 21 *supra*, p. 85.

31. See Spaeth and Peterson, *op. cit.*, fn. 12 *supra*.

32. *Ibid.*, pp. 429–431.

33. This definition of value differs from that of Rokeach. See *op. cit.*, fn. 13 *supra*, pp. 124, 159–161.

34. Maurice G. Kendall, *Rank Correlation Methods*, 2d ed. (New York: Hafner, 1955), pp. 34–48; Sidney Siegel, *Nonparametric Statistics* (New York: McGraw-Hill, 1956), pp. 213–219.

35. For the formula for tau *b* and examples of its calculation, see Siegel, *op. cit.*, fn. 34 *supra*, pp. 213–219.

36. *Ibid.*, pp. 220–222.

37. Guttman, *op. cit.*, fn. 21 *supra*, p. 79.

38. Spaeth, *op. cit.*, fn. 29 *supra*, pp. 299–303.

39. Allen L. Edwards, *Techniques of Attitude Scale Construction* (New York: Appleton-Century-Crofts, 1957), pp. 191–193.

40. John Morris, *Rank Correlation Programs* (East Lansing: Michigan State University Computer Institute for Social Science Research, 1967).

41. Leighton A. Price, *Hierarchical Clustering Based on a Criterion of Largest Average within Cluster Similarity* (East Lansing: Michigan State University Computer Institute for Social Science Research, 1969). The method is computer dependent. See Leighton A. Price, *LAWS*, Technical Report No. 70-1 (East Lansing: Michigan State University Computer Institute for Social Science Research, 1970).

42. *Ibid.*, p. 1.

43. *Ibid.*, p. 17.

44. Scott B. Guthery and Harold J. Spaeth, *DISFIT*, Technical Report No. 72-13 (East Lansing: Michigan State University Computer Institute for Social Science Research, 1971). Although nonmetric multidimensional scaling enjoys considerable popularity, especially in those programs utilizing the monotone criterion, it is not used in this analysis because of its theoretical and empirical shortcomings. See Harold J. Spaeth and Scott B. Guthery, "The Use and Utility of the Monotone Criterion in Multidimensional Scaling," *Multivariate Behavioral Research* 4 (1969): 501–515.

45. Gale Young and A. S. Householder, "Discussion of a Set of Points in Terms of Their Mutual Distances," *Psychometrika* 3 (1938): 19–22.

46. R. J. Rummel, *Applied Factor Analysis* (Evanston, Ill.: Northwestern University Press, 1970), pp. 338–345, 391–393.

5 | *Appointments to the Supreme Court*

> *By far the most important appointments [a President] makes are those to the Supreme Court of the United States. Presidents come and go, but the Supreme Court through its decisions goes on forever.*
>
> President Richard M. Nixon, October 21, 1971[1]

Most Presidents, especially those who have served in the twentieth century, would have agreed with this assessment by President Nixon. The Court, through its powers of constitutional and statutory interpretation, can have a substantial impact on the success of a President's programs. Thus, most Presidents have chosen their nominees with great care.

In this chapter[2] we examine the process by which appointments to the Court are made. Article II, section 2, clause 2 of the Constitution states that the President "shall nominate, and, by and with the Advice and Consent of the Senate, shall appoint . . . Judges of the Supreme Court." The power of appointment is, therefore, shared between the President and the Senate. We will consider the role of each in turn, and we will pay special attention to how the evidence gathered in this consideration bears on the theory of Supreme Court decision making that was presented in the preceding chapter.

The President and Nominations

When a seat on the Supreme Court falls vacant, the President is often bombarded with suggestions of names to fill the vacancy. Few of these suggestions have any impact, however, and most observers believe that the number of individuals and groups that may substantially influence the President's decision can fairly be limited to three: the Attorney General of the United States, members of the Senate, and justices currently sitting on the Court. This is not to say that all of these are important in the choosing of every nominee, but that each has had, from time to time, an important influence on the choice.

The one who is most likely to have an impact is the Attorney General. He is the top legal officer in the government and he is also often a major political adviser. Usually it is the Attorney General's responsibility to draw up a list of potential nominees from which the President will choose. The influence of senators and justices is less frequent, and of course depends upon the willingness of the President to seek or listen to their advice.

There seems to have been but one specific instance of influence by any of these groups during the last forty years—that of Chief Justice Burger, as evidenced by White House transcripts and two letters from Burger to former Attorney General John Mitchell. A close relationship between Mitchell and Burger had developed when Burger was still a judge on the Federal Court of Appeals for the District of Columbia. A similar relationship apparently also existed between Burger and Mitchell's successor, Richard Kleindienst. Burger reportedly was asked to recommend persons for advancement in the lower federal courts as well as to suggest names for the Supreme Court vacancies that occurred upon the resignation of Fortas in 1969 and John Marshall Harlan and Hugo Black in 1970. None of those nominated to the Supreme Court vacancies were persons recommended by Burger. Burger, however, may have indirectly influenced Nixon to nominate G. Harrold Carswell to the Supreme Court. Burger recommended Carswell to Mitchell as being worthy of advancement from the federal district court to the court of appeals in a letter to Mitchell in April 1969. Carswell was appointed to the court of appeals, but the Senate rejected him for the Supreme Court on April 8, 1970.[3]

Before Burger, the last previous instance of the influence of others on the appointment of Supreme Court justices seems to have been Senator Borah's influence on the nomination of Benjamin Cardozo in 1932, which we discuss in the following paragraphs. Earlier in United States history however, there had been a number of other instances.[4]

The factors any given President may take into account in choosing a nominee may be categorized in various ways, but we find most convenient the classification offered by Robert Scigliano.[5] He cites three sets of attributes as being important: representational qualifications, professional qualifications, and doctrinal qualifications.

Representational Qualifications

A Supreme Court nomination is not made in a vacuum. In addition to its potential impact on public policy, it also has implications for the political fortunes of the President and his party. Thus various political and sociological factors may have a bearing on the choice of a nominee.

The most obvious of these is a potential nominee's party affiliation. Of the 100 men who have served as Supreme Court justices from the beginning of the Republic through the confirmation of William Rehnquist in 1971, 90 have been of the same party as the President who first appointed them.[6] Of the 10 who were appointed across party lines, 9 were Democrats. The only Democratic President to appoint a Republican was Truman, who appointed Harold Burton of Ohio in 1946. It appears that the choice of nominees with the same party affiliation is less a means of rewarding party stalwarts (although this consideration is decidedly a factor) than it is a means of assuring a coincidence of views on important issues between the President and his nominee.[7]

Another consideration is geography. Most Presidents have believed that all major regions of the country should be represented on the Court. Geography assumes special importance when the region in question is part of (or is hoped to be made part of) the electoral coalition of the President's party. For example, many observers considered President Nixon's nominations of Clement Haynsworth, G. Harrold Carswell, and Lewis Powell, all Southerners, to be part of his much-discussed "Southern strategy."

In addition, there is a set of attributes, which may be labeled "sociopolitical," that are relevant. Such attributes include religion, ethnicity, and race, and are important because, like geography, they relate to the nature of party coalitions. The overwhelming majority of the justices have been Protestants;[8] Catholics and Jews have been the exception. The first Catholic to be appointed was Chief Justice Taney in 1835, and (except for the period 1949–1956) there has been a member of that faith on the Court from 1898 to the present. From 1898 to 1921, two Catholics, Joseph McKenna and Edward White, served simultaneously. White was the second and last Catholic Chief Justice, having been promoted from associate justice by President Taft in 1910. The nomination of Justice Brennan by President Eisenhower in 1956, a few weeks before the Presidential election, was viewed by some as an attempt to appeal to Catholic voters, most of whose previous voting patterns were Democratic.[9]

The first Jewish appointee was Justice Brandeis in 1916, and there was at least one Jew on the Court from that date until Justice Fortas' resignation in 1969. It is probably significant that all save one[10] of the five Jewish justices were nominated by Democratic Presidents, for the majority of Jews vote Democratic. When the tradition was broken in 1969, a Republican (Nixon) was in the White House. Similarly, the first and only black appointee (Thurgood Marshall, in 1967) was nominated by a Democrat, Lyndon Johnson.

Professional Qualifications

It would be a mistake to think that only political considerations influence the choice of a Supreme Court nominee. Presidents are conscious of their place in history and know that the type of person they nominate for high office will influence history's judgment. Thus, most Presidents have made an effort to ensure that their Court nominees were men of some professional eminence. Indeed, from time to time such considerations have controlled the choice. One example is Benjamin Cardozo, nominated by President

Hoover in 1932. By all the representational criteria we have mentioned, Cardozo was a bad choice. He was a Democrat (and a liberal one at that); he was a Jew (when there was already one Jew, Brandeis, on the Court); and he was from New York (when two sitting justices, Hughes and Stone, were from that state[11]). Cardozo was also, however, recognized as one of the finest judges in the country. (He was, at the time, Chief Judge of New York State's highest court.) Despite the representational problems, Hoover responded to strong pressure from Justice Stone, Republican Senator Borah of Idaho,[12] many members of the bar, and the public, and nominated Cardozo. The nomination was confirmed unanimously the day it reached the Senate.

Although membership in the bar is neither a constitutional nor a statutory requirement, all of the justices appointed since 1789 have been lawyers. In addition, some Presidents have considered previous judicial experience to be a desirable attribute for a nominee. Others have not, however, and many legal scholars and even justices have agreed with the latter view. Justice Frankfurter once wrote:

> One is entitled to say without qualification that the correlation between prior judicial experience and fitness for the Supreme Court is zero. The significance of the greatest among the Justices who had such experience, Holmes and Cardozo, derived not from that judicial experience but from the fact that they were Holmes and Cardozo. They were thinkers, and more particularly, legal philosophers.[13]

Indeed, many of the justices who have generally been regarded as "great" (e.g., Marshall, Story, Taney, Hughes, Warren, Brandeis) did not have previous judicial experience.[14] Such experience can be important, as we shall see, on another ground: it can provide the best possible indication of a justice's personal policy preferences.

Whether or not a nominee had judicial experience, almost all achieved considerable eminence in public service or the legal profession or both. Consider the following brief career sketches of the nine justices sitting at the beginning of the Court's 1973 term:[15]

> *William O. Douglas* (nominated by Roosevelt in 1939). A.B. Whitman College, 1920 (Phi Beta Kappa); LL.B. Columbia University Law School, 1925; taught law at Yale and Columbia; member of the Securities and Exchange Commission, 1936–1939 (chairman 1937–1939).

> *William Brennan* (nominated by Eisenhower in 1956). B.S. Wharton School of Finance and Commerce (University of Pennsylvania), 1928; LL.B. Harvard University Law School, 1931; judge of the New Jersey Superior Court, 1949–1952; judge of the New Jersey Supreme Court, 1952–1956.

> *Potter Stewart* (nominated by Eisenhower in 1959). A.B. Yale, 1937 (Phi Beta Kappa); LL.B. Cambridge University Law School, 1941; member of the City Council and Vice-Mayor, Cincinnati, Ohio; Judge of the U.S. Court of Appeals, 1954–1959.

Byron White (nominated by Kennedy in 1962). A.B. University of Colorado, 1938 (Phi Beta Kappa);[16] Oxford University, 1939 (as a Rhodes Scholar); LL.B. Yale Law School, 1946; Law Clerk to Chief Justice Vinson; deputy U.S. Attorney General, 1961–1962.

Thurgood Marshall (nominated by Johnson in 1967). A.B. Lincoln University, 1930 (with honors); LL.B. Howard University Law School, 1933 (first in class); legal counsel for the NAACP for 25 years; argued 32 cases before the Supreme Court, winning 29 (including *Brown* v. *Board of Education*); Judge of the U.S. Court of Appeals, 1961–1965; Solicitor General of the United States, 1965–1967.

Warren Burger (nominated by Nixon in 1969). LL.B. St. Paul College of Law, 1931 (magna cum laude); Assistant Attorney General of the United States; Judge of the U.S. Court of Appeals, 1954–1969.

Harry Blackmun (nominated by Nixon in 1970). B.A. Harvard University, 1929 (summa cum laude and Phi Beta Kappa); LL.B. Harvard University Law School, 1932; taught law at University of Minnesota Law School; Judge of the U.S. Court of Appeals, 1959–1970.

Lewis Powell (nominated by Nixon in 1971). B.S. Washington and Lee University, 1929 (Phi Beta Kappa); LL.B. Washington and Lee University, 1931; LL.M. Harvard University, 1932; President of the American Bar Association, 1964–1965; President of the American College of Trial Lawyers, 1969–1970.

William Rehnquist (nominated by Nixon in 1971). B.A., M.A. Stanford University, 1948; M.A. Harvard University, 1949; LL.B. Stanford, 1952 (Phi Beta Kappa); Law Clerk to Justice Robert Jackson, 1952–1953; Assistant United States Attorney General, 1969–1971.

Doctrinal Qualifications

In 1906, President Theodore Roosevelt wrote a letter to Senator Henry Cabot Lodge, discussing a potential Supreme Court nominee, in which he said:

> Nothing has been so strongly borne in on me concerning lawyers on the bench as that the nominal politics of the man has nothing to do with his actions on the bench. His *real* politics are all important.[17]

Most, if not all, Presidents have shared this view. They attempt to discern the policy views of potential nominees, and to put on the Court men who are, as Theodore Roosevelt stated (again writing to Senator Lodge), "absolutely sane and sound on the great national policies for which we stand in public life."[18]

More recently, in announcing the Supreme Court nominations of Powell and Rehnquist to the nation, President Nixon said:

> You will recall, I'm sure, that during my campaign for the Presidency, I pledged to nominate to the Supreme Court individuals who shared my judicial philosophy, which is basically a conservative philosophy.[19]

He went on to say that the nominees he was then proposing met this criterion, as did his previous nominees.

Of course, no President is (at least as far as we know) clairvoyant. Many Presidents have had cause to regret at least one of their nominations. At the end of this chapter we examine the question of how often the President has been successful in attempting to choose a nominee who shared his views on important policy questions. At this point, however, we only wish to point out that they *try* to do so. In making their choice, they draw on whatever clues to the views of a potential nominee are discernible. As we have seen, Presidents almost always choose a member of their own political party. In addition, they can examine the public record of the person in question; almost all justices, at the time of their nomination, had substantial records of public service, or were personally known by the President, or both. Of special value in this regard is a nominee's record as a judge. President Eisenhower, after having appointed Earl Warren (who had had no previous judicial experience), and presumably dissatisfied with Warren's liberal decisions, decided to appoint only men with experience on a state supreme court or a lower federal court. In his memoirs, Eisenhower said:

> My thought was that this criterion would ensure that there would then be available to us a record of the decisions for which the prospective candidate had been responsible. These would provide an inkling of his philosophy.[20]

The Senate and Confirmations

Once a President has chosen his nominee, the name is sent to the Senate for consideration and possible confirmation. In the majority of cases decided in this century, nominations of justices have been accepted by the Senate with little debate or opposition. A substantial minority of the decisions, however, were preceded by considerable conflict, and four twentieth-century nominees were not confirmed. An additional twenty failed to be confirmed in the eighteenth and nineteenth centuries—fourteen of them in the thirty years between 1844 and 1874. Three others, though initially rejected, were subsequently renominated and confirmed.

The confirmation process usually begins with hearings before the Senate Judiciary Committee. If the nominee is not controversial, the hearings are generally *pro forma*, offering representatives of the Administration, senators, and members of the public an opportunity to praise the candidate. If, on the other hand, there is substantial opposition to the nominee, the committee hearings become the initial focal point of the conflict, giving actors on both sides of the conflict a chance to make their case. Consider, for instance, the following partial list of witnesses present at the hearings on President Nixon's nomination of G. Harrold Carswell in 1970:[21]

For the Nomination

G. Harrold Carswell
LeRoy Collins, former Democratic governor of Florida
Mark Hulsey, president of the Florida Bar Association
James Moore, professor of law at Yale University

Against the Nomination

Clarence Mitchell, director of the Washington bureau of the NAACP
Thomas Harris, general counsel of the AFL-CIO
Rep. John Conyers (D., Michigan)
Rep. Patsy Mink (D., Hawaii)
Joseph Rauh, representing the Leadership Conference on Civil Rights
Leroy Clark, representing the National Conference of Black Lawyers
Betty Friedan, president of the National Organization of Women
Gary Orfield, professor of political science at Princeton University
William Van Alstyne, professor law at Duke University
John Lowenthal, professor of law at Rutgers University

When hearings are completed, the committee members vote on whether to report the nomination to the full Senate. If the nomination is reported, the Senate debates the nomination and then proceeds to vote on confirmation.[22]

Robert Scigliano's research on the confirmation process[23] indicates that in the course of the nation's history, three factors have had a bearing on the success or failure of Court nominations: partisanship, the timing of appointments, and the threat of senatorial courtesy. Partisanship, in this context, means whether the Senate majority is of the same party as the President. The President has been much more successful when it is (98 of 108 nominations confirmed, or 91 percent) than when it is not (11 of 26 nominations confirmed, or 42 percent).

By "timing of appointments," Scigliano means whether the nomination is made during the first three years of a President's term. If it is not, the President is either a "lame duck" or is on the verge of a re-election campaign. Presidents are in an apparently less powerful position in the latter case and are less successful. Of 100 nominations made during the first three years of a President's term, 87 (87 percent) were confirmed, whereas only 22 of 34 (65 percent) nominations made at other times were confirmed.

Scigliano points out that it is not simply either of these two factors alone, but their occurrence together, which is truly devastating to a nominee's chances. When the Senate was controlled by the opposition party, but the nomination was made during the first three years of a President's term, the nominee has usually been confirmed (7 of 11 confirmed, or 64 percent). When, however, an opposition Senate has received a nomination at another time, the President's nominees have been markedly unsuccessful (only 4 of 15 confirmed, or 27 percent).

The final factor Scigliano considered was the threat of senatorial courtesy. The theory here is that if a certain state seems to be entitled by tradition to the vacant seat, and if the President does not consult his party's senators from the state on the nominee, such nominees should be less successful than they otherwise would be. Scigliano examined seventeen instances where a state had "received at least the two immediately preceding nominations for the seat in question."[24] In eight of these instances the nominee failed to be confirmed. Lack of consultation with the state's senators was not the clear cause in all instances, but Scigliano does document a few cases when it was.[25] We should note, however, that all of these instances occurred before the twentieth century.[26]

In addition to these factors, one other must be considered: the nominee's personal policy preferences, which we found to be so important in the President's selection of a nominee. To analyze this point we selected the four most recent controversial nominations: Abe Fortas (for Chief Justice in 1968), Clement Haynsworth (1969), G. Harrold Carswell (1970), and William Rehnquist (1971).

The first step in our analysis was to construct a scale[27] of the votes in the Senate on these four nominations and then to determine whether a single dimension was present that could be used to explain the voting of senators on the nominations. (The details of the construction of the scale are presented in the Appendix to this chapter.)

We discovered that indeed an acceptable scale could be constructed. The question then presented is: What is the dimension that explains the senators' voting? We hypothesized that if the President selects nominees on the basis of his perception of their personal policy preferences, and if indeed such preferences determine the way a justice will decide cases on the Court (an assumption we discussed in Chapter 4), then this factor should explain Senate voting on contested nominations; that is, the more liberal a senator is, the more likely he should be to support liberal nominees and to oppose conservative ones.

The most widely used measure of the liberalism of members of Congress is the Conservative Coalition support score compiled annually since 1959 by Congressional Quarterly, Inc. We employed this index to classify senators into five categories from liberal to conservative (see the Appendix to this chapter). Then, to test our hypothesis, we related these categories to the scores that we assigned to the senators on our scale of nomination votes. The data are presented in Table 5.1. (A scale score of 4 indicates a perfect liberal[28] voting pattern on the nominations; a score of 0 indicates a perfect conservative pattern.)

The data demonstrate a clear and strong relationship between the liberalism of senators and their voting on Supreme Court nominations. Moreover, if we employ average scale scores of senators in the five categories

Table 5.1

*Liberalism of Senators and Their Votes on Supreme Court Nominations**

	SCALE SCORES					
SENATOR IS	4	3	2	1	0	TOTAL
Liberal	23	3	—	—	—	26
Moderate liberal	7	8	1	—	—	16
Moderate	—	4	1	1	2	8
Moderate conservative	—	1	6	3	5	15
Conservative	—	—	—	2	31	33
Total	30	16	8	6	38	98†

*Cells give the number of senators in each category.

†Only those senators who participated in at least three of the four votes are counted. See the Appendix to this chapter.

and control for the senators' party (see Table 5.2), we see that it is the degree of liberalism of a senator and not his party affiliation which is related to his voting on nominations. Liberal Republican senators are at least as likely to have a liberal voting pattern, and conservative Democrats are at least as likely to have a conservative pattern, as are senators from the other party in the same category.

These results should not be interpreted to mean that the policy views of senators tell the whole story in the matter of contested confirmations. The numbers in the categories demonstrate that neither the liberal senators nor the conservative senators had enough votes to confirm or defeat a nominee. It is the various kinds of moderates who determine the outcome. Presumably, since the views of moderates are less extreme, their perceptions of the policy preferences of nominees are less likely to be of determinative importance; moderates are correspondingly more likely to be moved by other considerations.

This fact can be illustrated by a comparison of the situations of the four nominees we have examined. The basic charge against both Fortas and Haynsworth was that they displayed unethical behavior while they were judges. The charge against Carswell was that he was racially prejudiced (both in private life and when sitting on the bench as a federal judge) and of less than minimal competence.[29] None of these three nominees was confirmed. On the other hand, the opposition to William Rehnquist was based almost entirely on the charge that he was too conservative; on that basis only 27 senators were willing to oppose his confirmation.

Table 5.2

*Liberalism of Senators and Their Votes on Supreme Court Nominations
(Controlling for Party)**

| | PARTY | | |
SENATOR IS	DEMOCRAT	REPUBLICAN	TOTAL
Liberal	3.87	4.00	3.88
	(23)	(3)	(26)
Moderate liberal	3.42	3.25	3.38
	(12)	(4)	(16)
Moderate	1.25	2.50	1.88
	(4)	(4)	(8)
Moderate conservative	1.75	1.18	1.20
	(4)	(11)	(15)
Conservative	0.00	0.10	0.06
	(13)	(20)	(33)
Total	2.54	1.19	1.94
	(56)	(42)	(98)

*The cells give the average scale scores of the senators in each category. (The number of senators in each category is given in parentheses.)

Presidential Success

The final matter we consider in this chapter is how successful Presidents have been in choosing nominees. In other words, have nominees, once confirmed, decided cases in general accord with the policy views of the Chief Executive who chose them?

Because of the ready availability of materials that would permit classification of the general voting patterns of justices, we selected for analysis all justices who were appointed between 1909 and 1971 (i.e., those appointed by Presidents from Taft through Nixon). We assumed that Republican Presidents wanted their appointees to be moderate to conservative, and that Democratic Presidents wanted their appointees to be moderate to liberal. The data on the general voting patterns of these nominees are presented in Table 5.3. (The categorization of justices and the data employed in the process are described in detail in the Appendix to this chapter.)

The data indicate that less than one-fourth of the nominees of both Democratic and Republican Presidents can be said to have generally voted contrary to the appointing President's views (as defined by our assumption). Moreover, the data indicate (see Table 5.4) that Presidents were much

Table 5.3

General Voting Patterns of Justices by Party of Nominating President, 1909–1971

PARTY OF NOMINATING PRESIDENT	GENERAL VOTING PATTERN OF JUSTICES							
	LIBERAL		MODERATE		CONSERVATIVE		TOTAL	
	N	*%*	*N*	*%*	*N*	*%*	*N*	*%*
Democrat	9	45	7	35	4	20	20	100
Republican	5	22	4	17	14	61	23	100
Total	14	33	11	26	18	42	43	101*

*Rounding error.

more likely to be successful in predicting the future voting behavior of a nominee when the nominee had a record of previous judicial experience that would provide a dependable clue to their probable future voting behavior on the Court. When such a record was available, the appointing Presidents made only two "unsuccessful" choices.[30] We should note, moreover, that these two unsuccessful choices were Justices Cardozo and Brennan, both of whom we discussed previously. Both of these nominees were from the opposition party, and both appear to have been selected *despite* their policy views rather than because of them.

These results should not, however, be viewed as conclusive. In the first place, the categorization of justices is general and gross. In addition, Presidents are likely to vary in their concern for the policy views of their nominees, depending on the situation. Robert Scigliano points out that

> those conditions under which Presidents are likely to be most interested in the specific views of their candidates are as follows. Public controversy over important matters, which, as we noted, usually assumes a form in which it may receive judicial treatment, must be at a high level of intensity; the President must have a policy for dealing with these matters; and the Supreme Court's position on the policy must be uncertain, if not hostile.[31]

Each of these conditions is met in the case of President Nixon's nominations to the Court. The "important matters" over which there was "public controversy" was the issue of crime. During 1968 (the year of Nixon's election), the issue of crime and lawlessness was ranked by the American people as either the first or second most important problem facing the nation, according to the Gallup poll.[32] In addition, the President had a policy for dealing with the problem and he viewed the Court's position on this policy as hostile. In his national address, made when he nominated

Table 5.4

*Previous Judicial Experience of Nominees to the Court and Presidential
Success in Predicting Nominees' Voting Behavior Once Confirmed*

	UNSUCCESSFUL		SUCCESSFUL		TOTAL	
APPOINTEE HAD	N	%	N	%	N	%
Previous judicial experience	2	9	21	91	23	100
No previous judicial experience	7	35	13	65	20	100
Total	9	21	34	79	43	100

Powell and Rehnquist, Nixon said:

> As a judicial conservative, I believe some Court decisions have gone too
> far in the past in weakening the peace forces as against the criminal
> forces in our society.
>
> In maintaining—as it must be maintained—the delicate balance be-
> tween the rights of society and defendants accused of crime, I believe
> the peace forces must not be denied the legal tools they need to protect
> the innocent from criminal elements.[33]

Thus we can examine President Nixon's success in choosing nominees
whose policy views agreed with his own by considering their voting record
on criminal procedures issues. We have analyzed the voting of the Court's
members in all such cases[34] from the appointment of Powell and Rehnquist
through the end of the Court's 1973 term (in July 1974). The voting pattern
of the "Nixon bloc" is detailed in Table 5.5. We find that *all* Nixon appointees participating voted against the claims of defendants in over three-
fifths of the criminal procedures cases, and all of the appointees participating voted for defendants' claims in less than one-fourth of the cases. In cases
where the majority of the Court found for defendants' claims, the Nixon
bloc voted with the majority in only slightly more than half of the cases,
and they voted as a group against the majority in almost one case out of
seven. In cases where the outcome was against defendants' claims, the Nixon
bloc voted together with the majority in all but two (or 97 percent) of the
cases. The presence of the four Nixon appointees produced case outcomes
against defendants' claims in about 57 percent of the cases (68 out of 120).

In Table 5.6 the same cases are analyzed from the slightly different
point of view of total votes cast by the Nixon nominees. The Nixon justices
cast almost three-fourths of their votes against defendants' claims. When the
case outcome was in favor of defendants, more than one-third of the votes of
Nixon appointees were against the majority view, and when a majority of

Table 5.5

Voting Patterns of the Nixon Bloc in Criminal Procedures Cases

| | VOTING PATTERN OF THE NIXON BLOC* | | | | | | | |
| CASE OUTCOME | ALL VOTED FOR DEFENDANTS | | ALL VOTED AGAINST DEFENDANTS | | OTHER | | TOTAL | |
	N	%	*N*	%	*N*	%	*N*	%
In favor of defendants	29	56	7	13	16	31	52	100
Against defendants	0	—	66	97	2	3	68	100
Total	29	24	73	61	18	15	120	100

*Of justices participating.

the Court found against the defendants' claims, a phenomenal 99.2 percent of the votes of Nixon's justices were in that direction. On the basis of this analysis, we believe that it is safe to conclude that Richard Nixon was markedly successful in choosing nominees for the United States Supreme Court whose voting behavior, after their confirmation, reflected policy views that were in agreement with his own.

Summary

In this chapter we have considered the process by which appointments to the Supreme Court are made. We first analyzed the factors that affect the President's choice of a nominee. Two sets of factors can be summarized by the terms *representational qualifications* (including such considerations as the potential nominee's party affiliation, regional background, religion, and ethnicity) and *professional qualifications* (including such matters as native ability and, for some Presidents, a record of prior judicial service). An analysis of statements of a number of Presidents, however, indicated that *doctrinal qualifications* are usually of primary importance; that is, Presidents select nominees who they think will decide important policy issues in the direction the President considers correct.

We next considered the confirmation process. We discussed research that indicates that the fate of a nomination depends primarily upon two variables: (1) whether the Senate majority and the President are of the same party, and (2) the point in a President's term at which the nomination is made. In addition, our own analysis of four contested nominations between 1968 and 1971 indicated that a senator's vote on a nomination is largely determined by the degree of coincidence between his own policy views and those of the nominee. The same analysis, however, showed that the actual

Table 5.6
Votes Cast by Nixon Nominees in Criminal Procedures Cases

| | VOTES CAST BY NIXON'S NOMINEES | | | | | |
| | IN FAVOR OF DEFENDANTS | | AGAINST DEFENDANTS | | TOTAL | |
CASE OUTCOME	N	%	N	%	N	%
In favor of defendants	124	66.0	64	34.0	188	100.0
Against defendants	2	0.8	256	99.2	258	100.0
Total	126	28.3	320	71.7	446	100.0

success or failure of a nomination does not depend solely on policy views. In other words, substantial divergence between the policy views of a significant number of senators and the perceived position of the nominee may set the stage for a fight, but this alone is probably not enough to lead to the nominee's defeat.

We examined the success Presidents have had in picking nominees whose policy views, as reflected in their voting behavior after confirmation, approximated their own. Our analysis indicated that (at least since Taft) both Democratic and Republican Presidents have been successful in choosing justices who shared their views in about three-fourths of the appointments. We also found that Presidential success was markedly improved when the nominee had a record of judicial experience that would provide a clue to his views. In addition, an analysis of the voting of the justices appointed by President Nixon in criminal procedures cases showed that he was very successful in his choices on that particular issue.

Finally, we simply wish to note that this analysis of the appointment process lends strong support to the primary assumption about the motivation of Supreme Court justices—that their decisions are a consequence of their personal policy preferences—that we made in the preceding chapter. At least, all of the evidence we have marshaled indicates that the major actors in the appointment process believe this to be true. In the next four chapters, we apply our theory to the four stages of Supreme Court decision making.

Appendix to Chapter 5

Senate Votes on Nominations

The votes analyzed were taken from *Congressional Quarterly Almanac 1968*, Vol. 24 (Washington, D.C.: Congressional Quarterly, 1969), p. 54-S (Fortas), and from the 1969–1971 volumes of *Congressional Roll Call* (also published by Congressional Quarterly): 1969, p. 29-S (Haynsworth); 1970, p. 21-S (Carswell); and 1971, p. 67-S (Rehnquist). Announced stands and pairs by senators were treated as being equivalent to roll call votes.

Any senator who was not recorded on at least three of the four votes was excluded from the analysis. There were 98 senators recorded on at least three of the votes. The order of the votes in the scale was: (1) Haynsworth, (2) Carswell, (3) Fortas, (4) Rehnquist. Votes against the confirmation of Haynsworth, Carswell, or Rehnquist, and a vote in favor of cloture (cutting off debate) on the Fortas nomination were classified as liberal (or +) votes.

In assigning scale scores where there were either nonscale responses or nonparticipations in the scale, we followed these conventions: (1) If there was a nonparticipation that would affect the scale score (e.g., a pattern of $+ + 0 -$, where + is a liberal vote, − is a conservative vote, and 0 is a nonparticipation), we treated the nonparticipation as if it were an actual vote, the nature of which was determined by the majority of other votes cast. (Thus, in the preceding example, the pattern was treated as if it were $+ + + -$, and the score assigned was 3, the last consistent positive vote.) (2) If there was a nonscale response that would affect the scale score (e.g., a pattern of $- + - -$), we assigned the more "moderate" scale score. (In this example, where the score could be either 0 or 2 depending on whether the first or second vote was counted as nonscale, we assigned a score of 2.)

Employing these rules, we found the full set of scale patterns to be as follows:

PATTERN				NUMBER WITH PATTERN	SCALE SCORE
PATTERNS WITH NEITHER NONPARTICIPATIONS NOR NONSCALE RESPONSES					
+	+	+	+	20	4
+	+	+	−	10	3
+	+	−	−	2	2
+	−	−	−	4	1
−	−	−	−	26	0
PATTERNS WITH NONPARTICIPATIONS BUT WITHOUT NONSCALE RESPONSES					
+	+	+	0	6	4
+	+	0	+	3	4
+	+	0	−	4	3
+	+	−	0	1	2
+	−	−	0	1	1
+	−	0	−	1	1
−	−	−	0	4	0
−	−	0	−	6	0

PATTERN	NUMBER WITH PATTERN	SCALE SCORE

PATTERNS WITH NONSCALE RESPONSES		

PATTERN				NUMBER WITH PATTERN	SCALE SCORE
−	+	0	+	1	4
+	−	+	−	2	3
−	+	−	+	1	2
−	+	−	−	2	2
−	+	0	−	1	2
−	+	−	0	1	2
−	−	+	−	2	0

TOTALS					
VOTES	VOTE 1	VOTE 2	VOTE 3	VOTE 4	TOTAL
+	54	52	40	25	171
−	44	46	42	60	192
0	0	0	16	13	29
Total	98	98	98	98	392

The coefficients for this scale are as follows. [Descriptions of the Coefficients of Reproducibility, or R, and of Minimal Marginal Reproducibility, or MMR, appear in the Appendix to Chapter 7. A description of the coefficient of scalability (S) is found in Glendon Schubert, *The Judicial Mind* (Evanston, Ill.: Northwestern University Press, 1965), p. 81.]

$$R = .970$$
$$MMR = .895$$
$$S = .711$$

The conservative coalition support scores employed in the analysis are for the 91st Congress (1969–1971) and were taken from the 1970 edition of *Congressional Roll Call*, p. 39. Since Congressional Quarterly computes the scores on the basis of all votes for which the senator was eligible, rather than only those in which he participated, the scores are biased for members who were often absent. To remove this bias we recomputed the scores by dividing the conservative coalition support score by the sum of the support and opposition scores.

Senators were then assigned to categories based on the recomputed support scores as follows: scores from 0 to 20 = liberal; scores from 21 to 40 = moderate liberal; scores from 41 to 60 = moderate; scores from 61 to 80 = moderate conservative; scores from 81 to 100 = conservative.

Presidential Success

Various sources were used to classify the general voting patterns of justices:

1. For justices appointed by Presidents Eisenhower through Nixon we used the voting patterns in our own scales, which form the basis for the analysis in Chapter 7.

2. For justices appointed by Presidents Truman and Roosevelt we used: Schubert, *The Judicial Mind* (Evanston, Ill.: Northwestern University Press, 1965); Peter G. Renstrom, *The Dimensionality of Decision Making of the 1941–1945 Stone Court: A Computer Dependent Analysis of Supreme Court Behavior* (unpublished Ph.D. Dissertation, Michigan State University, 1972); and C. Herman Pritchett, *The Roosevelt Court* (New York: Macmillan, 1948).

3. For justices appointed by Presidents Harding through Hoover we used the works referred to in (2), where helpful, and Alpheus Thomas Mason, *The Supreme Court from Taft to Warren* (Baton Rouge: Louisiana State University Press, 1958).

4. For justices appointed by Presidents Taft and Wilson we used Donald C. Leavitt, *Attitudes and Ideology on the White Supreme Court, 1910–1920* (unpublished Ph.D. Dissertation, Michigan State University, 1970).

We classified justices appointed by Presidents Eisenhower through Nixon according to their voting record on civil liberties issues; we classified justices appointed by Presidents Taft through Truman according to their voting record on economic issues. The information on prior judicial service was obtained from Henry Abraham, *The Judicial Process*, 2d ed. (New York: Oxford University Press, 1968), pp. 55–56.

The appointing Presidents, the justices, and their classifications are as follows (L = liberal; M = moderate; C = conservative; an asterisk indicates that the justice had prior judicial service):

Taft:	Lurton (C)*; White (C)*; Hughes (L); Van Devanter (C)*; Lamar (C)*; Pitney (M)*.
Wilson:	McReynolds (C); Brandeis (L); Clarke (L)*.
Harding:	Taft (C)*; Sutherland (C); Butler (C); Sanford (C)*.
Coolidge:	Stone (L).
Hoover:	Hughes (M)*; Roberts (M); Cardozo (L)*.
Roosevelt:	Black (L)*; Reed (M); Frankfurter (C); Douglas (L); Murphy (L)*; Stone (M)*; Byrnes (M); Jackson (C); Rutledge (L)*.
Truman:	Burton (C); Vinson (M)*; Clark (M); Minton (M)*.
Eisenhower:	Warren (L); Harlan (C)*; Brennan (L)*; Whittaker (C)*; Stewart (M)*.

Kennedy: White (M); Goldberg (L).

Johnson: Fortas (L); Marshall (L)*.

Nixon: Burger (C)*; Blackmun (C)*; Powell (C); Rehnquist (C).

Notes to Chapter 5

1. *New York Times*, October 22, 1971, p. 24.
2. In addition to specific works cited in the following section, our discussion in this chapter relies heavily upon Robert Scigliano, *The Supreme Court and the Presidency* (New York: Free Press, 1971), pp. 85–160; and Henry Abraham, *The Judicial Process*, 2d ed. (New York: Oxford University Press, 1968), pp. 50–87.
3. The report of Burger's influence is found in John P. MacKenzie, "Crossing the Judicial Line," *Washington Post*, June 13, 1974, p. A22.
4. See Scigliano, *op. cit.*, fn. 2 *supra*, pp. 90–91.
5. *Ibid.*, p. 105 ff.
6. The data on the 98 justices through Harry Blackmun are taken from Scigliano, *op. cit.*, fn. 2 *supra*, p. 111. Of the last two Nixon appointees, Lewis Powell was a Democrat and William Rehnquist was a Republican.
7. Although this is part of the reason. President Theodore Roosevelt had considered Horace Lurton, a Democrat, to fill a Court vacancy in 1906. Roosevelt wrote to Senator Henry Cabot Lodge, assuring Lodge that Lurton was "right" on the major policy questions of interest to the two men. Lodge replied that "he could not 'see why Republicans could not be found who hold these opinions as well as Democrats.'" Lodge instead supported the Republican Attorney General, William Moody, who received the nomination. Abraham, *op. cit.*, fn. 2 *supra*, p. 77.
8. 81 of the 91 Justices through 1957. See John R. Schmidhauser, "The Justices of the Supreme Court: A Collective Portrait," *Midwest Journal of Political Science* 3 (Feb. 1959): 22.
9. Brennan was, in addition to being Catholic, a Democrat.
10. Justice Cardozo, nominated by Hoover in 1932. Cardozo's tenure, 1932–1938, occurred during that of Justice Brandeis, 1916–1939.
11. The importance of geography was recognized when Stone offered to resign so that Cardozo could be appointed. Abraham, *op. cit.*, fn. 2 *supra*, p. 65.
12. Acknowledging the importance of geographic considerations, Borah told Hoover, "Cardozo belongs as much to Idaho as New York." *Ibid.*
13. Felix Frankfurter, "The Supreme Court in the Mirror of Justices," *University of Pennsylvania Law Review* 105 (1957): 781. Of course, it must be remembered that Frankfurter, himself, had no previous judicial experience.
14. Only 58 of the 100 justices had experience, and only 41 had served more than five years. See Scigliano, *op. cit.*, fn. 2 *supra*, p. 108.
15. From *The Supreme Court: Justice and the Law* (Washington, D.C.: Congressional Quarterly, 1973), pp. 62–64.
16. And an All-American football star.
17. Henry Cabot Lodge, *Selections from the Correspondence of Theodore Roosevelt and Henry Cabot Lodge, 1884–1918* (New York: Scribner's, 1925) 2: 228.

18. *Ibid.*, p. 519.

19. *New York Times*, October 22, 1971, p. 24.

20. Dwight D. Eisenhower, *The White House Years: Mandate for Change, 1953–1956* (New York: New American Library, 1965), p. 287.

21. From *Congressional Quarterly Almanac* (Washington, D.C.: Congressional Quarterly, 1971) 26 (1970): 157–158.

22. We should note in passing that Congress had earlier employed another means of checking the President (and, for that matter, the Court) besides rejecting nominees. As we noted in Chapter 3, Congress has the power to determine the size of the Court. Thus, if Congress is generally opposed to the President and does not trust him to make a "good" nomination, they can simply abolish the vacant seat. This was done in 1866. President Andrew Johnson was in the White House and the radical Republicans controlled the Congress. The size of the Supreme Court had been set at ten in 1863 and a vacancy occurred when Justice Catron died in May of 1865. President Johnson nominated Henry Stanberry of Ohio, the Attorney General of the United States and a personal friend. The Senate, instead of considering the nomination, passed a bill reducing the size of the Court to eight members, and the House of Representatives concurred. Later, when the Republican Ulysses Grant became President, the size was again increased to nine, where it has remained to the present day. See Charles Warren, *The Supreme Court in United States History* (Boston: Little, Brown, 1926) 2: 421–423, 501.

23. See Scigliano, *op. cit.*, fn. 2 *supra*, pp. 97–105.

24. *Ibid.*, p. 101. Such nominations were counted only if one or both of the senators from the state in question were of the President's party.

25. See *ibid.*, p. 102.

26. Henry Abraham adds three other considerations to those just mentioned. One is related to the point we will consider next, but the two others we will mention here. The first is the perception of limited ability of the nominee. As instances of this, Abraham cites President Grant's withdrawal of the nomination of George H. Williams in 1873 and the Senate's rejection of Alexander Wolcott, nominated by President Madison in 1811. (This factor also figured heavily in the Senate's rejection of G. Harrold Carswell in 1970.) The other factor is the perceived political unreliability of the nominee. President Grant withdrew the nomination of Caleb Cushing in 1874 after the Senate refused to act on it. Although Cushing claimed at the time to be a Republican, he had had at least four other party labels in the course of his career. See Abraham, *op. cit.*, fn. 2 *supra*, pp. 84–85. To these factors we may also add another, based on the failures of Abe Fortas in 1968 and Clement Haynsworth in 1969: the perception of unethical conduct by the nominee.

27. For a discussion of scaling of votes, see Chapter 4.

28. A perfect liberal pattern would be (if the senator voted every time) voting in support of cloture (ending debate) on the Fortas nomination and voting against confirmation on Haynsworth, Carswell, and Rehnquist. For a more detailed discussion, see the Appendix to this chapter.

29. One senator (who had voted for Haynsworth but against Carswell) said, in an interview with one of the authors: "I took a lot of time with both Haynsworth and Carswell. I think Haynsworth was very badly treated by the Senate, and I think Carswell had no business being a Justice of the Peace, and I voted accordingly."

30. We counted liberal justices appointed by Republican Presidents and conservative justices appointed by Democratic Presidents as "unsuccessful" choices.

31. Scigliano, *op. cit.*, fn. 2 *supra*, p. 117.

32. See Richard M. Scammon and Ben J. Wattenberg, *The Real Majority* (New York: Coward, McCann and Geoghegan, 1970), p. 39.

33. *New York Times*, October 22, 1971, p. 24.

34. Specifically, we selected for analysis any such case that was included in one of the following nineteen scales (the numbers correspond to the scales listed and described in the Appendix to Chapter 7): 1–7, 10–13, 22, 37–42, and 76.

6 | *What Cases for Decision?*

Methods of Access

Simply because an unsuccessful litigant or his attorney, in contesting a lower court decision, loudly proclaims that he will take his case "all the way to the Supreme Court" is no guarantee that the Supreme Court will hear the case. As explained in Chapter 3, the Court has complete control over its dockets. Consequently, no one actually has a right to have his case heard and decided by the Supreme Court.

Writs of Appeal

Theoretically, when a case is brought to the Court by means of a writ of appeal (as opposed to a writ of certiorari or by means of certification), the appellant is legally entitled to have his case reviewed by the Court. Such a "right" exists in the following situations:

1. Where the highest court of a state having subject matter jurisdiction over the controversy declares a federal law or treaty to be unconstitutional, or where such a state court upholds a state law or a state constitutional provision against the challenge that it violates a federal law, treaty, or constitutional provision.

2. Where a federal court of appeals declares a state's law or constitutional provision to be unconstitutional; or where a federal court of appeals, in a case to which the United States is party, declares a federal law to be unconstitutional.

3. Where a federal district court declares a federal law unconstitutional in a case to which the United States is party; or where the United

States is party to a civil suit brought in a federal district court under the federal antitrust, interstate commerce, or communication laws; or where a special three-judge federal district court has granted or denied an injunction in a proceeding that such a court is required to hear.

4. Where any federal court in a civil proceeding to which the United States is party declares a federal law unconstitutional.

The right to Supreme Court review in the foregoing situations, though statutorily guaranteed, does not necessarily exist because the Court remains capable of exercising discretion even over these sorts of cases. This it does by denying review "for want of a substantial federal question," "for want of jurisdiction," or for reasons stated in equivalent phraseology. What the Court means by these phrases is not spelled out, nor does the Court attempt to explain why a given case lacks a substantial federal question or why jurisdiction is found wanting. All that may be inferred is that fewer than four justices considered the case of sufficient importance to warrant the Supreme Court's attention; or, alternatively, that the case was a "hot potato" that ought to be avoided rather than handled.

From the standpoint of the appellant—the party appealing to the Supreme Court—several distinguishable outcomes may occur. The most important of these are listed in Table 6.1.

The outcome most favorable to the appellant is to have the decision of the lower court "reversed." Such an outcome rarely happens. (It happened only twice in the 876 appeals handled by the Supreme Court during the 1971–1973 terms.) But when it does, the appellant has won his case without the necessity of undergoing oral argument. A somewhat less favorable outcome for the appellant is that of "judgment vacated and case remanded." This means that the judgment of the court whose decision is appealed is returned to that court "for further consideration in light of" some specified decision of the Supreme Court. Approximately one out of every ten appeals is disposed of in this fashion. This outcome does not assure victory for the appellant, but the odds are heavily in his favor. He will lose only if the lower court, in subsequent proceedings, rules that his case is not covered by the specified Supreme Court decision. The remaining favorable outcome for the appellant—to have "probable jurisdiction noted"—is the most common. This means that the Court has accepted his appeal, will schedule oral argument, and in all likelihood will decide the merits of his case. But by no means does this disposition assure the appellant victory. The Supreme Court may well affirm the decision of the lower court that the appellant is appealing. In 1960, Justice Douglas observed that the Court notes probable jurisdiction of only about 15 percent of its writs of appeal.[1] The data in Table 6.1 also show that about 15 percent of the appeals have "probable jurisdiction noted." Presumably, then, 15 percent is a fairly constant proportion.

Table 6.1

Disposition of Appeals, 1971–1973 Terms

	TERM							
	1971		1972		1973		TOTAL	
OUTCOME	*N*	%	*N*	%	*N*	%	*N*	%
Reversed	1	<1	1	<1	0	0	2	<1
Judgment vacated and case remanded	19	8.1	49	14.1	24	8.2	92	10.5
Probable jurisdiction noted*	38	16.2	46	13.2	53	18.1	137	15.6
Subtotal (favorable outcomes)	58	24.7	96	27.6	77	26.3	231	26.4
Affirmed	56	23.8	100	28.7	61	20.8	217	24.8
Dismissed for want of a substantial federal question	53	22.6	87	25.0	89	30.4	229	26.1
Dismissed for want of jurisdiction	47	20.0	54	15.5	60	20.5	161	18.4
Dismissed on other bases†	21	8.9	11	3.2	6	2.0	38	4.3
Subtotal (unfavorable outcomes)	177	75.3	252	72.4	216	73.7	645	73.6
Total	235	100.0	348	100.0	293	100.0	876	100.0

*Includes "question of jurisdiction postponed to the hearing of the case on the merits." Two such dispositions occurred in the 1972 term, six in 1973.

†"Dismissed for want of a properly presented federal question"; "vacated and dismissed"; "dismissed"; "dismissed under Rule 60"; "dismissed for failure to docket case within time prescribed"; "dismissed as moot"; "dismissed for want of final judgment"; "dismissed for want of an appealable order."

All the other outcomes listed in Table 6.1 are unfavorable to the appellant. The lower court's decision may be summarily affirmed, or the appeal may be dismissed on any of a number of bases, the most common of which are dismissals "for want of a substantial federal question" or "for want of jurisdiction." The Court has never defined either of these phrases. As we noted earlier in this chapter, all that may be concluded from any dismissal of an appeal is that fewer than four of the justices considered the case sufficiently important to warrant the Court's attention. Approximately half of all appeals are "dismissed" on some basis or other; an additional quarter result in the lower court's decision being "affirmed."

In summary, then, the chances are three to one that an appellant will be denied relief. Of the 25 percent who gain access, two out of five will have the lower court's judgment vacated. The remainder will have their cases heard on their merits by the Supreme Court.

Writs of Certiorari

But what of those who perforce must seek access by means of a writ of certiorari? Those who have appeal available to them are the fortunate few. For the many, the only avenue is the writ of certiorari, and over this pathway the Court has formal as well as actual control. In the Judges Bill of 1925, Congress authorized an enlarged certiorari jurisdiction for the Court in which the votes of four of the nine justices (the votes of three if only seven justices are participating) are needed to advance the case for formal hearing and a decision on the merits.[2] Before passage of the Judges Bill, the Court had no discretion over some 80 percent of the cases that were docketed with it. These the Court had to hear and decide even though they were cases with an interest to and an impact upon none but the parties to the cases themselves.

How, then, do those seeking a writ of certiorari fare? Until the beginning of the Burger Court in the fall of 1969, the summary of the term printed in one of the privately published editions of the Supreme Court reports included a breakdown of the dispostion of writs of certiorari. For the last three terms of the Warren Court (1966, 1967, 1968) these data are as follows.[3]

On the Court's main docket (the Appellate Docket), certiorari was granted in 13.1 percent of the requests during the 1966 term, 17.0 percent in 1967, and 10.3 percent in 1968. The total for the three terms was 388 out of 2884 requests (13.5 percent). Of this total of 388, 246 (63.4 percent) were set for argument and the remaining 142 were summarily affirmed, reversed, or vacated.[4]

The other docket on which petitions for writ of certiorari are placed is the Miscellaneous Docket. Here are located the petitions of those proceeding *in forma pauperis*—persons, usually convicts, who are unable to bear the financial costs required to have their petitions placed on the Appellate Docket. Of these, 3.9 percent were granted in 1966, 5.9 percent in 1967, and 3.7 percent in 1968. The three-term total is 202 petitions granted out of a total of 4311 (4.7 percent). Of the 202 Miscellaneous Docket applications granted, 63 (31.2 percent) were set for oral argument and thereby transferred to the Appellate Docket, and the remaining 139 were summarily affirmed, reversed, or vacated.

Approximately 15 percent of the cases appealed to the Supreme Court are accepted for review, whereas only about 7.5 percent of certiorari petitions are accepted for review. The proportion of certiorari petitions on the Appellate Docket that are accepted is almost as high as the proportion of appeals that are accepted (13.5 percent as opposed to 14–15 percent). Miscellaneous Docket certiorari petitions are granted only one-third as frequently (about 4.5 percent of the time) as are certiorari petitions on the Appellate Docket.

Having established the proportion, albeit roughly, of those who secure access to the Supreme Court, we now turn to the types of issues and litigants most likely to be considered by the Court.

Criteria for Access

First, let us note the criteria that the Court itself has specified for access to its decision-making capabilities. With regard to certiorari, Rule 19 of the Rules of the Supreme Court of the United States reads:

> 1. A review on writ of certiorari is not a matter of right, but of sound judicial discretion, and will be granted only where there are special and important reasons therefor. The following, while neither controlling nor fully measuring the court's discretion, indicate the character of reasons which will be considered:
>
> (a) Where a state court has decided a federal question of substance not theretofore determined by this court, or has decided it in a way probably not in accord with applicable decisions of this court.
>
> (b) Where a court of appeals has rendered a decision in conflict with the decision of another court of appeals on the same matter; or has decided an important state or territorial question in a way in conflict with applicable state or territorial law; or has decided an important question of federal law which has not been, but should be, settled by this court; or has decided a federal question in a way in conflict with applicable decisions of this court; or has so far departed from the accepted and usual course of judicial proceedings, or so far sanctioned such a departure by a lower court, as to call for an exercise of this court's power of supervision.
>
> 2. The same general considerations outlined above will control in respect of petitions for writs of certiorari to review judgments of the Court of Claims, of the Court of Customs and Patent Appeals, or of any other court whose determinations are by law reviewable on writ of certiorari.[5]

As is typical of judicial guidelines, the criteria specified in this rule are nebulous. The only criterion that is clear is that pertaining to conflicting decisions on the same matter by a pair of federal courts of appeals. Rule 15 cf the Supreme Court, which governs jurisdiction on appeal, is similarly nebulous:

> If the appeal is from a state court, there shall be included a presentation of the grounds upon which it is contended that the federal questions are substantial . . . and shall include the reasons why the questions presented are so substantial as to require plenary consideration. . . .[6]

Consequently, the Court's own criteria leave discretion to the justices themselves. Upon whom this discretion is favorably exercised is the question now before us.

Which Cases Are Reviewed?

When a petition for certiorari arrives at the Supreme Court, it is initially placed on the Miscellaneous Docket. Such petitions do not immediately come to the justices' attention but are first screened by the Clerk of the Court. If he deems any certiorari petition to be "frivolous"—unworthy of consideration by the Court—he so informs the Chief Justice. The Chief Justice, in turn, has his staff of clerks prepare a brief digest of the case. Once this has been done, and if the Chief Justice agrees that the petitions are frivolous, the digest of these "deadlisted" cases is distributed to the justices for their information. Unless at least one of the justices so requests, the petition is not discussed in the justices' conference. Absent such a request, automatic denial results.[7]

The fact that a justice sometimes does request a petition to be removed from the deadlist does not guarantee that the Court will grant the petition for certiorari. For this to happen requires the vote of four of the justices, or three if the Court has fewer than eight members. This is the "Rule of Four," informally adopted by the Court as a result of the expanded control that Congress gave the Court in the Judges Bill of 1925.

Deadlisting appears to be the outcome of most petitions to the Supreme Court. Professor Sidney Ulmer reports that 53.4 percent of all certiorari petitions were deadlisted in the decade from 1947 to 1956.[8] The current scope of deadlisting as reported by Warren Weaver, the Supreme Court correspondent of the *New York Times*, from a speech of Justice Brennan is that the justices "discuss in their weekly closed conferences only about 1100 cases a year out of the 3500 to 4000 that are filed seeking review."[9] This seems to indicate an increase in the percentage of cases deadlisted, from the 53.4 percent between the mid-1940s and the mid-1950s to somewhere between 68.5 percent and 72.5 percent currently. The *New York Times* report, however, does not specifically state that this higher proportion is restricted to certiorari petitions. Hence, we may assume that the higher proportion may include deadlisted writs of appeals. In any event, deadlisting is the means whereby the majority of petitions for review are disposed of.

One way to ascertain whose cases escape deadlisting and overcome as well the hurdle imposed by the Rule of Four is to refer to the distribution of cases in the category scales that account for more than 96 percent of the cases decided by the Warren Court. As might be expected, the decisions constituting the typical category scale are relatively evenly distributed over the last eleven terms of the Warren Court. Thus, for example, antitrust decisions ranged from a low of 2 in 1964 to a high of 10 in both 1965 and 1966. Similarly, First Amendment freedom cases ranged from 1 in 1962 and 1967 to 4 in 1960. Scale categories with a small number of decisions follow the same pattern. No securities regulation decisions were handed down in four years, but 2 were decided in both 1959 and 1963.

On the other hand, a number of issues show a definite cyclical pattern. Cases involving the armed forces, for example, peaked in 1968 and 1969 with 6 decisions each year. The Vietnamese war had resulted in a reassessment of selective service procedures; in addition, the status of conscientious objectors produced considerable litigation. Reapportionment produced no decisions until 1962, peaked with 24 decisions in 1964, and then dropped off to 7, 6, and 9 in the next three years. In 1969, 23 bugging cases were decided, compared with only 12 between 1958 and 1968. Poverty law was another late arrival as a Supreme Court issue; 12 of 15 such cases were decided in 1968–1969. Legislative investigations, on the other hand, peaked early in the period under analysis; 23 of 29 such decisions were handed down between 1959 and 1962. This was undoubtedly due to the legacy of McCarthyism and the Red Scare of the middle and late 1950s. Finally, cases that concerned sit-in demonstrations peaked in the mid-1960s; 25 of 31 such decisions were reached in 1963–1965, but there have been none at all since 1966.

These data, then, suggest that the Court is responsive to new issues that come to a head, but that it also resolves issues that have something of a timeless character about them—for example, antitrust regulation. But what these data do not tell us is what proportion of cases dealing with the various category-scale issues the Court agreed to decide. The Court could have accepted for decision every antitrust case brought to it between 1958 and 1966, but such a result is most improbable. A more likely possibility is that many antitrust cases, in addition to the 73 it decided during this period, were denied review. Short of a careful, petition-by-petition analysis of the issues contained in each of the 3500 to 4000 petitions docketed with the court in a typical term, the question is unanswerable. Such a study could only be conducted in house—by the justices themselves or by their clerks.

Cue Theory

Some researchers, however, have attempted to discover whether there are some general indicators of the types of cases the Court will agree to review. They have termed their view of the process "cue theory." Until now their substantive examination has been limited to writs of certiorari, that is, it has excluded writs of appeal.

The assumptions underlying cue theory are essentially three in number. First, the criteria that the Court itself has specified for access to its decision-making capabilities (Rule 19 of the Supreme Court's Rules) provide no clear-cut guidelines. Second, the number of petitions is sufficiently large that the justices can give no more than cursory attention to most of these requests. Third, a substantial share of these petitions are so frivolous as to merit no serious attention.[10] These assumptions lead to the hypotheses that there exists some method for separating the wheat from the chaff, and that this method consists of a set of readily identifiable cues that signal that a petition deserves scrutiny. Absent such cues, the petition could safely be dismissed. Petitions containing cues could be studied "to determine which should be denied because of jurisdictional defects, inadequacies in the records, lack of ripeness, tactical inadvisability, etc., and which should be allotted some of the limited time available for oral argument, research, and the preparation of full opinions. Those remaining could then be disposed of by denying certiorari or by granting it and summarily affirming or reversing the court below."[11]

Tanenhaus and colleagues selected every fifth certiorari petition for the 1947–1951, 1953–1955, and 1957–1958 terms, and every petition for the 1952 and 1956 terms. These data were used to test the following hypothesis: When a petition contains only one of the four cues, the likelihood of certiorari being granted is greater to a statistically significant degree (probability less than .01) than when that particular cue is absent. The four cues tested were: petitions in which the federal government seeks review; those seeking review of a decision in which lower-court judges were divided; those in which a civil liberties issue was present; and those concerning an economic issue. The authors found that petitions containing all but the last of these cues were indeed granted to a statistically significant degree. The percentages of each type of petition that was granted were as follows: 47.1 percent of federal government certiorari petitions, 32.9 percent of those pertaining to a civil liberties issue, 12.8 percent of those in which the lower court was divided, and only 8.5 percent of those concerning an economic issue.[12]

Where the cues are found in combination, Tanenhaus theorizes that 80 percent of the petitions will be granted if all three of the statistically significant cues are present, 70 percent and 56 percent, respectively, will be granted where the federal government seeks review of a civil liberty decision or a decision involving lower-court division, and 43 percent of petitions involving a lower court divided over a civil liberty issue will be granted. Conversely, where none of the cues are present, only 7 percent of the petitions should be granted.[13]

In an effort to replicate the Tanenhaus study, Sidney Ulmer analyzed all the certiorari petitions that were not deadlisted during the 1955 term.[14] This term was one of those from which Tanenhaus had selected every fifth petition regardless of whether they were deadlisted. Ulmer found that only cases in which the federal government was the petitioning party proved to be statistically significant; lower-court dissension and civil liberty cases were not. In the 1955 term the Court granted 66 percent of the nondead-listed petitions in which the federal government was the petitioning party; only 29 percent of the petitions involving lower-court disagreement and 33 percent of the civil liberty petitions were granted.

Cue theory, then, appears to substantiate the hypothesis that a federal government petition for review of a lower-court decision is likely to be granted. The other cues tested produced either mixed or negative results. The willingness of the Court to allow the federal government access is not surprising. Tanenhaus notes that a special relationship exists between the Solicitor General's office and the Supreme Court.[15] As the federal government's attorneys, the Solicitor General's staff is mindful of the time constraints under which the Court labors. Consequently, they exercise restraint in petitioning for Supreme Court review of cases in which the federal government is party. Only those cases that concern a major public policy issue are placed before the Court. Because the Solicitor General requests review only of those government cases which he deems are important to the Court, the Court in turn, grants most such requests. This relationship between the Court and the Solicitor General is especially effective because, with few exceptions, no federal agency can take a case to the Supreme Court without the Solicitor General's authorization.[16] The members of the Solicitor General's staff also have the skills, resources, and experience to present persuasive arguments to the Court. Nor are they under pressure to seek Supreme Court review solely to satisfy a client or to gain the prestige of arguing a case before the nation's highest court.

One other basis on which the Court appears to grant review with a high degree of regularity is conflicting decisions on the same issue by two or more federal courts of appeals. This "conflict in circuits" may not invariably produce Supreme Court review, "but there is no question but that a clear conflict in circuits usually leads to a grant of the writ. In fact, universal recognition of the importance of this ground for access to the Court is reflected in the heroic efforts of skilled lawyers to work in some sort of conflict angle, however tenuous."[17]

This discussion of the question of which cases the Court accepts for decision has produced a less than specific answer. The most unequivocal answer is that the Court accepts all cases that four of the justices wish to decide. But though unequivocal, this answer is less than satisfactory. Empirical analyses have revealed that the Court is especially likely to decide cases in which two courts of appeals are in conflict about the meaning of a provision of the Constitution or an act of Congress. Also likely to receive Supreme Court decision are cases that the federal government has lost in the lower courts and that the Solicitor General requests the Supreme Court to decide. This is as far as empirical analysis has taken us. Beyond this point, the water is muddy.

Access Limited to Major Policy Issues

It is our judgment, however, that the Supreme Court has primarily responded, and is continuing to respond, to its perception of what are the
major public policy issues confronting American society.[18] In other words,
the Court acts compatibly with its own published criteria, nebulous though
these be, that govern the issuance of a writ of certiorari or appeal. We think
it fair to state that neither the Warren nor Burger Courts, at least, have
defaulted on their decision-making responsibilities. This is not to say that
the Court has responded to all major policy questions with alacrity or
that every case bearing on a major policy question has received the Court's
attention. What we do note is the *absence* of much public criticism of the
Court for refusing to decide major policy issues that have been brought to
its attention. Even in the absence of any public criticism for refusing to
decide this or that issue, there may nevertheless be policy questions that
the Court has not addressed. If so, the probable reason is that they have
not properly come to the Court's attention. Like all other courts, the Supreme Court cannot initiate litigation; it can only respond to cases properly
presented to it that lie within its jurisdiction. Hence, if a case is outside the
subject matter jurisdiction of the federal courts, or if it concerns an issue
that the lower courts have not had an opportunity to pass upon, the Court
will not resolve it.

Apart from issues improperly brought to the Court's attention, there
are those which the Court simply refuses to hear without explanation. A
recent example was the constitutionality of the Vietnam war. The Constitution gives Congress the power to declare war. In the absence of any
such declaration, may the President, in his role as commander in chief of
the armed forces, commit American troops to battle? The Court has had
several opportunities to answer this question; on each occasion it has refused to do so. Is refusal to decide a properly presented issue evidence
that the Court has abrogated its policy-making responsibility? Not at all.
A majority may simply believe that the lower courts have resolved the
issue in a satisfactory fashion and that it is inappropriate or unnecessary
for the Court to concern itself with the matter; or, alternatively, that discretion is the better part of valor—that it is sometimes unwise to resolve
all aspects of an issue in a short time span. Hence the Court's refusal to
decide the constitutionality of state laws prohibiting interracial marriage
or cohabitation until 1967, thirteen years after *Brown* v. *Board of Education*.

Although the Court's refusal to issue a decision in a case properly
before it does not necessarily mean that the Court agrees with the lower
court's disposition of the matter, the lower court's decision does stand as
the law of that part of the land over which the lower court has geographic
jurisdiction. And if there is no conflict among the decisions of lower courts

on a given issue, why is it necessary for the Supreme Court also to pass judgment upon the issue? A formal Supreme Court pronouncement would be more authoritative, of course. But the federal appeals and district courts and the various state supreme courts are not bereft of authority. Hence, given the facts that the Supreme Court's time is limited, that certain issues have a higher priority than others, and that the time may not be ripe for a given decision, it is reasonable for the Court to allow an occasional issue to be resolved by a forum other than its own.

If, then, in exercising its discretion, the Court does not abrogate its policy-making responsibilities by refusing to decide an occasional issue, nor does it shirk its responsibilities because it refuses to decide every properly presented case that pertains to a given public policy issue. Once the Court has enunciated its policy on some issue, it need not—and indeed it does not—respond to every subsequent plea bearing on the same issue. In cases where the lower courts are implementing the Court's policy, it would be silly for the Court to become an echo chamber, reiterating the same decision on the same issue over and over again. But if there be confusion among the lower courts because of lack of clarity in the Court's opinion, or if policy ramifications not covered by the Court's earlier opinions arise, then the Court may be expected to speak again.

For example, many questions were raised concerning the "with all deliberate speed" formula of *Brown* v. *Board of Education* with respect to the desegregation of public facilities. Was the formula to apply equally to different types of public facilities—schools, transportation, accommodations, recreational facilities? When would the period envisioned by the formula expire? It was obvious that the Court would have to answer these and related questions. This the Court did, but not knowing the ramifications of the Brown decision and the extent to which there might be resistance to it, the Court proceeded to treat the desegregation issue as the problems related to it arose rather than by attempting to guess which policy would resolve the matter in a single decision—assuming that the issue were resolvable with one sweep of the Court's policy-making pen.

The issue of obscenity provides another example. In *Miller* v. *California*,[19] Justice White joined with the Nixon appointees to form a conservative majority that halted the liberal tide of previous decisions. The Court ruled that the "community standards" that were determinative of whether material was obscene were not "national standards" but rather were more localized in nature. How localized they might be was not specified. The litigation and legislation to which this decision immediately gave rise will doubtless require some definition of "community standards," as well as further specification of other aspects of the Miller decision.

When the Court decides a case, technically only the parties to the litigation are bound by the Court's decision. In reality, however, all others similarly situated are also bound thereby. By virtue of the opinions that they express, the Court's decisions have applicability far beyond the parties involved in the cases that the Court agrees to decide. The opinion of the Court incorporates the broad constitutional and legal principles that govern its decisions, that guide and bind the lower courts in their subsequent decisions, and that serve as precedents for the resolution of future controversies.

Hence, direct access to the Court is not necessary for an issue to be resolved. Undoubtedly, a very large proportion of the Court's petitions concern a matter that the Court has adequately resolved. Unless the Court is disposed to alter, qualify, or reverse its previous policies, there is no need, as previously noted, for the Court to function as an echo chamber. Thus, although hope may spring eternally from unsuccessful litigants' breasts, it cannot be the function of the Court to realize such hopes. Where a substantial federal question has been implemented by the lower courts compatibly with Supreme Court mandates, a probability of access is all but nonexistent unless the Court desires a policy change.

Does this tightly restricted access to the Court not disadvantage the little person who seeks Supreme Court review? Not necessarily. There have been notable instances in which persons totally bereft of status and influence have not only secured access, but won their cases as well. Two of the more celebrated occurred in the early 1960s. In 1960, a handyman with a history of arrests for vagrancy appealed two $10 fines imposed by the Police Court in Louisville, Kentucky, for disorderly conduct and loitering. Because Kentucky law made no provision for state court appeal of a fine below $20, the case was taken directly to the Supreme Court. In a unanimous decision, the conviction was reversed; the Court ruled that it is a violation of due process of law to convict a person without evidence.[20] In 1962, a petty thief addressed a penciled petition to the Supreme Court requesting reversal of his breaking and entering conviction because he was not represented by counsel. In a decision that also was unanimous, the Court held that the states must provide counsel for all poor persons facing serious criminal charges.[21]

The Proposed Sub-Supreme Court

We have shown that only a small proportion of the petitions for Supreme Court review are granted, but that even so the Court arguably does address itself—sooner or later—to all properly presented issues that at least four of the justices deem significant. One question still remains. Should the Court exercise such discretion over its docket itself, or is it preferable that this task be performed by some other decision-making body? We consider the question of whether Supreme Court review should be a matter of right to be closed. The Judges Bill of 1925 answered that question negatively, and it is not now seriously proposed that every petition be accorded Supreme Court review.

But the question of whether the Court itself should screen its petitions has been the subject of significant national debate, precipitated by the report of a panel of noted legal authorities appointed by Chief Justice Burger in December 1972.[22] The panel, composed of four law professors and three lawyers, proposed the establishment of a new, seven-member court that would screen all petitions sent to the Supreme Court. The rationale behind this proposal is that the steady increase in the number of petitions brought to the Court has placed an excessive burden on the justices' time and energy. Between 1953, the first year of the Warren Court, and the 1972 term, petitions seeking Supreme Court review of lower-court decisions increased 350 percent—from approximately 1300 to 4500.

The petitions that the proposed sub-Supreme Court deemed most important would be sent to the Supreme Court for a formal hearing and decision. Those involving less important issues that had produced a conflict between two or more of the federal courts of appeals would be decided by the new court itself; all other petitions would simply be denied and thus would not reach the Supreme Court.

The new court would be staffed on a rotating, staggered three-year-term basis by seven judges from the eleven federal courts of appeals. No chief judge nor any judge with less than five years' service on a federal court of appeals would be eligible. Nor could any court of appeals have more than one representative on the sub-Supreme Court at any given time.

If Congress were to establish this proposed court, no longer would access to the Supreme Court be available to all who desired it; nor could the justices be sure that they were exposed to all issues raised and litigated in the lower courts. Nonetheless, Chief Justice Burger and a number of legal authorities, in addition to those who proposed the new court, support the proposal.

As noted, the chief justification for the proposal is that the steadily increasing number of petitions is overworking the Court. Related hereto is the argument of the panel that proposed the new court:

> The task of decision must clearly be a process, not an event, a process at the opposite pole from the "processing" of cases in a high-speed, high-volume enterprise. The indispensable condition for the discharge of the Court's responsibility is adequate time and ease of mind for research, reflection and consultation in reaching a judgment, for critical review by colleagues when a draft opinion is prepared, and for clarification and revision in light of all that has gone before.[23]

Opponents of the sub-Supreme Court scheme maintain that the Court is not overworked. Former Justice Goldberg and Chief Justice Warren deny that such is the situation.[24] Justices Stewart and Douglas agree. The former stated that "the very heavy caseload is neither intolerable nor impossible to handle."[25] Douglas has said that "it's about a four-day-a-week job."[26] Justices Powell and Rehnquist support the plan. Powell stated, "As a new member of the court . . . I can say without qualification that I find the situation disquieting."[27] Rehnquist declared that "periodic changes of this general nature are absolutely essential to its [the Court's] continued vitality. . . ."[28]

There is evidence that the Court is not overworked. First, the Court annually gives itself a solid three-month vacation, a period considerably longer than that taken by congressmen, officials in the executive branch, or judges on other courts—state or federal. Second, not only is the Supreme Court formally deciding as many cases as it did fifteen or more years ago, it also produces longer opinions (and the justices, individually, are writing more dissenting and concurring opinions) than it did in either the recent or the distant past. The opinion-writing aspect of the Court's activity is by far the most time-consuming. If the Court were actually overburdened, we might expect a diminution of separate opinion writing, or at least a substantial reduction in the length, if not the number, of opinions.

Meantime, the debate and discussions about the scheme continue.[29] But unless and until the justices themselves, the lower-court judges, and the legal profession approach consensus on the need for relief, Congress is not likely to act. And at this point in time, the possibility of such consensus is remote.[30]

Summary

In this chapter we attempted to identify the sorts of cases that the Supreme Court is most likely to accept for review. The disposition of writs of appeal and certiorari was noted and explained. Cue theory as an effort to identify the types of litigants and cases that the Court accepts for review was also explained and evaluated. The judgment was made that the Court is responsive to the major policy issues confronting American society. Lastly, we discussed the proposal to create a new sub-Supreme Court that would lessen the Court's responsibility to decide who shall have access to its dockets.

Notes to Chapter 6

1. William O. Douglas, "The Supreme Court and Its Case Load," *Cornell Law Quarterly* 45 (1960): 410.
2. Although four justices may wish to grant certiorari, tactical considerations may cause them not to insist that the case be decided on the merits. As an example, see the sixteen state and federal obscenity cases, some of which came to the Court on a writ of appeal and some on a writ of certiorari, at 41 L Ed 2d 1157–1160,

1163–1177 (1974); and nineteen others that came to the Court at the start of the 1974 term, at 42 L Ed 2d 148–150, 152–155, 159–161, 162–163, 173–174, 188–189, 281–282, 285, 288, 660, 671, and 828.

3. 89 S. Ct. 172 (1969).

4. The data do not distinguish among those affirmed, reversed, or vacated. Hence, we cannot determine the proportion of dispositions favorable to the petitioner as we can for those seeking a writ of appeal.

5. 398 U.S. 1030–1031 (1970).

6. *Id.* at 1026.

7. S. Sidney Ulmer *et al.*, "The Decision to Grant or Deny Certiorari: Further Consideration of Cue Theory," *Law and Society Review* 6 (1972): 643, fn. 6; Warren Weaver, Jr., "The Supreme Court at Work: A Look at the Inner Sanctum," *New York Times*, February 6, 1975, pp. 31, 57.

8. "The Decision to Grant Certiorari as an Indicator to Decision 'On the Merits,'" *Polity* 4 (1972): 439.

9. *New York Times*, May 24, 1973.

10. Joseph Tanenhaus *et al.*, "The Supreme Court's Certiorari Jurisdiction: Cue Theory," in Glendon Schubert, ed., *Judicial Decision-Making* (New York: Free Press, 1963), p. 118.

11. *Ibid.*

12. *Ibid.*, pp. 122–127.

13. *Ibid.*, p. 129.

14. Ulmer, *op. cit.*, fn. 7 *supra*, pp. 637–643.

15. Tanenhaus *et al.*, *op. cit.*, fn. 10 *supra*, p. 122.

16. For a detailed report of this special relationship, see Robert L. Stern, "The Solicitor General and Administrative Agency Litigation," *American Bar Association Journal* 46 (1960): 154–218; reprinted in Robert Scigliano, *The Courts* (Boston: Little, Brown, 1962), pp. 300–312.

17. Tanenhaus, *et al.*, *op. cit.*, fn. 10 *supra*, p. 115.

18. Indeed, the Court has demonstrated great willingness to accept review in some issue areas. Joel Grossman found that the Court granted 61 of 81 (75.3 percent) requests for review of sit-in cases between 1957 and 1967. See Joel B. Grossman, "A Model for Judicial Policy Analysis: The Supreme Court and the Sit-In Cases," in Joel B. Grossman and Joseph Tanenhaus, *Frontiers of Judicial Research* (New York: Wiley, 1969), p. 434.

19. 37 L Ed 2d 419 (1973).

20. *Thompson* v. *Louisville*, 362 U.S. 199 (1960).

21. *Gideon* v. *Wainwright*, 372 U.S. 355 (1963). The case resulted in the writing of three books by one author, Anthony Lewis: *Gideon's Trumpet* (New York: Random House, 1964); *The Supreme Court and How It Works* (New York: Random House, 1966); and *Clarence Earl Gideon and the Supreme Court* (New York: Random House, 1972). Gideon himself became something of a folk hero, so much so that shortly after his death a full-column epitaph appeared on the Op-Ed Page of the *New York Times*, February 12, 1972.

22. Chief Justice Burger appointed the panel acting in his capacity as chairman of the Federal Judicial Center, an institution that Congress established in 1968 and charged with researching and studying the activities of the federal courts.

23. *Report of the Study Group on the Caseload of the Supreme Court* (Washington, D.C.: Federal Judicial Center, 1972), p. 1.

24. Arthur J. Goldberg, "One Supreme Court," *The New Republic*, February 10, 1973, pp. 14–16; Warren Weaver, Jr., "Warren Attacks Plan to Screen Supreme Court Cases," *New York Times*, May 7, 1973.

25. Alan M. Dershowitz, "No More a Court of Last Resort?," *New York Times*, January 7, 1973.

26. Linda Charlton, "Douglas, Dissenter and Rights Champion, Sets Record for Tenures on Supreme Court," *New York Times*, October 29, 1973.

27. "Powell Says Justices on Court Overworked," *Washington Star*, April 11, 1973.

28. Warren Weaver, Jr., "Bar Association Members Cool to Proposal for New National Appeals Court," *New York Times*, February 12, 1973. By mid-1975, five of the nine justices had indicated their support for the concept of a national court of appeals—the four Nixon appointees and Justice White. See John P. MacKenzie, "5 Justices Back Second-Highest Court," *Washington Post*, June 13, 1975.

29. In addition to the references just cited, see Alexander M. Bickel, *The Caseload of the Supreme Court and What, If Anything, to Do about It* (Washington, D.C.: American Enterprise Institute for Public Policy Research, 1973); S. Sidney Ulmer, "Revising the Jurisdiction of the Supreme Court: Mere Administrative Reform or Substantive Policy Change?," *Minnesota Law Review* 58 (1973), 121–155; the opinion of Justice Douglas in *Tidewater Oil Co.* v. *United States*, 409 U.S. 151, at 174–178 (1972); Nathan Lewin, "Helping the Court with Its Work," *The New Republic*, March 3, 1973, pp. 15–19; Paul A. Freund, Arthur S. Miller, and Eugene Gressman, "National Appeals Court? Yes and No," *New York Times*, April 11, 1973; the columns of such nationally syndicated columnists as Jack Bell, December 23, 1972; Jack C. Landau, December 26, 1972; and James J. Kilpatrick, May 1 and December 4, 1973; and Warren Weaver, Jr., "Bar Group Backs Aid to High Court," *New York Times*, February 6, 1974. Proposals have also been made to make the jurisdiction of the federal courts more manageable and efficient. Chief Justice Burger, for example, has proposed elimination of the three-judge federal district courts, which hear challenges to the constitutionality of state and federal statutes, and abolition of the federal courts' diversity jurisdiction, as a result of which routine lawsuits are heard solely because the litigants are residents of different states. See Warren Weaver, Jr., "Burger Supports Proposal for a New National Court of Appeals," *New York Times*, June 4, 1975.

30. Justice Marshall added his voice to those opposing any plan to ease the Court's work load in a 1975 Law Day speech. See Warren Weaver, Jr., "Justice Marshall Rejects Plans to Ease High Court's Caseload," *New York Times*, May 2, 1975.

7 | *Why the Justices Vote as They Do*

In this chapter, we explain why the justices vote the way they do by identifying the attitudes and values that have motivated their behavior. The data to be analyzed for this purpose are drawn from decisions of both the Warren and Burger Courts. Inasmuch as the best measure of the adequacy of a theory is not merely how well it explained what *has* happened, but rather how well it predicts what *will* happen, we also report the results of predictions made of the outcome and voting alignment of a number of the more publicized Burger Court decisions. This chapter, then, applies the theory and methodology presented in Chapter 4 for the purpose of explaining and predicting the votes of the justices.

The Cases Analyzed

Observers commonly report that the Court decided *x* number of cases last term, that a given justice was a member of the majority coalition more frequently than any of his colleagues, that another justice dissented most often, or that certain of the justices voted as a bloc in all but a small percentage of the cases. However, the decisions and votes of the justices may be counted in a variety of ways, and the method chosen is virtually never reported.

Although there is no inherent superiority in counting cases and votes one way rather than another, the matter of method is sufficiently important to require specification. Accordingly, we adhere to the following decision rules to determine which cases are included in our analysis.

Two sets of data are analyzed: the last eleven terms of the Warren Court (1958–1968) and the first five terms of the Burger Court (1969–1973). Each term of the Court commences on the first Monday in October and terminates the following June or early July. We begin our analysis of the Warren Court period with the 1958 term because no personnel changes occurred during the next 3½ years. The construction of refined category scales becomes difficult if the Court is undergoing marked changes in membership. Too many justices who are here today and gone tomorrow prevent identification of voting behavior because of their lack of participation in the analyzed decisions.

Our cast of characters includes seventeen actors. Six justices performed during all of the last eleven terms of the Warren Court: Chief Justice Warren, Hugo Black, John Marshall Harlan, William O. Douglas, Potter Stewart, and William Brennan. The latter three—Douglas, Stewart, and Brennan—also were members of the five-year Burger Court period. Byron White replaced Charles Whittaker at the start of the 1962 term and has served since. Arthur Goldberg replaced Felix Frankfurter at the same time and served for three years. Abe Fortas replaced Goldberg at the start of the 1965 term and served the four remaining years of the Warren Court. Tom Clark served through the end of the 1966 term and was replaced by Thurgood Marshall, whose service on the Court spans the remaining terms being analyzed. Chief Justice Burger's tenure covers the first five terms of the Burger Court. Harry Blackmun filled the Fortas vacancy in 1970, and Lewis Powell and William Rehnquist replaced Black and Harlan midway through the 1971 term. On the average, each of the seventeen justices served for slightly more than half the period covered by our analysis—8.4 years. Three have held membership continuously since 1958: Douglas, Stewart, and Brennan. Warren, Black, and Harlan served throughout the first period. Burger, White, and Marshall—plus Douglas, Stewart, and Brennan—have served throughout the second period.

The source of the decisions that are included for analysis is the privately printed *Lawyers' Edition* of the *United States Supreme Court Reports*.[1] Of all the decisions reported therein, we have analyzed those that were orally argued—the so-called formally decided cases. To these we added those *per curiam* decisions (that is, those that were decided without the Court hearing oral argument) which the editors of the *Lawyers' Edition* saw fit to summarize. We excluded from analysis those formally decided cases and those summarized *per curiam* decisions that fall into one or the other of the following categories:

1. "Decrees" of the Court (e.g., *Texas* v. *New Jersey*[2]), which usually contain no summary anyway. Decrees usually result from the exercise of the Supreme Court's original jurisdiction and tend as well to be cases in which the Court appoints a "special master" who is usually a retired lower-court judge. More often than not the issue in such cases is determination of the boundary line between adjacent states—a determination necessary because of natural phenomena, such as an alteration in the course of a river that divides a pair of states.

2. Where the vote is unspecified (e.g., *Biggers* v. *Tennessee*[3]). This occurs when the decision of the lower court is upheld by reason of a tie vote, usually 4 to 4. Quite commonly, the Court does not report who voted which way. Without such information a case cannot be placed into the appropriate category scale.

3. Where a writ of certiorari has been dismissed as "improvidently granted" (e.g., *Smith* v. *Mississippi*[4]). The Court initially accepted each of these cases for decision and subsequently found that the record of the case lacked sufficient information to enable the Court to decide the merits of the case.

4. Where the case lacks a substantial or properly presented federal question (e.g., *Bohannon* v. *Arizona*[5]). These are cases within the Court's jurisdiction that the Court chooses not to hear because the issue is either insufficiently important or improperly presented to the Court. As in (3), the majority, in effect, refuses to decide the merits of the controversy.

When, however, one or more of the justices casts a vote on the merits under categories (3) or (4), the case is included for analysis. Also included are all the cases listed in the *Lawyers' Edition* as "Memorandum Cases," as well as those without a summary, in which both of the following conditions are present: (1) one or more of the justices dissented on the merits, and (2) the basis of dissent can be ascertained. The basis of dissent is determined from the opinion of the dissenting justice—frequently nothing more than a citation of a previously decided case—or, less commonly, the specification in newspaper reports of the substantive issue in the case. In perhaps a half dozen instances the preceding rule has been violated by using jurisdictional dissents—that is, dissents that do not address themselves to the merits of the controversy, but only disagree with the majority's refusal to decide the case—for the purpose of securing better rank-order discrimination among the justices in a category scale [e.g., *Murphy* v. *Butler*,[6] in the natural resources scale (number 47 in the Appendix at the end of this chapter), and *Pekao* v. *Bragalini*,[7] in the national supremacy scale (number 46)[8]].

When several cases, as identified by their docket numbers, are decided together in a single opinion of the Court, each docketed case is counted separately. In determining to which issue area a given case pertains, primary reference is made to the headnotes accompanying the opinions. In a case in which there were dissenting opinions, the thrust of which was addressed to an issue other than that focused upon by the majority, the dissenters' issue area controls placement of the case. The specification of the directionality of a case (i.e., whether it is pro or con the hypothesized motivating variable) also depends upon the dissenters' behavior. For example, a litigant in a civil liberties case may win because his conviction is reversed and remanded to the trial or lower appellate court for further proceedings. The two dissenters, however, may vote for reversal—period. Such a decision would be scored as 2 to 7 and be classified as anti the civil liberties issue to which it pertained. See the state obscenity cases, *Interstate Circuit* v. *Dallas* and *Dallas* v. *Interstate Circuit*,[9] for an illustration.

On the basis of these decision rules, 2129 cases were decided during the Warren Court period, and an additional 1187 cases were decided during the five-year Burger Court period. Using the procedures explained in Chapter 4, the Warren Court decisions were formed into 73 cumulative scales, each of which represents a discrete attitude. The smaller number of Burger Court decisions were formed into 64 cumulative scales. The 73 Warren Court scales contained 96.2 percent of the 2129 cases decided during the eleven-year period.[10] Because a number of the less common issue areas contained too few Burger Court cases to scale, the percentage of cases scaled for this five-year period is only 94.2 percent. The names, size, and other pertinent information about these scales are contained in the Appendix to this chapter. The data in the Appendix indicate that the scales, individually and collectively, form unusually valid and refined measures of the justices' attitudes.

We should mention here that a few cases were placed in two scales rather than only one because these cases related equally to two different scales. There are 33 such cases in the Warren Court scales, and 13 in those of the Burger Court.

Also to be noted is the division of the Warren Court's search-and-seizure decisions into three periods: 1958–1961 terms, 1962–1966 terms, and 1967–1968 terms. This division violates our longitudinal perspective to some extent. It was dictated, however, by the difficulty the justices had in formulating policies in this issue area as reflected in their erratic voting behavior. But with the passage of time, a sufficient number of search-and-seizure cases were decided so that they could be divided into periods, thus facilitating scale construction.

The Values Motivating the Justices' Behavior

In accordance with the procedure specified in Chapter 4, the rank order of the justices on each of the cumulative scales was correlated with their rank order on each of the other scales using Kendall's tau b correlation coefficient. For the 73 Warren Court scales, 2628 coefficients[11] were produced; for the Burger Court scales, 2016 coefficients were produced. The average correlation among the 73 Warren Court scales is .42; among those of the Burger Court, .52. Such a high average indicates that the attitudes of the justices are well structured and that a small number of values should explain the vast majority of the justices' decisions.

This is, indeed, true. All three of the data reduction techniques described in the Appendix to Chapter 4 (cluster analysis, metric multidimensional scaling, and factor analysis) revealed that three major values explain more than 85 percent of the Court's decisions during both the Warren and

Burger Court periods. Although each of the two periods was analyzed separately, the scales that clustered together to form the three major values are largely the same. This accords with our expectation that the justices' values would remain rather fixed and not subject to much change.

The scales that cluster together to form these three major values reveal that each has a distinguishable content. In one cluster are scales that concern civil liberties issues. The litigants in these scales are mostly persons accused of crime or political offenders of one sort or another (e.g., security risks or persons exercising their First Amendment freedoms). The situations to which these scales pertain involve the major procedural guarantees of the Bill of Rights, plus the limits upon use of governmental power to deprive individuals of their liberty—of their freedom of action. Given this content, it is reasonable to describe this cluster as a value that may appropriately be labeled "freedom."

The content of the second cluster of scales reveals that most of them concern persons who allege that they were subject to political, economic, or racial discrimination. Many of these scales, in addition, pertain to the equal protection of the laws clause of the Fourteenth Amendment. Given these features of this cluster, the label "equality" appears most descriptive of this value.

Examination of the content of the scales that form the third cluster shows that their most common characteristic is the presence of economic activity. This economic activity, moreover, is in the context of governmental regulation. Because of this regulatory aspect, it is perhaps most appropriate to label this value "New Deal economics" or "New Dealism." This label typifies the issues of the 1930s and 1940s[12] and, indeed, most of the economic regulation involved in these scales has remained prominent since the Great Depression of the 1930s.

In addition to these three major values, the data from the Warren Court period also show the presence of two minor values. The first of these is a cluster of three scales (numbers 42, 48, and 49 in the Appendix to this chapter) that form what may be called the value of privacy. The three scales are libel-privacy and the two obscenity scales, state and federal. The other minor value contains only two scales, numbers 29 and 54. Since the content of these two scales pertains to taxation, we use the label "taxation" to describe this value. The privacy value contains 2.4 percent of the Warren Court decisions; taxation accounts for 3.5 percent. Neither of these minor values appears in the analysis of the Burger Court data. The Burger Court has decided only one libel-privacy case; the federal obscenity scale has become part of the value of freedom; and state obscenity is a "mixed" variable that pertains equally to equality and New Deal economics. One of the taxation scales is now an outlyer, unassociated with any other scale; the other associates with the scales forming the value of equality.

A number of the scales appear as "mixed" variables according to the data reduction techniques. Those scales, instead of associating with a single value, correlated highly with two of them. Four of the Warren Court scales identified themselves as mixed, as did six of those of the Burger Court. Five of the Burger Court scales, for example, related to both freedom and equality: contempt of court (13), discovery and inspection (18), line-up (43), sex discrimination (68), and statutory interpretation (73). State obscenity (49) related to both equality and New Deal economics.

As for the major values, freedom encompasses 20 of the 73 Warren Court scales, equality encompasses 15, and New Deal economics encompasses 24. Adding the four "mixed" scales, the three values collectively account for 63 of the 73 Warren Court scales (86.3 percent) and 86.9 percent of the cases decided during this period. For the Burger Court period, freedom accounts for 20 of the 64 scales, equality accounts for 15, and New Deal economics also accounts for 15. Adding the six "mixed" scales, the three values collectively account for 56 of the 64 scales (87.5 percent) and 85.2 percent of the cases decided by the Burger Court.

What is significant here is that the same three values explain the overwhelming majority of the Court's decisions. That there are changes in the content of each of the values is not surprising and is readily explainable. Four of the Burger Court justices (the Nixon appointees—Burger, Blackmun, Powell, and Rehnquist) did not serve on the Warren Court. It is quite possible that one or more of these justices perceived a given attitude to pertain to a value different from that perceived by his predecessor. This possibility is heightened by the fact that the Conservative value systems of Burger and Blackmun differ markedly from the Liberal orientation of the value systems of their predecessors, Warren and Fortas. Nor is Justice Powell a pea from the same pod as his predecessor, Justice Black. And though Justice Harlan and his replacement, William Rehnquist, are both Conservatives, there is considerable evidence of differences in the degree as well as the character of their conservatism.

Additional reasons that may explain the shift of a given scale from one value to another may also be noted. A number of scales are small, which frequently precludes as much rank-order discrimination as tends to occur with larger scales. Such lack of rank-order discrimination could cause a scale to cluster with a value other than it did during the Warren Court period; for example, the shift of governmental corruption (32) from freedom to New Deal economics, the shift of discovery and inspection (18) from freedom to mixed status, and the shift of contempt of court (13) from New Deal economics to mixed status.

Another factor is that the content of a given scale may change over time. Many of the Warren Court's armed forces (5) decisions, for example, pertained to veterans' benefits. Those of the Burger Court, by comparison, have exclusively concerned provisions of the selective service statutes. In view of this change in content, the shift of the armed forces scale from New

Deal economics to freedom should occasion no surprise. Similarly, the Warren Court's statutory interpretation (73) decisions concerned traditional sorts of criminal laws. Those of the Burger Court, however, have pertained as well to criminal laws with a substantial civil rights focus. This content difference may well explain the shift of the statutory interpretation scale from freedom to a mixed variable relating to both freedom and equality.

Finally, the disappearance of the Warren Court's minor values from the Burger Court analyses necessarily affected the scales that constituted these minor values. Federal obscenity (48) and the priority of federal fiscal claims (54) now cluster with freedom and equality respectively. State obscenity (49) is a mixed variable and federal taxation (29) is an outlyer, unassociated with any other scale.

Not all shifts in scales are as plausibly explicated as the foregoing. The most notable exceptions are reapportionment (58), which moved from equality to (of all things) New Deal economics, and the shift of unions vis-à-vis business (80) from New Deal economics to an outlyer status.

Other shifts in the value location of the various scales may be found by consulting the Appendix to this chapter. Of the 55 scales that are common to both the Warren and Burger Court periods, 30 (54.5 percent) show no change between periods. Five additional scales (9.1 percent) move from positions outside the three major values to positions within a value or to a mixed status. Fifteen (27.3 percent) move within the major value structure. Only five scales (9.1 percent) that were originally part of a value are now unassociated with any cluster: federal taxation (29), libel-defamation (41), patents and copyrights (50), transportation (77), and unions vis-à-vis business (80).

Lastly, we cannot emphasize too much that our research methods neither inhibit nor compel the movement of attitudes from one value to another. If the rank order of the justices on one scale correlates closely with the rank orders on other scales, the data reduction techniques will reveal the existence of a value. On the other hand, if the correlation is low or nonexistent, the scale will appear as an outlyer or will relate to other scales (and hence to another value) with which its rank order correlates closely. But the most important point of the analysis is the discovery that the same three values—freedom, equality, and New Deal economics—explain the overwhelming majority of the Court's decisions during both the Warren and Burger Court periods.

The Justices' Value Systems

Having identified the three values that explain the bulk of the Court's decisions, we are now in a position to determine the value system of each of the justices. In Chapter 4, we defined value system as a justice's distinctive pattern of support or nonsupport of the relevant values that explain his votes. This definition was operationalized in terms of a justice's location on a numerical scale for each value that ranges from $+1.00$ to -1.00. A justice who invariably voted in support of a particular value would score $+1.00$. One who invariably voted against a particular value would score -1.00. A justice's location is determined by means of scale scores.

Scale scores are a function of a justice's scale position (P) in relation to the total number of cases in a scale (n). Scale position is defined as the midpoint between a justice's last consistent $+$ vote on a given scale and his first consistent $-$ vote. Thus, a justice's scale position in a scale containing ten cases in which he voted $+$ in the first four decisions, was not a member of the Court when the next two were decided, and voted $-$ in the last four, would be 5. In determining scale position, consideration is also given to nonscale or inconsistent votes. Thus, a justice would have a scale position of 9 in a ten-case scale in which he voted $+$ in all decisions except the eighth. Similarly, if, in the same scale, a justice voted $+$ in the first six cases, $-$ in the next three, and $+$ in the last, his scale position would be 7. To arrive at a scale score (S), scale position is multiplied by 2 and divided by the number of cases in the scale; 1 is then subtracted from this number: $S = 2P/n - 1$. The multiplication by 2 and subtraction are necessary to establish a range of $+1.00$ to -1.00. The average of a justice's scale scores on the scales that constitute the value specifies his support or nonsupport of the value in question.

Note that most of the justices did not serve during the entirety of the Warren or Burger Court periods. As a result, not every justice participated in enough decisions in every scale to allow us to rank order him or to calculate his scale score. Consequently, scale scores are calculated only for those justices who are rank ordered on a given scale. A justice's support or nonsupport of a given value is determined by averaging his scores on the appropriate scales. If he is rank ordered on only ten of a possible fifteen scales, the average of the ten scores is considered sufficient to rank order him.

We stated in Chapter 4 that the values discovered in our analyses would be dichotomous—that the justices would either support or oppose however many values were found. Because there are three major values, eight combinations of support ($+$) or nonsupport ($-$) are possible. Each of these eight combinations of support or nonsupport of our three values represents a value system. Table 7.1 lists these eight possible combinations and gives a label for each.

The description accorded each value system is subject to debate, but for the most part these descriptions accord with common usage. Liberals generally support demands for greater political and social freedom and for equality, and they also support governmental regulation favorable to labor and hostile to business. Conservatives, by contrast, oppose such demands. Civil Libertarians support noneconomic issues (freedom and equality); Individualists are the classic nineteenth-century-type liberals—they believe that that government is best that governs least. Hence, Individualists sup-

Table 7.1

Value Systems and Value Responses

VALUE SYSTEM DESCRIPTION	VALUES AND RESPONSES		
	FREEDOM	EQUALITY	NEW DEALISM
Liberal	+	+	+
Civil Libertarian	+	+	−
Individualist	+	−	−
Populist	+	−	+
Utopian Collectivist	−	+	−
Benevolent Authoritarian	−	+	+
New Dealer	−	−	+
Conservative	−	−	−

Legend: A + indicates support of the value in question; a − indicates nonsupport.
SOURCE: Copyright © 1972 by Chandler Publishing Co. From *Introduction to Supreme Court Decision Making*, by Harold J. Spaeth. By permission of Chandler Publishing Co., New York.

port freedom, but oppose governmental efforts to redress inequalities of either a social, political, or economic sort. Populists were the agrarian reformers of an earlier era. Supportive of personal freedom and economic reform, they had an impact in the West and South between the 1890s and the 1930s. The next two types, Utopian Collectivists and Benevolent Authoritarians, are most removed from the mainstream of American politics. Neither supports freedom for their opponents, but both are high on equality; various Marxist groups, the New Left, student radicals, and anti-establishment types might personify them. The remaining category, New Dealer, supports economic reform to the exclusion of personal freedom and political and social equality. This type had its heyday during the Great Depression of the 1930s.

Having identified the possible value systems into which the values of freedom, equality, and New Deal economics may be accommodated, we now specify which of these value systems typifies each of the justices.

Table 7.2 is a composite of both the Warren and Burger Court periods. Next to each justice's name is that part of the periods that he was a member of the Court. These periods are stated in terms rather than years. Hence, Chief Justice Warren served from the beginning of the periods analyzed until the end of the 1968 term, which was June of 1969. A number of the justices left the Court at a time other than the end of a term. The service of these justices is shown from the beginning of their appointment through the end of the terms closest to their appointment and departure. The three justices without a date next to their names have served during the entirety of both periods.

Table 7.2

The Justices and Their Value Systems

| JUSTICE | VALUES AND AVERAGE SCALE SCORES | | | |
	FREEDOM	EQUALITY	NEW DEALISM	VALUE SYSTEM
Douglas	.75	.79	.79	Liberal
Warren (through 1968)	.65	.61	.43	Liberal
Fortas (1965–1968)	.63	.64	.24	Liberal
Brennan	.38	.50	.61	Liberal
Goldberg (1962–1964)	.63	.63	.18	Liberal
Marshall (from 1967)	.52	.54	.34	Liberal
Black (through 1970)	.56	−.44	.56	Populist
Stewart	.08	−.12	−.13	Moderate
White (from 1962)	−.30	−.08	.16	Moderate
Clark (through 1966)	−.51	−.20	.25	New Dealer
Blackmun (from 1970)	−.33	−.43	−.29	Conservative
Powell (from 1971)	−.32	−.38	−.48	Conservative
Whittaker (through 1961)	−.38	−.67*	−.06	Conservative
Harlan (through 1970)	−.33	−.37	−.42	Conservative
Frankfurter (through 1961)	−.12	−.81*	−.36	Conservative
Burger (from 1969)	−.46	−.60	−.47	Conservative
Rehnquist (from 1971)	−.59	−.77	−.43	Conservative

*Based on two scale scores.

The order of the justices in Table 7.2 is from most to least Liberal and from least to most Conservative. This ordering was calculated simply by totaling each justice's scores across the three major values.[13] Douglas, consequently, appears as the most Liberal; Rehnquist appears as the most Conservative. In calculating the justices' average scale scores for each of the three major values, a few scales were either omitted or counted without including unanimously decided cases. This was done to prevent the justices' scores from being unduly inflated or deflated. Thus, for example, 26 of the 29 cases in the Warren Court's First Amendment freedom scale were decided favorably to those claiming that their First Amendment freedoms were abridged. This produced + scores even for those justices least sympathetic to the exercise of First Amendment freedoms. To portray the justices' attitudes more accurately, the 14 unanimous + decisions were excluded from consideration in calculating the justices' scale scores.

All but four of the justices listed in Table 7.2 have either a Liberal or a Conservative value system—13 of 17. Each group is of approximately equal size: six Liberals, seven Conservatives. An analysis of each justice's period of service shows this Liberal-Conservative balance to have been a shifting one. Until the end of the 1968 term, the Court had a definite Liberal cast. At this point in time, five of the justices were Liberals: Douglas, Warren, Fortas, Brennan, and Marshall. By contrast, Justice Harlan sat in solitary splendor as the Court's lone Conservative, a position he had occupied since the resignation of Whittaker and the retirement of Frankfurter at the end of the 1961 term. But with the accession of Warren Burger to the Chief Justiceship at the beginning of the 1969 term, the tide began to turn. Subsequent appointments of Blackmun to the Fortas vacancy, and the replacement of Black and Harlan by Powell and Rehnquist, brought the number of Conservatives to four, one short of a majority.

Actually, the Liberal majority of the last years of the Warren Court disappeared almost overnight. The departure of Warren and Fortas in the spring of 1969 reduced the number of Liberals to four and shifted the balance of power to the two Moderates, White and Stewart. These two justices have manifested a value system not shown in Table 7.1 because they neither support nor oppose any of the three major values. In using a scale of $+1.00$ to -1.00 to measure attitudes, it is conventional to consider scores in the middle of the range, from $+.20$ to $-.20$, as a zone of indifference—of neutrality with regard to the psychological determinants of behavior that are being tapped. Because White and Stewart lie primarily within this zone, it is inaccurate to consider their value systems as any of the eight listed in Table 7.1. Hence our characterization of them as Moderates.

During the Burger Court period, White and Stewart have been the Court's "swing men." Neither the Liberals nor the Conservatives command a majority of the Court's membership. The Conservatives are shy one vote, the Liberals are shy two. Obviously, a majority coalition is more likely to be formed by adding either or both of the Moderates than it is by securing a vote or two from justices whose value system is of an opposite pattern.

As for the three values themselves, a five-member majority supported freedom during the 1962–1966 terms: Douglas, Warren, Brennan, Goldberg (through 1964—his successor, Fortas, also supported freedom), and Black. Beginning with the 1967 term, Marshall provided a sixth vote in support of freedom. On New Deal economics, the foregoing justices, plus Clark (who was Marshall's predecessor), were supportive. Accordingly, during the entirety of the 1962–1968 terms, six of the nine justices supported New Deal economics.

Support for the value of equality fared less well. Neither the Populist, Justice Black, nor the New Dealer, Justice Clark, supported equality. Hence, the Court had a pro-equality majority for less than two years: from the appointment of Marshall at the beginning of the 1967 term until the resignation of Fortas in May 1969. These two individuals, plus Douglas, Warren, and Brennan, constituted the pro-equality majority.

As noted, with Burger's appointment as Chief Justice, the balance of power shifted to White and Stewart. During the 1969 and 1970 terms, the remaining Liberals—Douglas, Brennan, and Marshall—could count upon Justice Black's support of freedom and New Deal economics. To prevail, they needed to secure the vote of only one of the Moderates. On equality, the situation was reversed. The three Conservatives—Burger, Blackmun, and Harlan—plus Black, needed only the vote of either White or Stewart to command a majority. With the confirmation of Powell and Rehnquist in January 1972, only three supportive votes for the three values remained; the four Nixon appointees were in opposition. Thus, the Liberals needed the votes of both Moderates to constitute a majority; the Conservatives needed but one.

It is possible to calculate separate scores on each of the major values for the seven justices who served during both the Warren and Burger Court periods. Such separate scores show no appreciable change in the degree of support or nonsupport of the three major values. White, however, does appear to be slowly growing more opposed to the values of freedom and equality. If this trend continues, he may not qualify in the future as a Moderate but rather may be classified as a marginal New Dealer.

As a final comment on the justices and their value systems, we should note that the justices collectively mirror the value systems of most Americans. Fifteen of the seventeen are Liberals, Conservatives, or Moderates. We submit that the views of most Americans are similarly divided. The proportion of Liberals to Moderates to Conservatives in the general population undoubtedly differs from that in the Court. But regardless of the proportions found in any given population, these three value systems are commonplace. Nor is the Populism of Justice Black or the New Dealism of Justice Clark especially unusual. Even though Black and Clark were probably the last of their breed on the Court, they espoused a value system whose proponents lived during an earlier period in the nation's history. Hence, we may properly infer that these seventeen individuals share the same values as the overwhelming majority of Americans. They respond neither to alien nor to inscrutable influences. In this sense, the Court is a representative body, even though the justices serve for life and are accountable to no one, save their own consciences.

The Predictability of Supreme Court Decisions

In this chapter we have explained why the justices vote as they do. The attitudes, values, and value systems of the justices were identified and used to explain their voting behavior. Our concern now shifts to the question of whether the theory and methodology previously formulated can be used as well to predict the Court's decisions.

A major deficiency in social science research to date has been its inability to predict future happenings. Because of this inability, social scientists are considered less "scientific" than their colleagues in the so-called hard sciences, such as physics, astronomy, and biology, where accurate predictions are made routinely. The nonsocial sciences, of course, deal mostly with less complex phenomena than human activity, or, when dealing with human beings, concern themselves with the less distinctive aspects of man's existence, such as his physiology or anatomy. The fact that human activity is more complex than any other should not preclude predictive efforts, however.

Predicting Decisions

Commencing in the spring of 1970, the theory and methodology just described were used to predict the outcomes of decisions and how the justices would vote in some of the more important cases and issues coming before the Court.[14] "Important," in this sense, is defined as those cases that have received considerable attention in the news media or those that are likely to receive considerable attention after the Court's decision has been announced. Through the end of the 1973 term, several dozen predictions had been made. The results are summarized in Table 7.3.

The votes in Table 7.3 pertain to 73 decisions, in 64 of which (87.7 percent) the outcome was accurately predicted.[15] During the 1972–1973 terms, 33 of 34 decisions (97.1 percent) were accurately predicted.

Improvement in predictive accuracy during the 1972–1973 terms is a result of several factors. First, prediction was begun when the Burger Court was in its infancy—less than a year old. Predictions were thus necessarily based on Warren Court data (a risky undertaking as it turned out). Second, the appointment of Burger in 1969, Blackmun in 1970, and Powell and Rehnquist in 1972, brought to the Court individuals who were unknown quantities. Third, these appointments, particularly those of Burger and Blackmun, marked the end of the Liberal majority that had held sway during the last years of the Warren Court and meant a consequent shift in the balance of power to the Moderates, Stewart and White.

It may be noted initially that if all nine justices participate in a decision, any one of 512 different voting alignments may occur, ranging from a 9 to 0 victory for one of the litigants to a 0 to 9 loss for that same litigant. If less than the full Court participates, fewer than 512 combinations are possible. When eight justices vote, one of 326 alignments, from 8 to 0, through 4 to 4, to 0 to 8, must result.

The process of predicting the outcome of Supreme Court decisions and the voting of the individual justices poses a number of problems, chiefly as a result of the lack of information about the case. It is rare for the media to provide any but the most cursory information about a case before the Court

Table 7.3
Predicted Votes of Justices

JUSTICE	TOTAL			1972–1973 TERMS ONLY		
	RIGHT	WRONG	PERCENT	RIGHT	WRONG	PERCENT
Rehnquist	35	3	92.1	29	3	90.6
Powell	32	3	91.4	27	2	93.1
Blackmun	51	5	91.1	32	0	100.0
Douglas	50	6	89.3	30	3	90.9
Brennan	51	7	87.9	28	5	84.8
Burger	48	9	84.2	32	1	97.0
Marshall	47	9	83.9	27	6	81.8
Black	14	3	82.4	—	—	—
White	46	11	80.7	28	4	87.5
Stewart	46	11	80.7	28	5	84.8
Harlan	13	4	76.5	—	—	—
Totals	433	71	85.9	261	29	90.0

has announced its decision. The only major exception is *The United States Law Week*.[16] But even this publication is highly selective regarding the cases whose oral argument it reports. More often than not, coverage of oral argument is provided in cases that are of interest only to a small legal public. The briefs filed by the attorneys participating in Supreme Court cases are not available, and this, for all practical purposes, is also true of lower-court records. Nor is it feasible to be present during the Court's oral arguments.

This lack of all but the most sketchy information is a serious problem because inherent in the typical case that comes before the Court for decision is a number of issues, any one of which may be the basis for decision. More often than not, whether the Court chooses one basis for decision rather than another affects the votes as well as the outcome of the case. Thus, for example, in granting certiorari in *Maxwell* v. *Bishop*,[17] the Court limited its review to two questions: whether due process was violated by allowing a jury untrammeled discretion to impose the death penalty, and whether self-incrimination was violated by allowing a jury to determine guilt and punishment simultaneously. A prediction was made that on these bases, Maxwell would lose by reason of a 4 to 4 vote. But, as stated in its decision, the Court actually decided neither of these questions.[18] Instead, by a 6 to 1 vote (with Marshall not participating), it remanded the case to the federal district court for consideration of Maxwell's claim that opponents of capital punishment had been excluded from the jury that tried him in violation of the holding of a previously decided case.[19] Consequently, the outcome was wrongly predicted, as were the votes of Justices Burger, Harlan, and White who, along with Black, were expected to vote against Maxwell. When these questions were finally resolved, however, the outcome was accurately predicted and only Justice Stewart did not vote as had been expected.[20]

The lack of information about cases to be decided exists independently of our theory and methodology. The major problem in predicting, which is inherent in the model, is determining the "extremeness" of a case. Will it be decided 9 to 0, 0 to 9, or by some intermediate vote? The answer to this question pertains directly to the entire predictive process and will normally be a matter of judgment rather than a statistical probability.

In making a prediction, the initial task is to identify the most likely basis for the Court's decision. This is the point at which adequate information is vital. The ideal situation is one in which the issue is clear-cut and relates directly to only one of the cumulative scales into which the decisions of the Court have been apportioned. If this ideal situation exists (and frequently it does), the proportion of pro and con decisions in the relevant scale is ascertained, along with the scale scores of the participating justices. Attention is also paid any possible subset of the cases in the scale that bears especially directly upon the case to be predicted. Once these data have been obtained, the scores of the justices on the value of which the scale is a part are evaluated.

Thus, in the School Desegregation cases of 1971,[21] which presented a series of questions concerning Southern school desegregation, the fact that the decisions in 90 percent of the cases in the desegregation scale favored the black litigants, and that 25 of 26 decisions favored them in school desegregation litigation, strongly suggested a pro-desegregation result. And inasmuch as more than 92 percent of the justices' votes supported school desegregation, unanimous votes on most of the issues were likely. However, because only three of the participating justices strongly supported the value of equality, to which desegregation pertained, desegregation would be supported, but not unequivocally. The outcomes of all of the cases were predicted correctly. Douglas, the justice most supportive of the value of equality, was judged likely to require busing to eliminate the remnants of dual school systems, to oppose neighborhood schools, and, with Marshall, to vote to eliminate all-black schools. Neither he nor Marshall did so, however.

As an example of the judgment necessary to determine the extremeness of a case, reference may be made to the obscenity decisions of June 1973.[22] The basic question for decision was whether the states should be given greater authority to regulate alleged pornography. Analysis of the Burger Court's decisions revealed that the four Nixon appointees clearly supported the states in this endeavor. Douglas, Brennan, Marshall, and Stewart were as clearly opposed. A 5 to 4 vote was indicated, with White determining the outcome. During his service on the Warren Court, White was third most liberal in state obscenity decisions. On the Burger Court, however, he was ranked fifth. From a Warren Court scale score of $+.50$, he had dropped to $+.06$. This drop warranted a judgment that the Court's decision would support the states' regulatory authority, a judgment that proved to be accurate.

From what has been said, we may correctly infer the importance of the justices' past voting behavior in predicting future votes and case outcomes. Because of dependence upon past performance, some cases cannot be predicted, whereas others may markedly deviate from what has previously been decided. An example of the former type was a pair of parochiaid cases.[23] The relevant category scale, establishment of religion, showed that five of the nine justices who were ranked were tied with a scale score of .00. Consequently, analysis indicated that the justices' votes could not be predicted, with the exception of those of Douglas and Black, who were likely to vote that the governmental programs at issue were unconstitutional.

Illustrative of deviance from past performance was a set of poverty law cases decided in the spring of 1971.[24] The issues were clear-cut. In the *Java* case, the suspension of unemployment compensation benefits pending appeal by a former employer was predicted to be impermissible by a 5 to 4 vote. In *James*, a referendum requirement before low-cost housing could be constructed was predicted to be unconstitutional with only Justice Black dissenting; and in *Graham*, denial of welfare benefits to resident aliens was predicted to be unconstitutional by a 6 to 3 vote. In both *Java* and *Graham*, the outcome was as predicted, but by a unanimous vote. *Java* was closely related to a decision of the preceding year, in which the Court had held by a 5 to 3 vote that due process was violated by failure to provide notice and hearing upon termination of welfare benefits.[25] The federal district court that originally heard the *Java* case based its decision thereon. The Supreme Court, however, ducked the constitutional question and merely construed the relevant section of the Social Security Act in arriving at its decision. Even so, the unanimity of the Court's decision was totally unexpected. None of the 11 poverty law decisions of the first term of the Burger Court had been unanimous, and only 3 of the 15 Warren Court decisions had been unanimous. Moreover, 23 of the 26 decisions of both Courts had contained at least two conservative votes.

Graham, the second of these three cases, was closely related to a previously decided case in which a residency rule for welfare recipients was declared to be a violation of equal protection by a 6 to 3 vote.[26] But *James* was the most surprising of all. With Douglas not participating, the Court ruled by a 5 to 3 vote that the referendum requirement was constitutional. Again, a seemingly revelant precedent existed: *Hunter* v. *Erickson*.[27] Especially in view of the racial character of low-cost housing and the Court's strong opposition to *de jure* discrimination, a liberal outcome was highly probable. However, in the opinion of the Court (Black had been the sole dissenter in *Hunter*), Justice Black stated, albeit dissimulatingly, that: "Unlike the Akron referendum provision [which was at issue in *Hunter*], it cannot be said that California's Article 34 rests on 'distinctions based on race.' . . . The Article requires referendum approval for any low-rent public housing project, not only for projects which will be occupied by a racial minority."[28]

The foregoing are not the only examples of deviation from past performance. Closely related was *Flood* v. *Kuhn*,[29] the baseball antitrust case. In the first place, the Court agreed to review an issue decided in 1953.[30] In that year, the Court had held that professional baseball's reserve clause did not violate the antitrust laws. When the Court agrees to hear an issue previously resolved, the probability that the previous decision will be overturned is high. Secondly, 71 of the 79 antitrust decisions since 1957 had been pro-competition, anti-business decisions, and the 6 antitrust decisions of the Burger Court at the time the prediction was made were all unanimous pro-competition, anti-business decisions. Finally, since 1953 the Court had subjected all other professional sports to the operation of the antitrust laws. Not only was the predicted outcome (that baseball would be subject to the antitrust laws) incorrect, but so were the votes of four of the eight participating justices.

Such deviation from past performance as is exemplified by the foregoing examples is very much the exception to the rule. Rather, the justices are usually true unto themselves. Their personal policy preferences, as manifested in their attitudes and values, are highly stable and invariant. Their voting behavior is not random or quixotic. Viewed legalistically, the justices' choices do adhere to precedent. They will pick and choose among relevant precedents to be sure, but in exercising choice among alternative courses of action, each justice is personally consistent.[31] If they were not, predictive accuracy would be much less than 85.9 percent of their votes.

On the other hand, predictive accuracy is far from perfect. Nor indeed should perfect accuracy be expected. The inaccurate prediction of 14 percent of the justices' votes may in part be due to measurement error or bad judgment on our part. Just as likely an explanation is the likelihood that individual justices altered their attitudes and values because of changing circumstances and conditions. Human institutions are not unlike biological organisms in that if they fail to vary their activity in response to environmental changes, they have little chance of survival. The matter has been well stated:

> An organism learning is the analogue of a population adapting, but the population is required to maintain a high degree of variability no matter to what ecological niche it has adapted, whereas the organism, when learning, is expected to lose all response variety and become completely

uniform. I propose that any organism that did in fact behave as our theories suggest would be pathological and unfit. Rather than cursing the rat who breaks a sequence of seven consecutive correct runs through the maze with some exploratory behavior on the eighth trial, we should expect and appreciate that it is just such response variety that represents that organism's learning fitness. [32]

Hence, perfectly accurate predictions, though immensely gratifying, would signal deep trouble for the continued viability of the Supreme Court. This is especially so because our predictions are based upon the justices' *past* voting behavior. Because all human beings operate in a dynamic environment, they cannot be the prisoners of their pasts. Thus the necessity for unpredictable decision making such as the outcome in the poverty law and baseball antitrust cases, just mentioned. And the equally unpredictable outcome of such celebrated cases (which we incorrectly predicted) as abortion reform[33] and capital punishment.[34]

Illustrations of the Predictive Process

The final two decisions of the 1973 term, the Watergate Tapes case,[35] decided on July 24, 1974, and the Detroit Cross-District Busing case,[36] decided one day later, provide good illustrations of the process of predicting the Court's decisions. Prediction of the outcome of the Watergate Tapes case was "soft" in the sense that it was based upon very limited data and vaguely defined legal issues. The Detroit busing case, by comparison, concerned a single, sharply defined issue concerning which each of the justices had a detailed voting record.

In both cases, the outcome and the votes of all the participating justices were correctly predicted. Justice Rehnquist, who had been an Assistant Attorney General in the Department of Justice prior to his appointment to the Court in January 1972, disqualified himself from participation in the tapes case. The probable reason for his recusal seems to have been his several appearances before Congress to argue that the President's executive privilege precluded turning over confidential White House material to the legislative branch of government.

The issue in the Detroit busing case was the validity of a lower federal court ruling that ordered the busing of Detroit schoolchildren to the schools of 52 surrounding suburban school districts, and the busing of the children from these suburban districts to Detroit's schools. Detroit's school officials did not contest the finding that its schools were segregated. The precise question was what to do about it. Is desegregation to end at the city limits, or may surrounding suburban districts be added to achieve a more equal balance of black and white children?

The cumulative scale to which this issue pertains is desegregation. Although school desegregation is arguably an issue separate from other forms of segregation, not enough variation has occurred in the voting of the justices to allow for the formation of a separate school desegregation scale. As explained in Chapter 4, a cumulative scale should contain decisions that fairly completely range from 9 to 0 through 0 to 9. There has been a plentiful sufficiency of 9 to 0 school desegregation decisions (almost three dozen since 1958), but there has also been a decided lack of nonunanimous decisions, and a total absence, at the time the prediction was made, of any that held against desegregation, with the single exception of *Shuttlesworth* v. *Birmingham Board of Education*,[37] a 1958 decision concerned with pupil placement laws, which was decided 0 to 9. In any event, the voting patterns of the justices are such that they make no distinction between school desegregation and other sorts of desegregation, except that the Court has been more supportive of school desegregation than it has nonschool desegregation.

The data showed that the Burger Court had decided 17 school desegregation cases in which the votes of the justices were reported. All 17 of these decisions supported desegregation, as did a whopping 92 percent of the votes cast in these cases (108 of 117). On the basis of the justices' behavior in this set of the most directly relevant decisions, the vote in the Detroit case should have unanimously or nearly unanimously supported cross-district busing. Prediction, however, is not so simple.

The cumulative scale of desegregation clusters closely with others to form the value of equality, one of the three major values identified earlier in this chapter that, together with freedom and New Deal economics, account for approximately 85 percent of the Court's decisions. Given the extremeness of the desegregation ordered by the lower court, the justices' response to the value of equality was judged to be more predictive of the outcome than the voting pattern displayed in the school desegregation decisions.

Table 7.2 specified the response of each of the justices to the value of equality. Because of their support for the value of equality, Douglas, Brennan, and Marshall would support cross-district busing. The lack of support for equality shown by the four Nixon appointees indicated that they would vote against busing. The outcome of the case would turn, then, on the votes of White and Stewart. The data in Table 7.2 show that both these justices hold moderate views toward equality. During his dozen years as a member of the Supreme Court, Justice White had participated in twenty-eight school desegregation decisions. In each of them, he voted for desegregation. Justice Stewart, on the other hand, had twice dissented in opposition to school desegregation as a member of the Burger Court, and had dissented once as a member of the Warren Court.[38] Accordingly, White would vote with the liberals; Stewart would vote with the four Nixon conservatives.

Supporting this conclusion were three decisions that related especially closely to the Detroit busing issue. The first of these was a June 1972 decision, *Wright* v. *Emporia*,[39] in which the four Nixon appointees dissented from a ruling that a Virginia city could not separate itself from the county school district of which it was a part and which was under a court order to desegregate. Speaking through Chief Justice Burger, the dissenters protested that the majority was equating desegregation with racial balance. Once school officials have eliminated segregation, they said, judges should not impose their own plans to increase the ratio of black to white students.

The other decisions, *Richmond School Board* v. *Virginia Board of Education* and *Bradley* v. *Virginia Board of Education*,[40] were handed down in May 1973. Here the Court divided 4 to 4 and thereby upheld a lower-court ruling that two suburban districts could not be forced to consolidate with the Richmond schools. This outcome, incidentally, had been predicted by precisely this vote. Although the Court does not report how the individual justices vote when they are tied, there is little doubt that Rehnquist, Burger, Blackmun, and Stewart opposed consolidation, and that White and the three liberals were supportive. Justice Powell recused himself because of former membership on both the State and Richmond School Boards. These cases, then, further supported a prediction of 5 to 4 against cross-district busing, with Douglas, Brennan, Marshall, and White dissenting. The prediction was correct.

Predicting the Watergate Tapes decision involved a much softer set of assumptions. Initially, because a decision was possible within a day or two after oral argument was heard, the benefit of news reports of the oral argument in making a prediction was not possible. Inasmuch as the typical case contains a number of issues, on any one of which a decision may be based, oral argument frequently provides an indication of which is the most likely basis for decision. Oral argument does not, however, provide reliable clues as to how a given justice may vote.

The chief argument that Nixon's lawyers relied upon was separation of powers. Separation of powers is not a cumulatively scalable category, however, simply because it has not been a basis for any decisions of either the Warren or Burger Courts. But a search did disclose the existence of two peripherally related decisions that bore on the issue of executive privilege, which is based upon the constitutional principle of separation of powers. *Branzburg* v. *Hayes*[41] concerned the question of whether journalists have a First Amendment right to refuse to disclose the sources of their confidential information when called upon to testify as witnesses in grand jury proceedings. Justice White, speaking for himself and for the four Nixon appointees, said "no" and approvingly quoted "the long standing principle" that "the public has the right to every man's evidence." *Scheuer* v. *Rhodes*[42] was an outgrowth of the Kent State killings of 1970. The Court unanimously ruled that the parents of the victims could sue a former governor of Ohio and National Guard officials for damages. Speaking for the justices, Chief Justice Burger emphasized that the Constitution, not the dictates of public officials, is the law of the land, and that it is the responsibility of the courts to determine what materials must be produced in evidence and to what extent, if any, executive privilege applies.

Apart from the intertwined question of separation of powers and executive privilege was the fact that Nixon had voluntarily released portions of his Watergate conversations. For him subsequently to refuse to make further disclosures is analogous to a person who begins to testify on a subject and then refuses to answer additional questions on the ground that they may incriminate him. Although Nixon based his refusal to produce additional tapes upon executive privilege rather than possible self-incrimination, it was nonetheless possible that the Court's receptivity to claims of self-incrimination would prove to be relevant. Analysis did show that only 4 of the 23 Burger Court self-incrimination decisions (17 percent) support the claim. Furthermore, only Justice Douglas had a supportive, or liberal, voting record in this set of decisions.

In a much broader vein, Nixon had taken pains to appoint to the Court persons he described as "judicial conservatives." In October 1971, at the time he nominated Powell and Rehnquist to fill the Black and Harlan vacancies, Nixon, in a nationally televised address, said:

> As a judicial conservative, I believe some Court decisions have gone too far in the past in weakening the peace forces as against the criminal forces in our society.
>
> In maintaining—as it must be maintained—the delicate balance between the rights of society and defendants accused of crimes, I believe the peace forces must not be denied the legal tools they need to protect the innocent from the criminal elements.[43]

On criminal procedure issues, which form the greater part of the value of freedom, Nixon's appointees have been faithful to his position. Since January 1972, when Powell and Rehnquist took their seats, the four Nixon justices had cast approximately 75 percent of their votes in support of the "peace forces" and against "criminal elements."[44] As they were the four most Conservative members of the Court (see Table 7.2), it was not likely that the Nixon appointees would alter their stance simply because the President who had appointed them was now in the line of fire.

The course of Burger Court decision making shows that White and Stewart, the Court's two Moderates, align themselves more often than not with Nixon's appointees to produce conservative decisions in cases concerning the rights of persons accused of crime. Furthermore, neither tends to go his own way. In the almost 1200 cases decided by the Burger Court through the end of the 1973 term, White dissented alone only eight times, Stewart dissented seven, and only once were the two of them the only dissenters.

As for the three Liberal members of the Court, they were likely to take their cue from Douglas, with whom they are most often in agreement, and who is suspicious of executive prerogatives. In the famous Steel Seizure case of 1952 (*Youngstown Sheet and Tube Co.* v. *Sawyer*[45]), Douglas voted against President Truman's assertion of implied executive powers. Brennan and Marshall have each dissented alone only twice on the Burger Court, and in eleven other cases (decided by the Burger Court) they have been the only two dissenters.

Finally, and by no means least importantly, the tapes case constituted a "threat to the Court."[46] Normally, the Court forms minimum winning opinion coalitions (5 to 4, 5 to 3, 4 to 3) except when the justices perceive noncompliance with the Court's decision to be likely, or when Congress is threatening to sanction the Court by limiting its jurisdiction or changing the Court's personnel. In the face of such threats, instead of forming a minimum winning coalition, the Court's decision tends to be unanimous, with all the participating justices concurring in a single opinion. On several occasions, Nixon and his aides had suggested that he might not comply with an adverse decision from the Supreme Court. Consequently, a threat situation existed. Coupled with the indicators previously discussed, a unanimous decision was therefore deemed most probable. Again the prediction was correct.

Is Justice Blind?

Efforts to predict the outcome and voting alignment of pending Court decisions show that the justices base their decisions more on the situations that gave rise to the litigation and less on the characteristics of the litigants who brought the action. In other words, the justices' decisions are more a function of their attitudes toward situations than they are a function of their attitudes toward objects. This is a highly significant finding because of criticisms to which the Court has been subject in recent years.

The ideal, of course, is that justice should be "blind"—that judges, most especially those on appellate courts, should imbue their decisions with a certain myopia. This means that justice should be situationally determined, and that the personal attributes of litigants should never be relevant to a court's decision.

This normative expectation of judicial blindness has been subject to two sorts of attack. On one side, certain radicals maintain that achievement of "real" justice requires that decisions, at times, be partially predicated on personal characteristics. They assert that society has placed certain groups, such as blacks, women, and indigents, in a disadvantaged position. As a result, it ought to be the function of the judiciary to "correct" this imbalance by considering a litigant's color, social position, or degree of poverty as criteria relevant to courts' decisions. On the other side are those who maintain that the Supreme Court is not in fact living up to the standard of judicial blindness. They assert that many decisions of the Warren Court were based upon the litigants' personal characteristics. The Court thus stood accused of bias—of being "soft" toward such groups as blacks, communists, pornographers, and criminals.

Analyses have shown that neither criticism is valid.[47] The Warren Court, for example, did not decide its cases on the basis that a litigant was a business or a labor union, that he was a person exercising freedom of communication, or that he was a black. The Warren Court did, however, disregard the norm of judicial blindness in cases where the litigants were security risks or injured persons. But the Court's failure to adhere to the norm in such cases is explainable. Litigation involving security risks mostly dates from the McCarthy era, a period during which the fear of subversion and the threat of Soviet aggression loomed large in the public mind. No more damning indictment could be levied against an individual than that he was a "security risk" or a "subversive." Consequently, it may be argued that courts should not dispense justice blindly when a climate of fear and vigilantism pervades society. Rather, courts should heed another, equally important, norm—that victims of lawlessness should receive judicial protection, and that the actions of those attempting to punish "political" offenders should not be legitimated. The data indicate that this indeed was what happened, as approximately two-thirds of the Court's security risks decisions favored the accused.

The reason for the Court's failure to adhere to the blindness norm in cases concerning injured persons differs from that which explains the security risks decisions. Congress has never seen fit to enact a workmen's compensation law. Commentators,[48] as well as Supreme Court justices themselves,[49] have pointed out that the Court, at least since 1939, has been attempting to remedy congressional neglect by consciously functioning as a workmen's compensation commission for those fortunate few who managed to secure access to the Court. The data again indicate that this indeed is what has been happening, as approximately three-fourths of the Warren Court's decisions supported injured workmen.

Although mention of businesses, labor unions, persons exercising freedom of communication, blacks, security risks, and injured persons does not exhaust the list of persons seeking redress of grievances before the Supreme Court, we are reasonably confident that the Court deals with its other litigants compatibly with the normative ideal of judicial blindness, and that where the Court disregards the ideal it does so in preference to another equally important norm or because of inaction by other units of government.

Summary

In this chapter we applied the theory and methodology presented in Chapter 4 to the decision making of the last eleven terms of the Warren Court (1958–1968) and the first five terms of the Burger Court (1969–1973).

Compatibly with the operationalization of the construct "attitude," sets of cumulative scales were formed from the decisions of each period. Using three types of computer-dependent data reduction techniques, "values" were identified, three of which—freedom, equality, and New Deal economics—account for approximately 85 percent of the Court's decisions. On the basis of their voting in these category scales, the value systems of the justices were then identified. Thirteen of the seventeen justices were shown to be either Liberal or Conservative; two were Moderates—one each a Populist and a New Dealer. To test the adequacy of the theory and methodology, public predictions of some of the Court's more important decisions have been made. Approximately 86 percent of the votes of the justices in these cases have been accurately predicted. Almost 88 percent of the outcomes of these cases have been correctly predicted. During the 1972–1973 terms, 33 of 34 decisions (97.1 percent) were accurately predicted, including the two most widely publicized decisions of the 1973 term, the Detroit Cross-District Busing case and the Watergate Tapes case. As a by-product of our predictive efforts, analyses show that the Court adheres to the normative ideal of judicial blindness: that the decisions of the Court are based primarily upon the situations that gave rise to the litigation rather than upon the personal characteristics of the litigants themselves.

Appendix to Chapter 7

At the end of this Appendix is a table that lists the cumulative scales that reflect the attitudes that have motivated the justices' behavior. At the left are the number and name of the scale. These are followed by the attitude object (AO) and attitude situation (AS) that best describe the contents of the scale. In a few instances a subsidiary attitude situation (AS_1) is also listed in order to distinguish that scale from other scales with a similar content.

The data appearing to the right of the AO/AS listing for each scale are divided into two rows. The first row is the scale data for the 1958–1968 terms of the Warren Court. The second row is the scale data for the 1969–1973 terms of the Burger Court.

N refers to the total number of cases contained in the scale.

R is the coefficient of reproducibility, which measures the proportion of nonscale (or inconsistent) votes to consistent votes. In the calculation of R, votes in unanimously decided cases and votes with only a sole dissent are excluded. It is conventional to consider an $R \geq .90$ evidence of an acceptable scale. We have attempted to attain an $R \geq .95$ in our scales.

MMR is the minimum marginal reproducibility. It is the lowest empirical level that R can attain, given the maximum number of inconsistent votes that can occur in the actual voting of the justices in a particular scale. MMR can never be less than .50 or exceed 1.00.

$R - MMR$ is the difference between R and MMR for each scale. MMR is essentially meaningless except as a measure of the extent to which R is more than the empirically lowest level that could result from the justices' voting patterns. The greater the $R - MMR$ difference the better the scale. In general, a difference of at least .10 to .15 should occur except when R approximates 1.00.

"Value" refers to the value with which each scale associates. The three major values, as identified in the text of Chapter 7, are freedom, equality, and New Deal economics. The two minor Warren Court values, privacy and taxation, are also identified. The word "mixed" refers to a scale that clusters with at least two of the major values and thus cannot be identified as part of any single value. The word "outlyer" refers to a scale that is neither part of any of the major values nor of either of the two minor Warren Court values. These outlyers do not form part of any value, and no two of them cluster together by themselves.

Comparison of the legal and semantic content of some of the scales with the value with which it associates suggests that they would be better-positioned elsewhere. Thus, for example, reapportionment (58) clusters with New Deal economics in the Burger Court period rather than with equality, the value to which it is most closely related semantically. Some of these anomalous results occur because of the small size of the scale and/or the lack of rank-order discrimination among the justices. In scales where a majority of the justices are tied in rank with one another, or where several justices cannot be ranked at all because they were not members of the Court when the cases were decided, the existence of strange value relationships is not surprising.

Other deviations between a scale's legal and semantic content and the value of which it is a part are more apparent than real. Several Warren Court scales that cluster with New Deal economics appear semantically closer to freedom: libel-defamation (41), jury trial (37), Federal Rules of Civil Procedure (27), venue (81), and judicial administration (36). The majority of the cases in these scales, however, were civil, rather than criminal, litigation in which economic interests were at stake. The shift of statutory interpretation (73), from freedom in the Warren Court period to a mixed status in the Burger Court years, is similarly explainable. The statutes interpreted by the Warren Court pertained solely to personal freedom, whereas those interpreted by the Burger Court concerned political and social equality in addition to others that related to personal freedom. A similar difference in content explains the shift of subconstitutional fair procedure (75) and armed forces (5) from New Dealism to freedom. Approximately one quarter of these decisions were economically connected during the Warren Court—civil proceedings and various types of veterans' pension benefits. This economic aspect has virtually disappeared from the

Burger Court decisions: every armed forces case involving alleged violation of Selective Service (and all but two of the subconstitutional fair procedure cases) has related to criminal proceedings.

Apart from these explanations of deviance between the legal and semantic content of some of the scales and the values with which they associate, the basic point here is that our data reduction techniques pay no attention whatsoever to the contents of any scale. Whether a given scale clusters with others is simply a function of the scale's correlation coefficient, as derived from the rank order of the justices, with that of each of the other scales in the data set. Hence, even though the legal and semantic description of a given scale does not conform with what is considered freedom, equality, or New Deal economics, the fact remains that the justices treat the scaled cases as though they do pertain to an aspect of the value with which they associate.

The phrases "not scalable," "no decisions," and "no separate scale" that appear in place of the statistical data for some of the scales indicate that during either the Warren or Burger Court periods, the cases in the pertinent scale did not contain a sufficient number of different marginals (7–2, 6–3, 5–4, 4–5, 3–6, 2–7) to allow for the construction of a scale (numbers 25, 28, 34, 38, 57, 59, 71, 72, 79, and 81); that no cases were decided pertaining to the scale (numbers 1, 14, 16, 39, 42, 62, 63, 64, 65, 68, 69, and 78); or that the cases were combined with others so that no separate scale for one or the other of the periods was constructed (numbers 7, 21, 33, 55, and 70).

Eight of the ten "not scalable" scales pertain to the Burger Court period. The reason for this is that the Burger Court period covers less than half the length of time of the Warren Court period. The inclusion of a longer period would undoubtedly produce enough additional decisions to allow for the construction of these scales. Eight of the "no decisions" scales result because the Burger Court has rendered no decisions at all in those areas (numbers 16, 39, 42, 62, 63, 64, 69, and 78). Numbers 62, 63, and 64 result from the division of the Warren Court's search-and-seizure decisions into separate periods. There was no need to do this for the Burger Court. The remaining "no decisions" scales (numbers 1, 14, 65, and 68) are issues that the Warren Court did not address. Two of the five "no separate scale" scales, numbers 7 and 55, also result from the division of the Warren Court's search-and-seizure cases into their component parts. We did not treat numbers 21, 33, and 70 as separate scales for the Warren Court.

As a summary measure of the quality of the scales, the average and median R, MMR, and $R - MMR$ are listed at the end of this Appendix for the Warren and Burger Court periods.

Although it is not included in the data that follow, some discussion of the correlational characteristics of the three major values is in order. We limit our observations to the data on the Burger Court because they are more current and because they supply the primary data base from which predictions are made.

According to the operational definition of value specified in Chapter 4, the sum total of all the correlation coefficients between all the pairs of scales constituting a value should produce an average and median correlation $\geq .6$. This criterion has been met, with room to spare, by all three of the major values. Freedom produces an average correlation of .73 and a median of .76; equality produces an average of .71 and a median of .72; and New Deal economics produces an average of .69 and a median of .71.

The other aspect of the operational definition of a value is that each scale show an average and median rank-order correlation coefficient with the other scales that are part of the value $\geq .6$. This criterion is met in every case but one. Gifts (31) produces an average correlation of .58 and a median correlation of .59 with the other fourteen scales that constitute New Deal economics.

The other scales correlate with the others in their respective values at a level ranging from the low sixties to the low eighties. Correlating highest among the freedom scales are retroactivity (60) with an average correlation of .79 and a median of .81, subconstitutional fair procedure (75) at .80 and .79, and federal obscenity (48) at .79 and .80. Lowest are abortion (1) with an average and median correlation of .62, and creditors' rights (14) with an average and median of .63. Among the equality values, comity (11) is highest at .81 and .83, followed by extralegal jury influences (24) at .80 and .80, and indigents (35) at .79 and .81. Lowest are judicial administration (36) at .60 and .63, and cruel and unusual punishment (15) at .61 and .63. Correlating highest within New Deal economics are election of remedies (22) at .80 and .83, and mergers (44) at .78 and .79. Lowest are gifts (31), as previously noted, and business vis-à-vis unions (8) at .60 and .60.

Finally, a word about the six scales identified as "mixed." All produce an average and median correlation with both of the values to which they relate $\geq .6$. Both line-up (43) and statutory interpretation (73) correlate with both freedom and equality at a level $> .75$. At the other extreme is sex discrimination (68), which correlates with equality at an average of .66 and a median of .69, and with freedom at an average of .62 and a median of .61.

160

SCALE	AO/AS	N	R	MMR	R − MMR	VALUE
1. Abortion	AO: fetuses	4	1.00	No decisions		
	AS: abortion legislation			.828	.172	freedom
2. Administrative procedure	AO: administrative agencies	54	.957	.787	.170	outlyer
	AS: autonomy of administrative agency regulation	30	.959	.774	.185	outlyer
	AS$_1$: judicial supervision of administrative agency decision making					
3. Antitrust	AO: restrictive business activities	73	.978	.865	.113	New Deal
	AS: federal antitrust regulation	12	.968	.875	.093	New Deal
4. Arbitration	AO: labor contracts	16	1.00	.900	.100	outlyer
	AS: arbitration	5	.939	.826	.113	outlyer
5. Armed forces	AO: military personnel: potential, actual, or former	31	.947	.831	.116	New Deal
	AS$_1$: civil and/or economic rights	30	.960	.812	.142	freedom
6. Bankruptcy	AO: debtors	16	.987	.818	.169	New Deal
	AS: federal regulation	5	.963	.901	.062	New Deal
7. Bugging	AO: criminal defendants	35	.953	.800	.153	equality
	AS: search and seizure					
	AS$_1$: electronic eavesdropping			No separate scale		
8. Business/unions	AO: labor unions	16	.971	.825	.146	mixed
	AS: legal rights of business vis-à-vis unions	8	.970	.849	.121	New Deal
9. Citizenship, immigration, and naturalization	AO: citizens, naturalized persons, or persons seeking naturalization	15	.981	.850	.131	freedom
	AS: citizenship	8	.963	.834	.129	freedom
10. Coerced confession	AO: criminal defendants	39	.987	.852	.135	freedom
	AS: voluntariness of confession	9	1.00	.944	.056	freedom

(*Continued*)

SCALE	AO/AS	N	R	MMR	R − MMR	VALUE
11. Comity	AO: persons negatively sanctioned by state judicial systems	28	.986	.892	.094	equality
	AS: comity	41	.955	.844	.111	equality
12. Confrontation	AO: criminal defendants	28	1.00	.925	.075	equality
	AS: right to confront and cross-examine witnesses	12	.968	.833	.135	equality
13. Contempt of court	AO: litigants negatively sanctioned by the judicial system	17	.988	.860	.128	New Deal
	AS: contempt of court	6	1.00	.833	.167	mixed
14. Creditors' rights	AO: creditors	5	1.00	No decisions		freedom
	AS: right to property		.986	.934	.066	freedom
15. Cruel and unusual punishment	AO: persons convicted of crime	8	.986	.789	.197	equality
	AS: cruel and unusual punishment	11	1.00	.906	.094	equality
16. Deportation	AO: aliens	18	.977	.868	.109	freedom
	AS: deportation			No decisions		
17. Desegregation	AO: blacks	45	.987	.843	.144	equality
	AS: desegregation	48	1.00	.894	.106	equality
18. Discovery and inspection	AO: criminal defendants	20	.994	.906	.088	freedom
	AS: access to governmental testimony	5	1.00	.853	.147	mixed
19. Double jeopardy	AO: criminal defendants	19	.990	.837	.153	freedom
	AS: double jeopardy	30	.980	.870	.110	freedom
20. Due process	AO: litigants negatively sanctioned by the judicial system	30	.992	.768	.224	freedom
	AS: due process	32	.955	.817	.138	freedom
21. Due process hearing	AO: litigants negatively sanctioned by the judicial system	7	1.00	.861	.139	New Deal
	AS: right to hearing			No separate scale		
22. Election of remedies	AO: injured persons	32	.983	.854	.129	New Deal
	AS: election of remedies	13	1.00	.852	.148	New Deal

#	Topic		Description	N				Category
23.	Establishment of religion	AO:	persons exercising religious freedom	12	1.00	1.00	.000	New Deal
		AS:	establishment of religion	20	1.00	.920	.080	freedom
24.	Extralegal jury influences	AO:	criminal defendant	54	.978	.876	.111	equality
		AS:	extralegal influence upon jurors	39	.963	.800	.163	equality
25.	Fair Labor Standards Act	AO:	employees	10	.925	.781	.144	freedom
		AS:	Fair Labor Standards Act	3		Not scalable		
26.	Federal internal security legislation	AO:	security risks	25	1.00	.908	.092	freedom
		AS:	federal internal security legislation	3	1.00	.900	.100	freedom
27.	Federal Rules of Civil Procedure	AO:	persons negatively sanctioned by the legal system	25	.954	.810	.144	New Deal
		AS:	Federal Rules of Civil Procedure	8	.963	.851	.112	freedom
28.	Federal Rules of Criminal Procedure	AO:	criminal defendants	27	1.00	.878	.122	freedom
		AS:	Federal Rules of Criminal Procedure	3		Not scalable		
29.	Federal taxation	AO:	taxpayers	55	.979	.893	.086	taxation
		AS:	federal taxation	21	.939	.735	.154	outlyer
30.	First Amendment	AO:	persons exercising freedom of communication	16	1.00	.889	.111	freedom
		AS:	"harmful" beliefs or ideas	29	.981	.899	.082	freedom
31.	Gifts	AO:	taxpayers	18	.977	.856	.121	New Deal
		AS:	federal taxation of gifts, professional and personal expenses	5	1.00	.889	.111	New Deal
32.	Governmental corruption	AO:	governmental wrongdoing	11	.966	.755	.211	freedom
		AS:	federal regulation	2	1.00	.833	.167	New Deal
33.	Habeas corpus	AO:	persons convicted of crime	11	1.00	No separate scale	.867	.133	equality
		AS:	writ of habeas corpus					
34.	Indians	AO:	Indians	2		Not scalable		
		AS:	government regulation	10	.938	.824	.114	freedom
35.	Indigents	AO:	indigents	35	.974	.900	.074	equality
		AS:	legal aid	29	.957	.876	.081	equality

(*Continued*)

SCALE	AO/AS		N	R	MMR	R − MMR	VALUE
36. Judicial administration	AO:	persons seeking federal judicial redress	35	.946	.763	.183	New Deal
	AS:	Supreme Court supervision of the judicial system	29	.985	.803	.182	equality
	AS₁:	federal court jurisdiction					
37. Jury trial	AO:	litigants negatively sanctioned by the judicial system	28	.984	.816	.168	New Deal
	AS:	right to trial by jury	16	.941	.894	.047	freedom
38. Juveniles	AO:	juveniles	4		Not scalable		
	AS:	legal rights	6	.952	.825	.127	equality
39. Legislative investigations	AO:	security risks	29	.989	.876	.113	freedom
	AS:	legislative investigations			No decisions		
40. Liability	AO:	injured persons	42	.964	.817	.147	New Deal
	AS:	liability	16	.962	.876	.086	New Deal
41. Libel-defamation	AO:	persons exercising freedom of communication	16	1.00	.806	.194	New Deal
	AS:	defamation	9	.967	.831	.136	outlyer
42. Libel-privacy	AO:	persons exercising freedom of press communication	3	1.00	No decisions	.176	privacy
	AS:	privacy					
43. Line-up	AO:	criminal defendants	5	.978	.833	.145	mixed
	AS:	line-up identification	3	.962	.927	.035	mixed
44. Mergers	AO:	mergers	57	.995	.895	.100	New Deal
	AS:	federal regulation	11	.981	.928	.053	New Deal
45. Mootness	AO:	persons seeking judicial redress	15	.968	.813	.155	freedom
	AS:	mootness	20	.930	.784	.146	New Deal
46. National supremacy	AO:	federal-state conflict	28	.983	.743	.240	outlyer
	AS:	national supremacy	11	.953	.749	.204	outlyer

			N				
47. Natural resources	AO:	natural resources	12	.955	.829	.126	New Deal
	AS:	governmental regulation	14	.984	.833	.151	New Deal
48. Obscenity—federal	AO:	persons exercising freedom of communication	8	1.00	.833	.167	privacy
	AS:	federal regulation of obscenity	30	1.00	.967	.033	freedom
49. Obscenity—state	AO:	persons exercising freedom of communication	39	.990	.832	.158	privacy
	AS:	state regulation of obscenity	99	.999	.988	.011	mixed
50. Patents and copyrights	AO:	patents and copyrights	19	.944	.749	.195	New Deal
	AS:	creativity	8	.932	.722	.210	outlyer
51. Plea bargaining	AO:	criminal defendants	7	1.00	.865	.135	equality
	AS:	plea of guilty to lesser offense than that charged	9	.985	.897	.091	equality
52. Poverty law	AO:	indigents	15	.938	.841	.097	equality
	AS:	poverty law	50	.970	.852	.118	equality
53. Pre-emption	AO:	state court jurisdiction	27	.974	.844	.130	freedom
	AS:	labor union activities	8	.940	.788	.152	freedom
	AS_1:	federal pre-emption of state jurisdiction					
54. Priority	AO:	federal fiscal claims	16	.958	.752	.206	taxation
	AS:	priority of federal fiscal claims	4	.944	.778	.166	equality
55. Privacy	AO:	criminal defendants	14	.990	.894	.096	freedom
	AS:	search and seizure			No separate scale		
	AS_1:	privacy					
56. Protest	AO:	demonstrators	18	.951	.859	.092	equality
	AS:	protest demonstrations	29	.968	.853	.115	equality
57. Public utilities	AO:	public utilities	55	.982	.833	.149	New Deal
	AS:	federal regulation	9		Not scalable		
58. Reapportionment	AO:	persons seeking equitable governmental representation	56	.993	.909	.084	equality
	AS:	legislative reapportionment or districting	19	.974	.851	.123	New Deal

(Continued)

SCALE	AO/AS		N	R	MMR	R − MMR	VALUE
59. Religious freedom	AO:	persons exercising religious freedom	9	.981	.831	.150	outlyer
	AS:	religious freedom	3		Not scalable		
60. Retroactivity	AO:	criminal defendants	35	.982	.913	.069	outlyer
	AS:	retroactive application of constitutional and statutory guarantees	16	.941	.857	.084	freedom
61. Right to counsel	AO:	criminal defendants	20	.986	.786	.200	freedom
	AS:	right to counsel	8	.952	.870	.082	freedom
62. Search and seizure (1958–1961 terms)	AO:	criminal defendants	15	.975	.843	.132	mixed
	AS:	search and seizure			No decisions		
63. Search and seizure (1962–1966 terms)	AO:	criminal defendants	20	.957	.848	.109	freedom
	AS:	search and seizure			No decisions		
64. Search and seizure (1967–1968 terms)	AO:	criminal defendants	21	.940	.816	.124	equality
	AS:	search and seizure			No decisions		
65. Search and seizure (Burger Court)	AO:	criminal defendants	50	.993	.915	.078	equality
	AS:	search and seizure			No decisions		
66. Security risks	AO:	security risks	17	.983	.896	.087	freedom
	AS:	public employment or benefits	11	1.00	.903	.097	New Deal
67. Self-incrimination	AO:	criminal defendants	188	.992	.891	.101	New Deal
	AS:	self-incrimination	26	1.00	.900	.100	freedom
68. Sex discrimination	AO:	women	10	.987	No decisions		
	AS:	sex discrimination			.848	.139	mixed
69. Sit-ins	AO:	demonstrators	31	.986	.882	.104	equality
	AS:	sit-in demonstrations			No decisions		
70. Standing to sue	AO:	persons seeking judicial redress			No separate scale		
	AS:	standing to sue	10	.983	.920	.063	freedom
71. State business regulation	AO:	business	23	1.00	.834	.166	New Deal
	AS:	state regulation	1		Not scalable		

72. State taxation	AO: business	24	.988	.804	.184	mixed
	AS: state taxation	7		Not scalable		
73. Statutory interpretation	AO: criminal defendants	17	.931	.809	.122	freedom
	AS: interpretation of federal statutes	25	.945	.780	.165	mixed
74. Stocks	AO: securities industries	9	1.00	.843	.157	equality
	AS: federal regulation	7	.976	.875	.101	New Deal
75. Subconstitutional fair procedure	AO: persons negatively sanctioned by the legal system	35	.968	.843	.125	New Deal
	AS: subconstitutional fair procedure	10	.981	.840	.141	freedom
76. Sufficiency of evidence	AO: injured persons	35	.993	.845	.148	New Deal
	AS: sufficiency of evidence	12	.986	.959	.027	New Deal
	AS_1: jury determination					
77. Transportation	AO: transportation industries	66	.969	.805	.164	New Deal
	AS: federal regulation	8	.976	.907	.069	outlyer
78. Union and closed shop	AO: labor unions	13	.960	.807	.153	freedom
	AS: union membership as a condition of employment		No decisions			
79. Union antitrust	AO: restrictive union activities	10	.964	.878	.086	New Deal
	AS: federal antitrust regulation	1		Not scalable		
80. Unions/business	AO: labor unions	46	.952	.820	.132	New Deal
	AS: legal rights of unions vis-à-vis business	17	.941	.774	.167	outlyer
81. Venue	AO: persons seeking judicial redress	18	.971	.775	.196	New Deal
	AS: venue	1		Not scalable		
82. Voting	AO: persons seeking to vote	32	.960	.801	.159	equality
	AS: right to vote	32	.995	.854	.141	equality

(*Continued*)

SUMMARY DATA

COURT	R		MMR		R – MMR	
	AVERAGE	MEDIAN	AVERAGE	MEDIAN	AVERAGE	MEDIAN
Warren Court (73 scales)	.977	.982	.843	.843	.134	.139
Burger Court (64 scales)	.974	.975	.858	.853	.116	.122

Notes to Chapter 7

1. Published by the Lawyers Co-Operative Publishing Co., Rochester, New York.

2. 14 L Ed 2d 49 (1965).

3. 19 L Ed 2d 1267 (1968).

4. 10 L Ed 2d 321 (1963).

5. 19 L Ed 2d 1 (1967).

6. 4 L Ed 2d 747 (1960).

7. 5 L Ed 2d 222 (1960).

8. The numbers in parentheses following the names of the scales refer to the table of cumulative scales at the end of the Appendix to this chapter.

9. 20 L Ed 2d 415 (1968).

10. Among the 80 cases not located in any one of the 73 category scales are 20 that formed three quasi-scales. These are excluded from analysis because of lack of rank-order discrimination among the respondent justices. If these 20 cases are excluded from consideration entirely, 97.1 percent of the remaining cases locate in a category scale.

11. $n(n - 1)/2$, where $n = 73$.

12. Mary R. Mattingly, *The Hughes Court 1931–1936: Psychological Dimensions of Decision Making* (unpublished Ph.D. Dissertation, Michigan State University, 1969); and Peter G. Renstrom, *The Dimensionality of Decision Making of the 1941–1945 Stone Court: A Computer Dependent Analysis of Supreme Court Behavior* (unpublished Ph.D. Dissertation, Michigan State University, 1972).

13. The scores of Douglas, Brennan, Marshall, Stewart, and White are based upon their votes in Burger Court decisions only. This was done to ensure accuracy of their current response to the three major values. The scores of the other justices cover the entirety of the 1958–1974 period during which they were members of the Court.

14. Most of these predictions have appeared in an occasional newspaper column entitled, "The Supreme Court Computer," distributed by R-Squared, Inc. of Los Angeles, and published in the *Los Angeles Herald-Examiner*.

15. Not every outcome that was predicted pertained to every justice. Thus, contrary to other published reports, we predicted in May 1970 that Stewart and White would be the Court's "swing men," who would be in the majority more frequently than any of the other justices in closely decided cases (i.e., 5 to 4, 5 to 3, and 4 to 3). The prediction still holds five years later.

16. Washington, D.C.: Bureau of National Affairs.

17. 393 U.S. 997, 21 L Ed 2d 462 (1968).

18. 398 U.S. 262, 26 L Ed 2d 221 (1970). "In the action we take today, we express no view whatever with respect to the two questions originally specified in our grant of certiorari." 398 U.S. 262, at 267.

19. *Witherspoon* v. *Illinois*, 391 U.S. 510, 20 L Ed 2d 776 (1968).

20. *McGautha* v. *California* and *Crampton* v. *Ohio*, 402 U.S. 183, 28 L Ed 2d 711 (1971).

21. *Swann* v. *Charlotte-Mecklenburg Board of Education*, 402 U.S. 1, 28 L Ed 2d 554; *Davis* v. *Mobile County Board of School Commissioners*, 402 U.S. 33, 28 L Ed 2d 557; *McDaniel* v. *Barresi*, 402 U.S. 39, 28 L Ed 2d 582; and *North Carolina State Board of Education* v. *Swann*, 402 U.S. 43, 28 L Ed 2d 586.

22. *Miller* v. *California*, 37 L Ed 2d 419; *Paris Adult Theatre* v. *Slaton*, 37 L Ed 2d 446; *Kaplan* v. *California*, 37 L Ed 2d 492; *Heller* v. *New York*, 37 L Ed 2d 745; and *Roaden* v. *Kentucky*, 37 L Ed 2d 757.

23. *Lemon* v. *Kurtzman*, 403 U.S. 602, 29 L Ed 2d 745; and *Tilton* v. *Richardson*, 403 U.S. 672, 29 L Ed 2d 790 (1971).

24. *California Department of Human Resources* v. *Java*, 402 U.S. 121, 28 L Ed 2d 666; *James* v. *Valtierra*, 402 U.S. 137, 28 L Ed 2d 678; and *Graham* v. *Richardson*, 403 U.S. 365, 29 L Ed 2d 534.

25. *Goldberg* v. *Kelly*, 397 U.S. 254, 25 L Ed 2d 287 (1970).

26. *Shapiro* v. *Thompson*, 394 U.S. 618, 22 L Ed 2d 600 (1969).

27. 393 U.S. 385, 21 L Ed 2d 616 (1969).

28. 402 U.S. 137, at 141; 28 L Ed 2d 678, at 682.

29. 407 U.S. 258, 32 L Ed 2d 728 (1972).

30. *Toolson* v. *New York Yankees*, 346 U.S. 356, 98 L Ed 64.

31. As evidence, see the work of Reed C. Lawlor: "Personal Stare Decisis," *Southern California Law Review* 41 (1967): 73–118; "Fact Content Analysis of Judicial Opinions," *Jurimetrics Journal*, June 1968, pp. 107–130; "The Chancellor's Foot: A Modern View," *Houston Law Review* 6 (1969): 630–665; "Axioms of Fact Polarization and Fact Ranking—Their Role in Stare Decisis," *Villanova Law Review* 14 (1969): 703–726; and his unpublished 1971 papers, "Theory of Applicability" and "Fact Content of Cases and Precedent—A Modern Theory of Precedent."

32. M. J. Klingsporn, "The Significance of Variability," *Behavioral Science* 18 (1973): 443.

33. *Roe* v. *Wade*, 35 L Ed 2d 147 (1973); and *Doe* v. *Bolton*, 35 L Ed 2d 201 (1973). The state abortion laws were predicted to be constitutional by a 5 to 2 vote, Stewart and Douglas dissenting. The actual vote was 7 to 2 against their constitutionality, White and Rehnquist dissenting. The votes of Burger, Blackmun, Marshall, and Brennan were incorrectly predicted. No prediction of the votes of Powell and Rehnquist was made because they did not participate in the original arguments.

34. *Furman* v. *Georgia*, 408 U.S. 238, 33 L Ed 2d 346 (1972). The constitutionality of capital punishment was predicted by a 6 to 3 vote with Douglas, Brennan, and Marshall dissenting. The actual vote was 5 to 4 against constitutionality, with the four Nixon appointees dissenting. The incorrectly predicted votes were those of Stewart and White.

35. *United States* v. *Nixon* and *Nixon* v. *United States*, 41 L Ed 2d 1039.

36. *Milliken* v. *Bradley, Allen Park Public Schools* v. *Bradley*, and *The Grosse Pointe Public School System* v. *Bradley*, 41 L Ed 2d 1069.

37. 358 U.S. 101, 3 L Ed 2d 145. In 1973, the Court upheld a pair of anti-desegregation decisions by a 4 to 4 vote. See p. 153.

38. *Singleton* v. *Jackson School District* and *Carter* v. *West Feliciana Parish School Board*, 396 U.S. 290, 24 L Ed 2d 477 (1970); and *Sweet Briar Institute* v. *Button*, 387 U.S. 423, 18 L Ed 2d 865 (1967).

39. 407 U.S. 451, 33 L Ed 2d 51.

40. 36 L Ed 2d 771.

41. 408 U.S. 665, 33 L Ed 2d 626 (1972).

42. 40 L Ed 2d 90 (1974).

43. *New York Times*, October 22, 1971, p. 24.

44. For more detail on this point see Chapter 5.

45. 343 U.S. 579.

46. For a full discussion of this concept and examples of its application, including this case, see Chapter 9.

47. Harold J. Spaeth and Douglas R. Parker, "Effects of Attitude toward Situation upon Attitude toward Object," *Journal of Psychology* 73 (1969): 173–182; Harold J. Spaeth et al., "Is Justice Blind: An Empirical Analysis of a Normative Theorem," *Law and Society Review* 7 (1972): 119–137.

48. For example, James C. Connor, "Supreme Court Certiorari Policy and the Federal Employers' Liability Act," *Cornell Law Quarterly* 43 (1958): 451–468; Glendon Schubert, "Policy Without Law: An Extension of the Certiorari Game," *Stanford Law Review* 14 (1962): 284–327.

49. For example, *Bailey* v. *Central Vermont R. Co.*, 319 U.S. 350 (1943), at 354–359; *Stone* v. *N.Y.C. & St. L.R. Co.*, 344 U.S. 407 (1953), at 410–413; *McAlister* v. *United States*, 348 U.S. 19 (1954), at 23–25; *Rogers* v. *Mo. Pacific R. Co.*, 352 U.S. 500 (1957), at 559–564.

8 | *The Assignment of the Majority Opinion*

When John Marshall became Chief Justice of the United States, he did away with the practice of delivering opinions *seriatim* (each justice writing and delivering an opinion in every case), believing that the power and prestige of the Supreme Court would be enhanced if it spoke with a single voice.[1] Since that time the Chief Justice, if he is in the majority, has had the authority to write the majority opinion himself or to assign it to one of the other justices in the majority. If the Chief Justice has dissented, or did not participate, this power passes to the senior associate justice in the majority.

Opinion Assignments and Policy Goals

The Opinion of the Court is the core of the policy-making power of the Supreme Court. The vote on the merits in conference determines only whether the decision of the court below will be affirmed or reversed. It is the majority opinion which lays down the broad constitutional and legal principles that govern the decision in the case before the Court, which are theoretically binding on lower courts in all similar cases, and which establish precedents for future decisions of the Court.

The primary responsibility for formulating the policy to be made in a case rests with the justice to whom the majority opinion is assigned. He is not, however, a free agent who can simply write the opinion to satisfy solely his own preferences. If there is to be an Opinion of the Court, he must fashion his opinion so that it will gain the assent of at least four of his colleagues (if eight or more justices are participating). Often the preferences of other justices are taken into account during the drafting of an opinion. At other times demands for changes are made after a draft opinion has been circulated to the other members of the Court, and such demands are often quite explicit. Justice Stone once wrote the following note to Justice Frankfurter:

> If you wish to write, placing the case on the ground which I think tenable and desirable, I shall cheerfully join you. If not, I will add a few observations for myself.[2]

The writing of the majority opinion has important implications for the achievement of policy goals by the opinion assigner, the opinion writer, and the other justices on the Court.[3] The opinion assigner knows that the justice to whom he assigns the majority opinion will be forced to bargain and make policy concessions, and the important question to him is, with whom will bargains be struck and precisely what concessions will be made? He also knows, however, that the justice to whom he assigns the opinion will use that opinion to achieve his (the writer's) policy goals. Thus the rational strategy for the assigner would be to assign the opinion to the justice in the majority whose views are closest to the assigner's.

Obviously, the person whose views are most congruent with those of the assigner is the assigner himself, and thus the safest strategy would be for the assigner to write all opinions himself. It is clear, however, that the assigner operates under a constraint that makes this impossible. An expectation exists among the members of the Court that the work load of majority opinion writing will be spread fairly evenly among the justices. A departure from this expectation can produce serious disharmony within the Court. During Hughes' Chief Justiceship, Stone felt slighted because Hughes did not assign him as many important opinions as he felt he should have received. Justices Murphy and Rutledge apparently felt the same with regard to Stone during his tenure as Chief Justice.[4]

Chief Justice Warren noted the importance of this point in discussing his opinion assignments (and it was the only factor he mentioned as influencing them):

> I do believe that if [assigning opinions] wasn't done with regard to fairness, it could well lead to great disruption in the Court.
> During all the years I was there . . . I did try very hard to see that we had an equal work load, that we weren't all writing in one field where one person would be considered the expert. Everybody, regardless of length of time they were on the Court, had a fair opportunity to write important cases.[5]

Thus there exists a source of tension: the assigner attempts to satisfy both his own policy goals and the expectations of the other justices.

If the opinion assigner must, in order to equalize the work load among the justices, assign most of the majority opinions to others, to whom should he assign them? Remembering our assumption that the motivation of each justice is the achievement of his policy goals, and that, therefore, the justice who writes the majority opinion will try to use it to that end, we can say that the rational strategy for the assigner is to assign the opinion to the justice whose views are most like his own on the issue being decided. Thus our theory implies a general decision rule for opinion assigners: *The justice who assigns the majority opinion will either write the opinion himself or assign it to the justice whose position is closest to his own on the issue in question.*

We discuss the application of this decision rule in detail in the following paragraphs, in connection with an examination of data on opinion assignments in the Warren Court. First, however, we consider some other potential influences on opinion assignments.

Other Influences on Opinion Assignments

Many students of the Court have noted factors that may influence opinion assignments. These may be grouped into two categories: considerations that relate to intra-Court persuasion and satisfaction, and considerations that relate to extra-Court influences.

Intra-Court Factors

In addition to the expectation, just discussed, that majority opinion writing will be spread equally among the justices, a frequently noted influence on opinion assignments is the desire to hold together a majority opinion coalition or to expand agreement within the Court or both.[6] According to this view, the majority opinion may be used both as a "side payment," that is, a reward to a justice to induce him to join in, or remain in, a majority opinion, and as an influence toward moderation of views within the Court—an effort to increase group cohesion with regard to policy.

The influence of this "persuasion" factor will thus be directed primarily toward one of two goals: (1) to hold together a tenuous majority, or (2) to increase the size of a solid majority. If the effort is directed at holding a majority, the opinion will be assigned to a wavering or unsure justice, "hoping that this task—if not further reflection and research— will strengthen the Justice's resolve and perhaps sway the minority."[7] Alternatively, if the purpose is to gain additional adherents, the opinion will be assigned to the most moderate member of the majority. "The theory here is that the justice would, in this case—and probably in others—be a 'center justice,' whose 'middle' approach would be acceptable, more or less, to both majority and minority."[8]

In line with this second purpose, Danelski has hypothesized two assignment rules for the persuasion of would-be dissenters:

> *Rule 1:* Assign the case to the Justice whose views are closest to the dissenters on the ground that his opinion would take a middle approach

upon which both majority and minority could agree.
Rule 2: Where there are blocs on the Court and a bloc splits, assign
the case to a majority member of the dissenters' bloc on the ground
that he would take a middle approach upon which both the majority
and minority could agree with him because of general mutuality of
agreement.[9]

Analyzing Supreme Court decisions from the period 1921 to 1946,
Danelski found that Taft and Stone did not follow either of these rules
with any consistency, but that "an analysis of Hughes' assignments from
1932 to 1937 indicates that he probably did."[10] Danelski found the evidence strong that Hughes followed Rule 1 whenever the right or left bloc
dissented intact.

> When the liberal bloc dissented, Roberts, who was then a center judge,
> was assigned 46.5 percent of the opinions. The remaining 53.5 percent
> were divided among the conservatives, apparently according to their
> degree of conservatism: Sutherland, 25 percent; Butler, 17.8 percent;
> McReynolds, 10.7 percent. When the conservative bloc dissented,
> Hughes divided 63 percent of the opinions between himself and Roberts.[11]

Another intra-Court factor is the importance of the decision as a
precedent. Even if the Court agrees on a decision, there may be differing
opinions as to whether the decision should be based on a broad or narrow
construction of the issue. As Mr. Justice Frankfurter once put it, the Chief
Justice may pick the man "who will write in the narrowest possible way . . .
[or] take the chance of putting a few seeds in the earth for future flower-
ing."[12] If there is a large number of alternatives available, the Chief Justice
must select an opinion writer who will choose the ground most likely to
hold five justices.

Extra-Court Influences

Another group of influences that are hypothesized to affect the assignment
of opinions are those that involve the relationship between the Court and
the rest of the political system. The first of these is the assertion that the
Chief Justice will tend to write the majority opinion himself in the "big"
or "important" constitutional cases.

> The Chief Justice's retention of "big Cases" is generally accepted by
> the Justices. In fact the expectation is that he would write in those cases
> so as to lend the prestige of his office to the Court's pronouncement.
> In varying degrees, Chief Justices have fulfilled this expectation.[13]

Danelski found that during their terms as Chief Justice, Taft wrote
the majority opinion in 34 percent of the "important constitutional cases,"
Hughes wrote 28.9 percent of them, and Stone wrote 17.9 percent.[14]
Among the most obvious recent examples of this are Chief Justice Warren's
opinions in *Brown* v. *Board of Education*[15] (the School Desegregation case)

and *Reynolds* v. *Sims*[16] (the State Legislative Reapportionment case), and Chief Justice Burger's opinion in *U.S.* v. *Nixon*[17] (the Watergate Tapes case).

The second of the extra-Court influences is that the Chief Justice is conscious of the element of "public relations" in his selection of an opinion writer. Such considerations would be particularly important if the resulting decision would be unpopular to a sizable segment of the public. "In other words, he is not unmindful of the importance of making a decision acceptable to the public, or, when applicable of coating the bitter pill about to be swallowed."[18]

Perhaps the clearest example of this influence was in the case of *Smith* v. *Allwright*[19] (the Texas White Primary case). The majority opinion was originally assigned by Chief Justice Stone to Justice Frankfurter. A few days later Justice Jackson, after discussing the problem with some of his associates, wrote a letter to Stone in which he argued that the nature of the case was so important and emotional that the fact of Frankfurter's authorship was bound to "grate on Southern sensibilities." He stated further:

> Mr. Justice Frankfurter unites in a rare degree factors which unhappily excite prejudice. In the first place, he is a Jew. In the second place, he is from New England, the seat of the abolition movement. In the third place, he has not been thought of as a person particularly sympathetic with the Democratic party in the past.[20]

Jackson stated that he discussed these factors with great reluctance, but had talked about the matter with Frankfurter. Apparently Stone was persuaded, for he reassigned the opinion to Justice Reed, who was a Protestant, from a border state (Kentucky), and a former Democratic office holder.[21]

The relationship between the decision rule implied by our theory and a number of these other influences on opinion assignments will be discussed later in this chapter. First, however, some brief comments on the data to be employed and the method of presenting the data are appropriate.

Opinion Assignments in the Warren Court

The data we will use to examine the predictions of our theory regarding opinion assignments are derived from a set of 616 civil liberties cases decided by the Warren Court between 1953 and 1969.[22] The cases were organized into 34 issue scales and yielded a total of 480 opinions assigned.[23]

Each scale orders the justices from "left" to "right" (or liberal to conservative) on that issue. In each case we can compare the scale score of the opinion assigner to the score of any other justice, and thereby determine whether the assigner in fact assigned the opinion to the justice who was closest to him on that issue.

176

Table 8.1

Majority Opinion Assignment by Warren, Frankfurter, and Black

ASSIGNER	TOTAL ASSIGNED	NUMBER ASSIGNED TO CLOSEST GROUP	ACTUAL PROPORTION OF OPINIONS ASSIGNED p	EXPECTED PROPORTION OF OPINIONS ASSIGNED π	DIFFERENCE $p - \pi$
Warren	393	219	.557	.439	+.118
Frankfurter	48	26	.542	.444	+.098
Black	25	12	.480	.386	+.094

It is unlikely that we will find our predictions supported in every case. We will, therefore, need some yardstick against which we can measure our predictions to determine how accurate our theory is. It seems to us that the most appropriate yardstick to employ is to assume that in every case, each justice in the majority is equally likely to be assigned the majority opinion. This assumption captures the essence of the necessity of equalizing the opinion-writing work load that we discussed previously. Thus, in any set of cases, we can compare the actual proportion of majority opinions assigned to a justice or a group of justices to the proportion we would expect if opinions were simply randomly assigned among justices who were in the majority. In order for us to accept our predictions as supported by the data, we would have to find that the proportion of opinions assigned in accord with our predictions is substantially greater than the proportion that we would expect to result from random assignment.

For convenience we will employ a couple of symbols to describe these proportions. The letter p indicates the proportion (or percent) of opinions in a set of cases that were actually assigned to a justice or a group of justices, and the Greek letter π indicates the proportion that we would expect to result from random assignment. Thus subtracting the second value from the first $(p - \pi)$ will show us whether our predictions have been either more or less accurate than we expected.

We are now able to make an initial assessment of how well the decision rule we derived from our theory predicts opinion assignments. To recapitulate, we predict that in each case the assigner will either write the majority opinion himself or assign it to the justice who is closest to him on that issue. Thus, if an opinion is to be predicted correctly, it must go to one of a specified group of justices numbering two or more.[24] We will refer to such a group of justices as "the closest group."

Table 8.1 presents the data on the three major opinion assigners in the Warren Court (Warren, Frankfurter, and Black).[25] We can see that for each of the assigners the prediction of our decision rule is supported.

In each instance, about 10 percent more of the majority opinions go to the closest group than we would expect if assignments were made randomly.

Thus the initial hypothesis is supported by the data. However, to be confident about the predicted relationship between ideological closeness and opinion assignment, we would also want to find the relationship holding across issue areas and across individual assignees. In other words, perfectly consistent support for the theory would be that the closest group is advantaged (in terms of being assigned opinions) in each individual issue area, and each individual justice is advantaged when he is closest to the assigner and disadvantaged when he is not closest.

Table 8.2 presents the data on opinion assignments by Warren controlled for issue area. The hypothesis is supported in 29 of the 34 issue areas. Moreover, in 19 of the issue areas, the magnitude of $p - \pi$ is .10 or more. We may therefore conclude that the decision rule, although not perfectly supported, holds consistently across issues.

Before we proceed further, one interesting point about the issue area data should be noted. There is, unfortunately, no way to measure the saliency of the various issue areas to the assigners. The logic of the theory indicates that we should expect the prediction to hold more strongly as the saliency of the issues increases. We do have, however, one datum that bears on this point. In an interview just after his resignation as Chief Justice, Warren was asked what was the Supreme Court's most important decision during his tenure. He replied:

> I think the reapportionment, not only of state legislatures, but of representative government in this country, is perhaps the most important issue we have had before the Supreme Court.[26]

In addition, he cited the pornography issue as the "most difficult" policy question the Court considered. The data on Warren's assignments in these two areas are consistent with our theoretical expectation. The magnitude of $p - \pi$ for the censorship cases is $+.42$ (ranking second); for the reapportionment cases it is $+ .34$ (ranking fifth).

Table 8.3 shows the data on Warren's assignments to individual justices, controlling for when those justices are closest to Warren and when they are not. Again there is systematic support for the primary hypothesis. Of the 26 data points (10 justices who are on some issue closest to Warren, and all 16 justices when they are not closest), 20 are in the predicted direction.[27] Furthermore, if we restrict our consideration to the 8 justices who were present on the Court for 6 or more of the 16 terms (and whose positions as measured by the scales we may have the most confidence in), there are 15 data points, 13 of which are predicted correctly.[28]

Thus the prediction regarding assignments to the closest group is supported not only in the aggregate, but also when considered in relation to individual issues and individual assignees. We may now turn, therefore, to a consideration of other predictions that follow from the theory.

Table 8.2
Warren's Assignments by Issue Area

ISSUE AREA	TOTAL ASSIGNED	NUMBER ASSIGNED TO CLOSEST GROUP	OPINION ASSIGNMENT		
			ACTUAL p	EXPECTED π	DIFFERENCE $p - \pi$
Political expression: speech, press, and association	23	16	.70	.57	+.13
Political expression: nonverbal	10	4	.40	.28	+.12
Sit-ins	12	7	.58	.42	+.16
Censorship	13	9	.69	.27	+.42
Internal security: federal criminal regulation	9	3	.33	.30	+.03
Internal security: federal administrative regulation	14	4	.29	.31	−.02
Internal security: legislative investigations	7	3	.43	.67	−.24
Internal security: state regulation	7	5	.71	.66	+.05
Religion	10	7	.70	.39	+.31
Reapportionment	17	14	.82	.48	+.34
Courts martial	7	4	.57	.48	+.09
Selective service	8	7	.88	.53	+.35
Aliens: 1953–1955	11	10	.91	.43	+.48
Aliens: 1956–1957	12	2	.17	.30	−.13
Aliens: 1958–1968	12	6	.50	.39	+.11
Racial discrimination: 1953–1961	11	7	.64	.35	+.29
Racial discrimination: 1962–1968	21	8	.38	.47	−.09
Voting rights	11	10	.91	.74	+.17
Civil rights acts	10	6	.60	.46	+.14
Discovery and inspection	7	4	.57	.50	+.07
Contempt	12	8	.67	.46	+.21
Indigents	6	4	.67	.59	+.08
Double jeopardy	7	2	.29	.49	−.20
Self-incrimination: 1953–1957	16	8	.50	.37	+.13
Self-incrimination: 1958–1961	7	3	.43	.31	+.12
Self-incrimination: 1962–1966	19	10	.53	.51	+.02
Self-incrimination: 1967–1968	11	5	.45	.37	+.08
Right to counsel: 1953–1961	11	7	.64	.49	+.15
Right to counsel: 1962–1968	14	9	.64	.63	+.01
Confrontation of witnesses	9	4	.44	.28	+.16
Wiretapping and electronic eavesdropping	10	7	.70	.34	+.36
Search and seizure: 1953–1961	13	4	.31	.30	+.01
Search and seizure: 1962–1966	15	5	.33	.30	+.03
Search and seizure: 1967–1968	11	7	.64	.51	+.13
Total	393	219	.56	.44	+.12

Table 8.3
Warren's Assignments to Individual Justices, Controlled for Closeness

	WHEN CLOSEST			WHEN NOT CLOSEST		
	ACTUAL	EXPECTED	DIFFERENCE	ACTUAL	EXPECTED	DIFFERENCE
JUSTICE	p	π	$p - \pi$	p	π	$p - \pi$
Brennan	.135	.099	+.036	.018	.027	−.009
Douglas	.092	.071	+.021	.028	.054	−.026
Black	.061	.050	+.011	.043	.065	−.022
Clark	.031	.010	+.021	.066	.069	−.003
Fortas	.015	.018	−.003	.018	.021	−.003
Frankfurter	.013	.007	+.006	.025	.034	−.009
Stewart	.013	.003	+.010	.081	.073	+.008
White	.010	.010	.000	.025	.051	−.026
Marshall	.010	.009	+.001	.013	.014	−.001
Goldberg	.010	.010	.000	.028	.025	+.003
Harlan	—	—	—	.056	.074	−.018
Whittaker	—	—	—	.023	.021	+.002
Reed	—	—	—	.003	.009	−.006
Burton	—	—	—	.013	.021	−.008
Minton	—	—	—	.003	.009	−.006
Jackson	—	—	—	.000	.003	−.003

The theory predicts that the closest group should be advantaged in terms of opinion assignments, and includes as a logical corollary the prediction that justices in other positions should be, *as a group*, disadvantaged. What, however, does the theory have to say about the other positions *individually*?

We have already discussed the fact that the opinion writer is constrained in making policy by the need to gain the adherence of a majority of the Court for his opinion. The Court makes no general policy unless an Opinion of the Court is agreed upon. Moreover, once an opinion is accepted by a majority, there is no need for further adherents, at least as far as the actual policy making is concerned. Thus, if we consider the possible positions from position 1 (the opinion assigner) to position 9 (the justice farthest from the assigner in a unanimously decided case), the theory predicts that positions 1 and 2 should be advantaged. In addition, since the assigner is trying to build an opinion coalition whose position will be as close as possible to his most preferred position, there usually is no reason why he should try to include any justice beyond position 5.[29] We would also, therefore, predict that positions 6 through 9 should be individually

Table 8.4
Assignments to Positions (All Assigners)

			OPINION ASSIGNMENT		
POSITION	ASSIGNED	NOT ASSIGNED	ACTUAL p	EXPECTED π	DIFFERENCE $p - \pi$
1	186	819	.388	.314	+.074
2	74	303	.154	.119	+.035
3	29	243	.060	.092	−.032
4	46	364	.096	.132	−.036
5	72	373	.150	.139	+.011
6	28	287	.058	.088	−.030
7	22	190	.046	.054	−.008
8	15	153	.031	.040	−.009
9	8	87	.017	.022	−.005

disadvantaged. This leaves positions 3 through 5 to be considered. All three of these positions are necessary to the formation of a minimum winning opinion coalition, for the defection of even one justice will make a majority opinion impossible. In terms of the assigner's preferred position, the justice who is most likely to defect is the one who occupies the fifth position. The surest way to hold him in an opinion coalition would be to let him write the majority opinion himself. Therefore, we would expect that if any one of positions 3 through 5 should be advantaged, it would be the fifth (or pivotal) position. We can summarize our predictions about the nine positions as follows: for positions 1 and 2, p should be greater than π; for positions 3, 4, and 6 through 9, p should be less than π; and for position 5 we might expect p to be greater than π.

Table 8.4 presents the aggregate data on assignments to positions for all assigners and shows that the predictions just described are supported. For positions 1 through 4 and 6 through 9, the predicted direction of $p - \pi$ is correct. For position 5, $p - \pi$ is positive, but the magnitude is small compared with that for positions 1 and 2. We will consider the special case of the fifth position further later in this chapter.

To this point the data have provided considerable support for the predictions of the theory, but the support has been far from perfect; that is, we have not found that the assigner gives 100 percent of the opinions to the closest group. It is in the explanation of this fact that the impact of the equal work load constraint, which we discussed previously, becomes clear. If all justices occupied the closest position in relation to Warren with approximately equal frequency, then Warren could have assigned the majority opinion to the closest justice in every case, and he still would have satisfied the equal work load constraint. However, as Table 8.5 shows, all justices were not equally likely to be closest to Warren when they were in the majority. Some justices (such as Brennan) were almost always closest to Warren, whereas others (Harlan, for example) were never closest to Warren. It was, therefore, impossible for Warren invariably to assign the majority opinion to the closest justice *and* equalize the work load. If he had always followed the decision rule, Harlan would never have received an opinion assignment, at least not in this set of cases.

Since all justices were not closest to Warren with equal frequency, we may view his decision about whether to assign the majority opinion to the closest group in a given case to be a judgment concerning the allocation of a scarce resource. In other words, the theory predicts that Warren should always have wanted to follow the decision rule, but observance of the equal work load constraint meant that he could not. Since he could not, then whether the decision rule was followed in a particular case should have been governed by various strategic considerations that would have made it more or less desirable to do so in that instance.

Indeed, this consideration, in conjunction with research completed by another student of the Court, sheds further light on the empirical results we have obtained so far. Gregory Rathjen has recently reported the results of a study that attempted to replicate the research we have been describing, by examining the opinion assignments made by Warren in all *economics* cases decided by the Court between 1959 and 1969.[30] Rathjen found that the predictions of our theory were in general *not* supported by the data on economics cases. If, however, we accept an additional factual assumption— that civil liberties cases were more important to Warren, in general, than economics cases—then a plausible interpretation of the failure of our predictions in Rathjen's analysis may be offered.

It should not be surprising to the reader to discover that the justices who were frequently closest to Warren in the economics cases were the same justices who were frequently closest in the civil liberties cases.[31] We saw in our examination of the value systems of the justices in Chapter 7 that most of the justices can be described as liberals or conservatives. This means that most members of the Court had the same orientation (either positive or negative) on both civil liberties and economics issues. Thus Warren, because of the equal work load constraint, could not follow the decision rule across the board. If civil liberties issues were indeed more salient to Warren, a reasonable strategy for him to follow would have been to follow the decision rule relatively often in civil liberties cases and seldom in economics cases. This would explain why we found the theory's prediction supported and Rathjen did not.

Rathjen's analysis provides some support for this view. In Chapter 7, we found that one justice for whom neither the term "liberal" nor the term

Table 8.5

Individual Justices and Their Frequency
of Being Closest to Warren

JUSTICE	TIMES IN MAJORITY	PERCENT CLOSEST
Brennan	343	80
Douglas	343	55
Fortas	109	48
Black	321	45
Marshall	63	38
Goldberg	94	30
White	180	18
Frankfurter	117	15
Clark	230	11
Stewart	229	4
Reed	26	0
Harlan	228	0
Whittaker	64	0
Burton	57	0
Minton	25	0
Jackson	10	0

"conservative" was an accurate description was Justice Clark. Clark was termed a "New Dealer," which meant he was positively oriented on the value of New Dealism (involving economics cases) and negatively oriented on the values of freedom and equality (involving civil liberties cases). Thus we would expect Clark to appear closest to Warren more often in economics cases than in civil liberties cases. This was in fact the situation. Although our data indicate that Clark was closest to Warren in only 11 percent of the civil liberties cases in which he was in the majority (see Table 8.5), Rathjen's data found Clark to be closest 51 percent of the time—more than any other justice.[32]

Thus Clark was one justice for whom Warren *could not* follow the decision rule in civil liberties cases, but *could* follow it in economics cases. If our previous argument were correct, we would, therefore, expect Clark to be advantaged in terms of opinion assignments in economics cases. And the data do, in fact, show that, as Rathjen states,

> We find that Clark is, indeed, assigned the majority opinion more often than would be expected. In fact, the magnitude of Clark's $p - \pi$ evidences the strongest support for Rohde's primary hypothesis among individual justices.[33]

The next strategic consideration we will discuss is the effect of the size of the decision coalition (i.e., the majority on the merits) on the application of the decision rule. In a given issue area, as the size of the decision coalition increases, the range of preferred policy alternatives within the majority increases. Generally speaking, then, as the size of the decision coalition increases, so does the likelihood that a majority opinion can be created that is substantially different from the preferred position of the assigner (if the decision rule is not followed)—that is, if the assigner does not assign the opinion to the closest group, then as the size of the majority increases, the likelihood that his agreement will be necessary to the creation of a majority opinion decreases, and consequently so does the likelihood that his preferences will be taken into account in the final outcome. Thus if the decision rule is to be followed differentially, then the assigner should follow the decision rule to a greater degree as the size of the majority increases.

Another way in which the size of the decision coalition should affect opinion assignments is in regard to the importance of the pivot (that is, the justice in the fifth position relative to the assigner). We noted previously that the pivotal justice is important because he is the most likely to defect from the formation of a minimum winning opinion coalition based on the preferences of the assigner. But the likelihood of his defection would seem to vary inversely with the size of the majority. A justice would be more likely to defect if his defection would further the possibility of achieving his policy goals, so long as there were other justices with whom he could join to achieve a different result. As the size of the majority decreases, the size of the group of opposition justices increases, thus increasing the possibility that they will achieve their intended result. The pivot is in a unique position (and the effect of his defection would be maximized) when there is a 5 to 4 division on the Court, since the pivot may determine the outcome by switching from one side to the other.[34] We would therefore expect the proportion of opinions assigned to decrease as the size of the majority increases, and we would expect the value of $p - \pi$ to be positive in five-member majorities.

The preceding discussion enables us to make two sets of predictions about assignments to positions when the size of the decision coalition is controlled. The first set of predictions concerns whether the value of $p - \pi$ should be positive or negative (i.e., whether the position should be advantaged or disadvantaged). Our theory predicts that $p - \pi$ should always be positive for positions 1 and 2, it should always be negative for positions 3 and 4 and positions 6 through 9, and it should be positive for position 5 in five-member majorities and negative in other majorities. Table 8.6 presents the data that relate to these predictions; $p - \pi$ is in the correct direction in 33 of our 35 predictions.

The second set of predictions we can make concerns the relationship between the magnitude of $p - \pi$ and varying sizes of majorities with regard

Table 8.6
Assignments to Positions, by Size of Majority (All Assigners)

MAJORITY SIZE AND OPINION ASSIGNMENT

POSITION	MAJORITY = 5			MAJORITY = 6			MAJORITY = 7			MAJORITY = 8			MAJORITY = 9		
	p	π	$p-\pi$	p	π	$p-\pi$	p	π	$p-\pi$	p	π	$p-\pi$	p	π	$p-\pi$
1	.382	.377	+.005	.358	.326	+.032	.328	.278	+.050	.438	.285	+.153	.424	.270	+.154
2	.163	.145	+.018	.138	.135	+.003	.188	.128	+.060	.172	.084	+.088	.127	.093	+.034
3	.089	.153	−.064	.083	.101	−.018	.063	.090	−.027	.016	.057	−.041	.025	.039	−.014
4	.146	.169	−.023	.156	.167	−.011	.031	.108	−.077	.078	.111	−.033	.034	.085	−.051
5	.220	.156	+.064	.138	.150	−.012	.234	.168	+.066	.094	.119	−.025	.085	.108	−.023
6				.128	.122	+.006	.078	.135	−.057	.031	.119	−.088	.059	.107	−.048
7							.078	.094	−.016	.109	.131	−.023	.085	.097	−.012
8										.063	.094	−.031	.093	.113	−.020
9													.068	.089	−.021

Table 8.7

Assignments to Closest Group and Pivot, by Size of Majority

SIZE OF MAJORITY	CLOSEST GROUP			PIVOTAL GROUP		
	p	π	$p - \pi$	p	π	$p - \pi$
5	.545	.522	+.023	.340	.244	+.096
6	.496	.461	+.035	.257	.265	−.008
7	.516	.406	+.110	.328	.249	+.079
8	.610	.369	+.241	.109	.182	−.073
9	.551	.363	+.188	.110	.177	−.067

to both the closest group and the pivotal group.[35] The argument just stated, about the connection between assignments and majority size, leads to the prediction that the magnitude of $p - \pi$ for the pivotal group should decrease as the size of the majority increases. As the data in Table 8.7 indicate, these predictions are basically supported. The magnitude of $p - \pi$ does tend to increase for the closest group as majority size increases, and it tends to decrease for the pivotal group as majority size increases.

The final strategic consideration that we will discuss is the impact of the importance of individual cases on whether the decision rule is followed. As we discussed earlier in this chapter, David Danelski has argued that the members of the Court expect that the Chief Justice will write the majority opinion in "important constitutional cases"; Danelski presented data on Chief Justices Taft, Hughes, and Stone that support the argument. This argument fits well within our theory, but our prediction is somewhat broader. We would expect the decision rule to be followed more often in "important" cases than in less important ones. The more important the case is, the more important it should be for the assigner that the policy enunciated by the Court be close to his own position. Thus, we would expect $p - \pi$ to be greater in important cases than in less important ones for *both* the assigner *and* other members of the closest group, and we would expect this result whether or not the assigner was the Chief Justice.

Table 8.8 presents data that compare assignments by the Chief Justice and other justices, controlled for whether the cases are "important."[36] We find that the magnitude of $p - \pi$ for Warren in "important constitutional cases" is almost four times as large as in those cases which do not meet the definition of importance. However, on the basis of the same comparison, $p - \pi$ for the other assigners is almost three times as large, and furthermore, the magnitude of $p - \pi$ in important cases is less for Warren than for the other assigners. Moreover, if we consider assignments to other members of the closest group, the same pattern repeats itself. For both Warren and other assigners, the rest of the closest group is more favored in important cases than in other cases. Thus, our predictions are supported.

Table 8.8
Assignments in "Important Constitutional Cases"

JUSTICE AND TYPE OF CASE	TO ASSIGNER			TO CLOSEST JUSTICE		
	p	π	$p - \pi$	p	π	$p - \pi$
Warren: important cases (120)	.200	.145	+.055	.391	.302	+.089
Warren: other cases (194)	.160	.146	+.014	.366	.281	+.085
Other justices: important cases (24)	.250	.189	+.061	.250	.213	+.037
Other justices: other cases (56)	.214	.191	+.023	.214	.246	−.032

Summary

In this chapter, we considered what our theory has to say about the third stage of Supreme Court decision making, the assignment of the majority opinion. We argued that our assumptions imply a general decision rule for opinion assigners: he should either write the majority opinion himself or assign it to the justice whose views are most like his own on the issue in question.

After an initial examination of data on assignments in civil liberties cases in the Warren Court, which generally supported the prediction of the decision rule, we noted that it was not possible for Warren to follow the decision rule in every case and, at the same time, maintain the approximately equal work load of majority opinion writing that is expected by the other justices. We therefore proceeded to examine various factors that, we argued, ought to affect whether the decision rule would be followed in a particular case. These factors were the nature of the issue, the size of the decision coalition, and the importance of the case.

Although the predictions of the theory are not overwhelmingly supported, there is consistent support for each of them. We can, therefore, now turn to a consideration of the theory's predictions with regard to the final stage of Supreme Court decision making—the building of the majority opinion coalition.

Appendix to Chapter 8

In this Appendix we present a more detailed description of the data and methods employed in the analysis discussed in this chapter.

The Data

The data employed here include all orally argued civil liberties cases decided by the Supreme Court by full or *per curiam* opinion during the tenure of Earl Warren as Chief Justice (1953–1968 terms). This yielded a set of 821 cases. The cases were then classified into issue areas, made up of 616 (75 percent) of the total set of civil liberties cases that were acceptable for scale analysis.[37] Since we are, for the purposes of this study, interested in cases that were decided by full opinion, it should be noted that these 616 cases included 498 cases decided by full opinion (81 percent) and that the remaining 205 cases included only 135 full opinion cases (66 percent).

The set of 616 cases was then subjected to Guttman scale analysis.[38] In order to increase the reliability of the scales, issue areas were, when possible, broken down into periods shorter than the full sixteen years. This procedure resulted in a substantial decrease in the number of non-participations in the scales. It further allowed for the possibility that a justice might change his views over time, thus additionally increasing the reliability of the scales. In addition, one issue area (internal security) was found to contain four discrete subissues. There were enough cases to enable us to construct separate scales for each of the subissues. The final result was 34 scales.

When the scales were constructed, they were examined to see if they met minimally acceptable levels of unidimensionality. The minimum accepted levels for the two coefficients that are conventionally employed are .9 for the coefficient of reproducibility (CR), and .60–.65 for the coefficient of scalability (CS).[39] All scales surpassed the minimum level for CR, and all but three exceeded the minimum level for CS.

From the scales we obtained an ordinal ranking of each justice along a "left–right" continuum in each policy area. Each justice was awarded a scale score based on his placement on the continuum.[40] These scale scores were employed to measure the proximity of each justice to the opinion assigner. The operational definition of "closest" was: If a justice in the majority had the same scale score as the opinion assigner, he was considered closest to the assigner; if no justice had the same scale score as the assigner, the justice in the majority who was the smallest distance from the assigner in terms of the scale score was considered closest.

By using the scale scores in this fashion, we are obviously treating the ordinal scales as if they afforded an interval measure—that is, as if they not only ordered the justices along a continuum, but also indicated how far apart the justices were. Clearly, this raises questions about the validity of the measurement. If, however, we had limited our analysis to those cases in which only an ordinal assumption was necessary (i.e., those in which the closest justice had the same scale position as the assigner), the size of the data set would have been reduced by half and we would have been precluded from considering the predictions concerning the pivot. To avoid these restrictions, we decided to treat the scale scores as interval measures. As a check on the problem, however, data were analyzed that were available under only the ordinal assumption.[41] Similar results were obtained, and the predictions were even more strongly supported.

The Null Hypothesis

"Null hypothesis" is the technical term for the yardstick against which we chose to measure our theoretical predictions. As we stated previously, the null hypothesis that we employed assumes that in each case the majority opinion is assigned randomly. More formally, if the null hypothesis were correct, then in any set of cases, p_i (the proportion of majority opinions actually assigned to justice i) should be equal to π_i (the proportion of majority opinions we would expect if opinions were randomly assigned). The latter proportion is computed as follows:

$$\pi_i = \frac{1}{N} \sum_{n=4}^{9} \frac{m_{in}}{n},$$

where N = the number of cases in the set; n = the number of justices in the majority in a case; and m_{in} = the number of participations by justice i in majorities of size n in the set of cases.

Notes to Chapter 8

1. *Seriatim* opinions are still handed down occasionally, although more by happenstance than by design. For example, in both the Pentagon Papers cases (*New York Times Co.* v. *U.S.*, 403 U.S. 713, 29 L Ed 2d 822, 1971) and the death penalty cases (*Furman* v. *Georgia*, 408 U.S. 238, 33 L Ed 2d 346, 1972), all nine justices wrote separate opinions. In both sets of cases, however, there were brief *per curiam* opinions for the majority.

2. Quoted in Walter F. Murphy, *The Elements of Judicial Strategy* (Chicago: University of Chicago Press, 1964), p. 59.

A case that clearly illustrates the fact that majority opinions often do not completely accord with the views of their authors is *Abbate* v. *U.S.*, 359 U.S. 187 (1959). The case involved the issue of double jeopardy and Justice Brennan was assigned the majority opinion. Brennan succeeded in gaining the agreement of five other justices, but apparently he was not successful in getting them to accept all of his views, because he also proceeded to write a separate concurring opinion! We discuss the bargaining over the content of the majority opinion in detail in the next chapter.

3. One indicator of the importance of the assigning power is the reported friction that has developed within the Court over recent alleged attempts by Chief Justice Burger to deviate from traditional assignment procedures. As we noted previously, the Chief Justice has, in the past, assigned the opinion only if he was in the majority. If he was not, the power to make the assignment passed to the senior associate justice in the majority. It has been reported by some, however, that after becoming Chief Justice, Burger attempted to assign opinions in cases in which he was in the minority. (Other reports dispute this claim.)

These reports surfaced in connection with the Court's consideration of the abortion cases in 1972 (*Roe* v. *Wade*, 35 L Ed 2d 147, 1973). The Court heard arguments on these cases in December 1971, when (due to the resignations of Justices Black and Harlan) the Court had only seven members. Some sources claim that the Chief Justice was in a 5 to 2 minority with Justice White, but assigned the majority opinion to Justice Blackmun anyway. This allegedly caused a vigorous protest by Justice Douglas, who normally would have assigned the opinion.

We will perhaps never know whether the facts were as described. Justice Blackmun took a long time drafting his opinion. Near the end of the 1971–1972 term the Court decided to hold the cases over until the next term. They were re-argued in October 1972 before a nine-member Court. When the decision was finally announced, Justice Blackmun was the author of the majority opinion, but the Chief Justice was a member of the majority.

For a discussion of this controversy, see "Abortion Cases Creating Friction on High Court," *New York Times*, July 7, 1972; and Joel B. Grossman and Richard S. Wells, eds., *Supplemental Cases for Constitutional Law and Judicial Policy Making* (New York: Wiley, 1973), p. 26.

4. For a discussion of the attitudes of members of the Court in this regard see Alpheus Thomas Mason, *Harlan Fiske Stone: Pillar of the Law* (New York: Viking, 1956), pp. 602–603, 793; and Felix Frankfurter, *Of Law and Men: Papers and Addresses*, ed. by Philip Elman (New York: Harcourt Brace, 1956), p. 137.

5. Anthony Lewis, "A Talk with Warren on Crime, the Court, the Country," *New York Times Magazine*, October 19, 1969, p. 130.

6. See Henry Abraham, *The Judicial Process*, 2d ed. (New York: Oxford University Press, 1968), pp. 211–212; David Danelski, "The Influence of the Chief Justice in the Decisional Process of the Supreme Court," in Thomas P. Jahnige and Sheldon Goldman, eds., *The Federal Judicial System* (New York: Holt, Rinehart and Winston, 1968), p. 156; S. Sidney Ulmer, "The Analysis of Behavior Patterns on the United States Supreme Court," *Journal of Politics* 22 (Nov. 1960): 644; and Murphy, *op. cit.* fn. 2 *supra*, p. 84.

7. Murphy, *op. cit.*, fn. 2 *supra*, p. 84.

8. Abraham, *op. cit.*, fn. 6 *supra*, p. 210.

9. Danelski, *op. cit.*, fn. 6 *supra*, p. 157.

10. *Ibid.*

11. *Ibid.* A problem with these hypotheses concerning "persuasion" is the assumption that the opinion assigner *wants* to persuade the dissenters to join the majority. This would probably be true if there were no costs involved, but, as we shall see in the next chapter, our theory would predict that in most circumstances the author of the opinion will seek to achieve a majority of only five justices.

12. Felix Frankfurter, "Chief Justices I Have Known," *Virginia Law Review* 39 (1953): 904.

13. Danelski, *op. cit.*, fn. 6 *supra*, p. 157.

14. Danelski operationalized this concept by surveying four leading works on the Constitution. If a case was discussed in any two of these works, it was considered an "important constitutional case." See *ibid.*, p. 157, note 59.

15. 347 U.S. 483 (1954).

16. 377 U.S. 533 (1964).

17. 41 L Ed 2d 1039 (1974).

18. Abraham, *op. cit.*, fn. 6 *supra*, p. 209.

19. 321 U.S. 649 (1944).

20. The discussion of this case is taken from Mason, *op. cit.*, fn. 4 *supra*, pp. 614–615.

21. A large number of other cases could be cited as examples of this factor, among them: *Korematsu* v. *U.S.*, 323 U.S. 214 (1944), which involved the constitutionality of the relocation of Japanese-Americans in World War II, and in which Justice Black, one of the foremost civil libertarians on the Court, wrote the majority opinion upholding the government's action; *Abington School District* v. *Schempp*, 374 U.S. 203 (1963), the School Prayer case, in which the majority opinion was written by Justice Clark, a prominent Presbyterian layman; and *Mapp* v. *Ohio*, 367 U.S. 643 (1961), which applied the Fourth Amendment fully to the states, and in which Justice Clark, a former Attorney General, wrote the majority opinion.

22. A more detailed discussion of the data is included as an Appendix to this chapter.

23. The main reason the number of opinions is 480 and not 616 is that most of the other cases were decided *per curiam*. See the Appendix for details.

24. The reader will note that it is "two or more" because a number of justices may be equally close to the assigner in terms of their scale scores. See Chapter 7 for a discussion of the calculation of scale scores.

25. In addition to these three, four other justices made assignments: Reed (8), Clark (4), Douglas (1), and Harlan (1). The number of opinions is clearly too small to allow us to analyze these assigners individually. However, these data are included in the later analysis of total opinions assigned.

26. *New York Times*, June 27, 1969, p. 17.

27. It is obvious that the magnitude of $p - \pi$ in Table 8.3 is in many instances very small. This is, however, a result of the testing method. The p's are proportions of all opinions assigned and the π's are proportions of all participations divided into 27 separate units, making it impossible for either the individual p's and π's or the difference between them to be very large. We would, therefore, argue that it is not the magnitude of $p - \pi$ that is important, but whether its direction is systematically in accord with the prediction. We have already shown that it is.

28. These justices are Black, Douglas, Clark, Brennan, Harlan, Frankfurter, Stewart, and White.

29. See Chapter 9 for an extended discussion of this point.

30. Gregory James Rathjen, "Policy Goals, Strategic Choice, and Majority Opinion Assignments in the U.S. Supreme Court: A Replication," *American Journal of Political Science* 18 (Nov. 1974): 713–724.

31. See *ibid.*, p. 724.

32. *Ibid.*

33. *Ibid.*

34. An alternative strategy, instead of joining with the dissenters, would be simply to refuse to join a majority opinion. This strategy would also have maximum impact when there was a five-member decision coalition, because the defection of a single justice would mean there could be *no* majority opinion.

35. The definition of the closest group has already been discussed. The term "pivotal group" does not refer simply to the justice who occupies the fifth position in relation to the assigner, but is analogous to the definition of the closest group. When we coded the justices according to their positions, a justice was assigned position five only if there were three other justices occupying different scale positions who were closer to the assigner; that is, if the rank order was (1) the assigner,

(2 and 3) two other justices, followed by two justices occupying the same scale position, then the two latter justices were *both* coded as occupying position 4. They are, however, both pivotal in relation to the assigner. *Pivotal group* is thus defined as any justice (or group of justices occupying the same scale position or scale positions equidistant from the assigner) who, according to his (their) rank order from the assigner, would be included in a minimum winning opinion coalition built around the preferences of the assigner, and who, according to his (their) rank order, would be most likely to defect from such a coalition. The only exception to this definition occurs when the closest group has five or more members. Then all members of the closest group (or at least all members but the assigner) would fit the definition of pivotal. They would not seem, however, to fit our intuitive notion of a pivot. We have, therefore, classified such justices only as being members of the closest group. This is not much of a problem since such a situation arose in only 21 of the 480 cases.

36. Our operationalization of "important constitutional cases" is analogous to that used by Danelski (see footnote 14). We selected four sources: Henry J. Abraham, *Freedom and the Court* (New York: Oxford University Press, 1967); M. Glenn Abernathy, *Civil Liberties under the Constitution* (New York: Dodd, Mead, 1968); Robert F. Cushman, *Cases in Civil Liberties* (New York: Appleton-Century-Crofts, 1968); and Harold J. Spaeth, *The Warren Court: Cases and Commentary* (San Francisco: Chandler, 1966). Any case mentioned in the tables of cases in two or more of the sources was classified as "important." Since one of our sources was published in 1966 and another was published in 1967, cases from the 1967 and 1968 terms were excluded from this part of the analysis.

37. The other 205 cases were considered unacceptable for scale analysis because they fell into issue areas made up of fewer than ten cases.

38. For a discussion of the techniques of scale analysis see Chapter 6.

39. The coefficient of reproducibility is described in the Appendix to Chapter 7. A description of the coefficient of scalability may be found in Glendon Schubert, *The Judicial Mind* (Evanston, Ill.: Northwestern University Press, 1965), p. 81.

40. The calculation of scale scores is discussed in Chapter 7.

41. See David W. Rohde, "Strategy and Ideology: The Assignment of Majority Opinions in the United States Supreme Court" (unpublished Ph.D. Dissertation, The University of Rochester, 1971), pp. 134–139.

The Formation of the Majority Opinion Coalition | 9

In this chapter we consider the fourth and final stage of Supreme Court decision making, the formation of the majority opinion coalition. In the majority opinion, a group of justices joins in support of the Court's policy statement, which justifies and elaborates the decision in a particular case. The predictions of our theory that we will discuss relate to two aspects of this stage of decision making: the number of justices who will support a given policy (i.e., the size of the opinion coalition), and the pattern of agreement among the justices on that policy. In addition, the predictions concerning these matters will distinguish between two types of situations the Court may face in making decisions. We will refer to these as "threat" and "nonthreat" situations.

The formation of the opinion coalition is the crucial stage of Supreme Court decision making. When the justices vote on the merits, the result of the vote determines only which party before the Court wins. However, the importance of the Supreme Court in our political system rests to a substantial degree on the fact that its decisions have policy impacts that reach far beyond the particular parties involved in a case. It is in the majority opinion that the Court lays down the broad constitutional and legal principles governing the outcome in the instant case, which are binding on lower courts in all similar cases and which establish precedents to guide future Court decisions. For the Court to decide, for example, that a lower-court decision that upheld a congressional district apportionment was in error is one thing; to decide that the constitutional standard by which apportionments are to be judged is precise mathematical equality of districts is quite another.[1]

Some Theoretical Concepts

Before we proceed further in our discussion of opinion coalitions, we need to introduce and discuss some additional theoretical considerations that we will use in making our predictions.

Robert Axelrod has developed a theory of decision making built around the concept of conflict of interest.[2] The basic theme of his analysis is that the amount of conflict of interest in a particular situation can be a useful predictor of behavior in that situation.

Axelrod informally defines conflict of interest as "the state of incompatibility of goals of two or more actors."[3] The more the preferences of a number of actors are in disagreement, the higher is the conflict of interest between them, and therefore, he argues, the amount of conflictful behavior among them will be greater. After offering a formal definition of conflict of interest, he employs his concept to examine a number of specific political situations, including congressional conference committees and bureaucratic decision making.

The specific application of Axelrod's theory that is most relevant here is his treatment of the formation of governing coalitions in multiparty parliamentary democracies. He assumes that there exists an ordinal, "left–right" policy dimension along which the political parties can be ordered, that the payoffs to the parties are determined by which policy along the dimension is chosen for society, and that the preferences of the parties across the policy dimension are "single-peaked."[4] Axelrod then argues that "the less dispersion there is in the policy positions of the members of a coalition, the less conflict of interest there is. And, "the less conflict of interest there is in a coalition, the more likely the coalition will form."[5] Although it is not possible to measure dispersion precisely on an ordinal space, a number of properties that affect the dispersion can be ascertained.[6]

Consider a five-member group, whose members are labeled *A*, *B*, *C*, *D*, and *E* from left to right on the policy dimension. Although we cannot compare the dispersion of coalition *ABC* as opposed to coalition *BCD*, we can say that *ABC* is less dispersed than *ABD*; that is, "a coalition consisting of adjacent [members] or a *connected* coalition as it can be called, tends to have relatively low dispersion and thus low conflict of interest for its size."[7]

In addition to connectedness, we may consider the property of size of a coalition. Coalition *ABC* has less dispersion (and thus less conflict of interest) than *ABCD*, although both are connected.

A final property to be considered is strategic in nature. If coalitions form to achieve policy objectives, then which coalitions form will be determined, in part, by whether they can control policy outcomes. In other words, whether or not a coalition is *winning*, in terms of the rules, will determine whether or not it will form.

Threat Situations

Another concept that is important to our subsequent discussion of coalition formation is that of a "threat to the Court." In earlier research on coalitions in the Court,[8] where the concept of a threat was introduced, it was argued that these threats could be of two types: threats to the Court's power and threats to the Court's authority.

> Threats to the Court's power will be defined as serious pending attempts by Congress to limit the Court's jurisdiction in an issue area (as in the removal of the Reconstruction Acts from the Court's jurisdiction in the late 1860's . . .), or to change the Court's personnel (as in the Court-packing attempt or by impeachment). Threats to the Court's authority will be defined to exist in issue areas in which it is probable that there may be serious resistance or disobedience to the Court's mandate by those to whom it will apply (as in the school desegregation cases of 1954–55).[9]

The role of the concept of a threat within our theory will be discussed later in this chapter. At this point we wish only to describe the data we will employ in this chapter and to specify the issue areas that fit our definition of a threat. The basic data we use are the same 821 civil liberties cases we used in the preceding chapter.[10] The organization of the cases is, however, somewhat different. For this analysis the cases were classified into 25 issue areas comprising 636 (77 percent) of the total number of cases.[11] These cases were then subjected to Guttman scale analysis.[12] Each of the 27 sets of cases was found to meet the criteria for an acceptable scale.[13]

It does not seem possible, short of interviewing the justices, to derive an objective indicator of threat situations. Thus we are left with some kind of subjective judgment. However, some of the issues listed in footnote 12 seem to fit the definition fairly well. With regard to threats to the Court's authority, the many interrelated issues surrounding the questions of segregation and discrimination are especially appropriate examples of issues where the probability of disobedience was high.[14] Therefore, the issues of racial discrimination (both scales) and civil rights acts, and those cases in the voting rights, protest, and freedom of association scales which involve the rights of blacks are classed as threat situations. In addition, two other issue areas seem to fit our definition of a threat to the Court's authority: first, the School Prayer cases, in which the Court said that prayers in public schools were unconstitutional and to which there was substantial resistance,[15] and second, two criminal procedures issues (involuntary confessions and search-and-seizure cases relating to warrantless searches), where the Court tried to place limits directly on police behavior. Thus, the appropriate cases from the freedom of religion, involuntary confessions, and search-and-seizure scales will be included as threat situations.

Threats to the Court's power occur less frequently and are of shorter duration than threats to the Court's authority. Two serious attempts were made during the Warren Court period to alter the Court's jurisdiction. The first was the 1958 Jenner-Butler Bill, which proposed that a number of internal security issues be removed from the Court's jurisdiction. The second was the 1968 Omnibus Crime Bill, which contained sections (eventually deleted) that would have prevented the Court from considering certain questions of criminal procedure. With regard to threats to the Court's power, the only relevant cases are those internal security cases decided during the consideration of the Jenner-Butler Bill. We include no cases on the basis of the Omnibus Crime Bill of 1968, because the attempts by congressmen, in debate, to alter the Court's jurisdiction related to involuntary confessions and searches and seizures, which are already classed as threat situations.

The Size of Opinion Coalitions

We have assumed that the justices are motivated by their own policy preferences. Their goal is to make the policy output of the Court approximate as closely as possible those preferences. After the vote on the merits is taken in conference, one of the members of the majority on the merits (which we have termed the *decision coalition*) is assigned the task of writing the majority opinion. The opinion he drafts is shaped by his own preferences, but he is not a free agent. If he is to form a winning coalition, he must gain the assent of at least four other justices in the opinion. The opinion writer is thus forced to bargain with the other justices. Because he is trying to make the opinion approximate his own position, he will accept those proffered bargains that are most attractive to him and reject others. Moreover, since he only needs the agreement of four justices in addition to himself, he has to accept compromises only until he achieves that result, after which he can reject further proposals to change the opinion. By rejecting bargains after he has obtained the agreement of a majority, the opinion writer minimizes the conflict of interest within the coalition *and* the deviation from his preferred policy position.

Therefore, in general, we would expect opinion coalitions to be minimum winning size. It is here, however, that the concept of a threat to the Court becomes relevant. Although in a normal policy-making situation we would expect coalitions to be minimum winning, the presence of a threat alters this expectation.

> When such a threat exists, the nature of the game changes. It is no
> longer primarily an intra-Court game, but a game between the Court
> and another part of the political system or society. Glendon Schubert,
> . . . in analyzing such a threat situåtion (the "court-packing" fight of
> 1937), has shown how the threat brought about a change in the be-
> havior of certain members of the Court. . . . It seems probable that
> when a threat to the Court exists, at least some of the members will
> become more concerned with protecting the Court than with having
> the Court espouse their own value position.[16]

When there is a threat to the Court, a number of strategic alternatives
are available. First, the justices can accede to the threat and decide in
favor of the side that is threatening them. This is the course Hughes and
Roberts followed in the famous "switch in time that saved nine."

Second, the Court may simply refuse to decide any more cases involving the issue that produced the threat, or at least refuse cases that
involve similar issues and that, if decided, would exacerbate the threat.
An example of this latter course was the Court's refusal to decide (in the
years immediately following the decision in *Brown* v. *Board of Education*)
a number of cases concerning antimiscegenation statutes. After leaving a
conference in which the Court refused to decide this issue, one of the justices
is alleged to have remarked, "One bombshell at a time is enough."[17]

Third, the justices may restrict their policy making by deciding *per
curiam* the cases they actually agree to hear in a threat area. This usually
limits the policy in the case to the parties at hand, or at least does not
extend previous policy further. The Court may have chosen this option
with regard to involuntary confessions cases; during the 1967 and 1968
terms the Court decided five such cases—four in favor of the defendants
and all *per curiam*.[18]

Finally, the Court can persist in its previous course and hope to
weather the storm. It is this last strategy that is most relevant at this point
in the discussion. If a majority of the Court chooses this course, some of
the justices will be likely to acquiesce silently in spite of their disagreements, in order to present a united front against the threat. The reasons
for this behavior may be illustrated by examining the school desegregation
controversy, probably the prototype of a threat to the Court's authority.
In considering this point, we must first recognize that much of the Court's
effectiveness as a policy maker stems from the fact that its decisions are
usually obeyed without enforcement by other nonjudicial agencies.[19] A
good example of this is the reapportionment issue. The Court said the
states must redistrict and, in spite of the criticism of the Court's decisions
in Congress and from the states, the states did redistrict. This semi-auto-
matic obedience is, however, probably fragile and is endangered by instances of public disobedience, and it is clear that the relative unity of the
Court affects the probability and degree of such disobedience.

Certainly the enforcement of the desegregation decisions was a slow and difficult process. The reader can imagine, however, how much greater the problem could have been had there been a minority of justices willing publicly to support the maintenance of segregated schools.[20] Resistance would surely have been stronger and more widespread, and would therefore have further endangered the Court's authority with regard to other issues. As important as any single issue may be to a justice, it is probably not important enough to risk the Court's ability to make policy in many other areas. Hence, we argue that at least some justices will suppress their disagreements in an attempt to lessen the threat, hoping that it will thus end more quickly.

In summary, our theory predicts that in those issue areas where there is a threat to the Court and the Court chooses to persist in the policy direction that produced the threat, the opinion coalitions formed will tend to be larger than minimum winning; in other situations, opinion coalitions will tend to be minimum winning.

Before presenting the data relevant to these hypotheses, a comment on the decision-making context of the Court is appropriate. Public disagreement within appellate courts is generally frowned on in the legal community. Canon 19 of the Canons of Judicial Ethics clearly admonishes judges that such disagreement should be an occasional thing.[21] Although justices would certainly differ about what frequency of dissent is proper, many justices seem to have followed the admonition of Canon 19 quite closely.[22] This comment, moreover, applies only to dissents. It appears that the writing of concurring opinions may be held in even lower esteem.[23]

The point of this discussion is that, insofar as these norms are operative in the Court, we should not expect perfect support of our prediction regarding minimum winning coalitions. Also, the effect of these norms would be to bias the data in support of the prediction regarding threat situations.

Table 9.1 presents data on nonthreat and threat situations.[24] There are two ways in which a justice may exclude himself from the opinion coalition. First, he may dissent from the Court's decision on the merits. Second, he may agree that the Court reached the correct result (e.g., he may agree that the decision of the lower court should be reversed), but disagree with the policy of the majority opinion and therefore write a separate concurrence. The data in Table 9.1 reflect both of these alternatives.

Clearly, there is support for both predictions. In nonthreat situations fully 40 percent of the opinion coalitions are minimum winning—the most frequently occurring single coalition size by a large margin. Unanimous opinion coalitions, moreover, occur in only 8 percent of the cases. In threat situations, on the other hand, the most frequently occurring single size of coalitions is the nine-member coalition (26 percent), whereas only 23 percent of the coalitions are minimum winning. In addition, if we make

Table 9.1

Size of Decision and Opinion Coalitions in Threat and Nonthreat Situations

SIZE OF DECISION COALITION	SIZE OF OPINION COALITION							
	9	8	7	6	5	NONE	TOTAL	PERCENT-AGE
NONTHREAT SITUATIONS								
9	31	11	12	6	5	1	66	16.6
8	—	23	8	14	6	0	51	12.8
7	—	—	41	10	7	2	60	15.1
6	—	—	—	62	25	10	97	24.4
5	—	—	—	—	116	8	124	31.2
Total	31	34	61	92	159	21	398	—
Percentage	7.8	8.5	15.3	23.1	39.9	5.3	—	—
THREAT SITUATIONS								
9	29	10	5	3	1	0	48	43.6
8	—	12	0	2	1	0	15	13.6
7	—	—	5	3	4	1	13	11.8
6	—	—	—	14	6	0	20	18.2
5	—	—	—	—	13	1	14	12.7
Total	29	22	10	22	25	2	110	—
Percentage	26.4	20.0	9.1	20.0	22.7	1.8	—	—

some allowance for an "information effect"[25] and combine five- and six-member coalitions (calling them, perhaps, "minimal" winning coalitions) the difference is even more striking. In nonthreat situations 63 percent of the coalitions are minimal winning, but in threat situations only 43 percent attain this size.

These data are illustrated by Figure 9.1, which is a graph of the proportions of the various sizes of coalitions in the two situations. In nonthreat situations there is a progressive tendency toward small coalitions. In threat situations, on the other hand, the tendency is for coalitions to be either large (9 or 8 members) or small (6 or 5 members), and in about equal proportions. A plausible explanation for this tendency is that although threat situations do exert a fairly strong push toward unanimity, once two members decide to express their disagreements, other members have little to gain by maintaining silence, and hence they tend to go their own ways. In any event, the data demonstrate that the behavior of the Court is markedly different in the two situations.

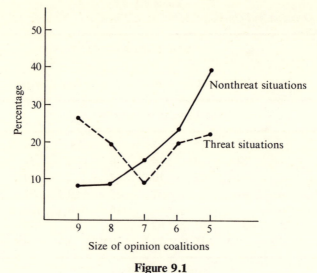

Figure 9.1
Size of opinion coalitions in threat and nonthreat situations.

Before proceeding, one more point should be noted from these data. We have demonstrated a tendency toward minimum winning coalitions; however, there is little tendency for decision coalitions to fractionalize and result in no opinion coalition. Only 5 percent of the nonthreat cases and 2 percent of the threat cases produced no opinion coalition. The theory hypothesizes that the writer of the majority opinion *will* make bargains until a minimum winning coalition is attained and will then refuse other bargains, thus excluding other members. The data are consistent with this hypothesis.

The Court's Response to Two Threat Situations

In this section we examine in some detail the Supreme Court's response to two situations involving threats to the Court's authority. One is from the early years of the Warren Court (involving the School Desegregation cases); the other is from the Burger Court's 1973 term (involving the subpoena for the White House tapes).

The School Desegregation Cases

In December 1953, the Supreme Court heard oral arguments in the case of *Brown* v. *Board of Education*,[26] which involved a challenge to the constitutionality of segregated public schools in Topeka, Kansas. Arguments had been heard in the case during the preceding term, when Fred Vinson was Chief Justice, but the case was held over without decision and the Court now had a new Chief—Earl Warren.

When, after argument, the justices met in conference to discuss the case, there appears to have been general agreement among them concerning the difficulty of the matter and the potential resistance to a decision ruling segregation unconstitutional.[27] Initially, not all of the justices were inclined toward making such a ruling. Two or three of the justices were inclined to uphold school segregation as perhaps reprehensible, but constitutional.[28] A number of justices foresaw problems. Justice Clark "noted South Carolina Governor Jimmy Byrnes' threat to abolish public schools," and Justice Jackson "predicted that trouble would occur when white children were sent to colored schools and colored teachers."[29]

Thus the justices recognized that there was substantial probability of resistance and even disobedience if the Court ruled segregation unconstitutional and ordered desegregation. The situation, therefore, fits our definition of a threat to the Court's authority. How, then, did the Court respond?

The Court's decision was not announced until May 17, 1954, in an opinion written by the Chief Justice. This was more than five months after the Court's initial conference on the case—a long time, considering that Warren's opinion runs only eleven pages. Ulmer's analysis demonstrates that what took so long was not getting a majority to agree in the opinion, but the achievement of Warren's more ambitious goal: getting a unanimous opinion.

Warren apparently redrafted his opinion a number of times. He met with the other justices, individually and in groups, many times to discuss the case, gathering information about their views and planning his strategy. Although the matter was apparently in doubt until just before the announcement of the decision,[30] Warren finally achieved what he sought. In May of 1954, the Court ruled, in a unanimous opinion, that segregated public schools were unconstitutional.

In the *Brown* case then, the Court clearly faced a threat situation. There was, throughout the consideration of the case, disagreement among the justices over what should be the Court's ruling. Yet, in the end, the members closed ranks and produced a unanimous opinion.[31]

The Watergate Tapes Case

During its investigation of the break-in at the headquarters of the Democratic National Committee in the Watergate Hotel in Washington, the Senate Select Committee on Presidential Campaign Activities (better known as the Ervin Committee) discovered that conversations in the White House oval office had been automatically tape-recorded for a couple of years.

Following the discovery of the White House taping system, various tapes were sought by the Senate Committee, the House Judiciary Committee, and the Watergate Special Prosecutor. After much conflict and maneuvering, the controversy reached a head when Special Prosecutor Leon Jaworski sought a subpoena for a number of tapes and other records. On May 20, 1974, District Judge John Sirica ruled that President Richard Nixon was obligated to turn over the subpoenaed materials. The President refused and stated he would appeal the ruling.

In order to expedite matters, Jaworski applied to the Supreme Court for immediate review, bypassing the Court of Appeals. The Court agreed, and on July 8, 1974, the justices heard oral arguments in the historic case of *United States* v. *Richard M. Nixon*.[32]

The importance of this case for this discussion is not so much the legal issues it involved but the attempt by the President to create the impression that he might defy an adverse Supreme Court ruling. Both before and after oral argument, spokesmen for the President refused to state that he would obey an order to turn over the tapes. Even in the argument before the Court, the President's lawyer, James St. Clair, hedged. St. Clair had asserted that the doctrine of executive privilege gave the President the right to withhold the subpoenaed material, and Justice Marshall, in an exchange with the lawyer, pressed him to admit that that was a legal question that was up to the Court to decide.

> MARSHALL: And you are still leaving it up to this court to decide it.
>
> ST. CLAIR: Yes, in a sense.
>
> MARSHALL: In what sense?
>
> ST. CLAIR: In the sense that this court has the obligation to determine the law. The President also has an obligation to carry out his constitutional duties.
>
> MARSHALL: You are submitting it for us to decide whether or not executive privilege is available in this case.
>
> ST. CLAIR: Well, the problem is the question is even more limited than that. Is the executive privilege . . . absolute or is it only conditional?
>
> MARSHALL: I said "in this case." Can you make it narrower than that?
>
> ST. CLAIR: No, sir.
>
> MARSHALL: Well, do you agree that that is what is before this court, and you are submitting it to this court for decision?
>
> ST. CLAIR: This is being submitted to this court *for its guidance* and judgment with respect to the law. The President, on the other hand, has his obligations under the Constitution.[33]

To many observers, the implication of this exchange was that if the President did not agree with the "guidance" from the Court, he might not feel obligated to obey its ruling.

After the completion of the oral argument, the justices retired to reach their decision. A number of news publications reported that initially the Court was divided 6 to 2 (Justice Rehnquist did not participate) against the President, with the Chief Justice and Justice Blackmun in the minority.[34] These reports may or may not be correct; in any event, when the Court's decision was announced it was through an Opinion of the Court written by Chief Justice Burger. And that opinion left no doubt as to the Court's view of the binding nature of its decision:

> We therefore reaffirm that it is "emphatically the province and the duty" of this Court "to say what the law is" with respect to the claim of privilege presented in this case.[35]

The decision was unanimous, with neither a concurring nor a dissenting opinion.

Thus we have seen that in two cases the Court was faced with the possibility of disobedience to its decisions. In one case the Court was initially divided as to what should have been the decision, and some reports indicate that this was also the situation in the second case. Yet in both cases, when the Court announced its judgment, the members were unanimous and united behind a single policy statement. This is precisely the response that our theory predicts in situations in which there is a threat to the Court's authority.[36]

Membership in Opinion Coalitions

The final aspect of coalitions to be considered here is the pattern of membership in opinion coalitions. Earlier in this chapter we discussed the bargaining process by which an opinion coalition is formed. The opinion writer accepts those bargains which are most attractive in terms of his own policy preferences and rejects those bargains which are less attractive. If the justices can, as we have argued, be ranked ordinally on each policy issue, then any opinion coalition that is formed should include only justices who are adjacent on the issue dimension (i.e., opinion coalitions should be connected).

In order to test this hypothesis, we must define one more concept: a *reduced opinion coalition*, which is an opinion coalition that is smaller than the decision coalition from which it results.[37] To test whether coalitions are connected, a number of alternative methods are available. We might, for example, compare the membership in the opinion coalition to the ordering of all justices who participated in the case. This, however, would make all unanimous opinions automatically connected. Furthermore, even if we restrict our consideration to cases in which there was at least one dissent, we know that because our scales meet the criteria of unidimensionality, almost all nonreduced coalitions will be connected. Therefore, in order to make our test more stringent, we will restrict our attention to reduced opinion coalitions and compare their membership to the membership in the decision coalition from which they resulted.

When we attempt to operationalize the concept of a connected coalition, a problem is presented by the fact that there are ties in the rank order of justices in some of the issue scales. If no ties were present and all the justices occupied discrete positions, the probability of any given coalition being connected could be compared with the expected proportion.[38] When ties exist, however, we must decide what we will define as a connected coalition. Two choices are possible. Consider nine justices labeled *A* through *I* in accord with their ranking on an issue dimension. Assume that Justices *A* and *B* are tied in rank order. Given a nine-member decision coalition and an eight-member opinion coalition, we could impose a strict definition of connectedness and accept as connected only the coalition from which *I* is excluded. (We can call a coalition whose members are tied in rank order, and are either all excluded or all included, *strictly connected.*) We could, on the other hand, apply a less strict definition of connectedness and accept as connected those coalitions from which either *A*, *B*, or *I* is excluded.

For our purposes, the latter definition seems the more appropriate, especially if we recall that because policy differences sometimes are not expressed publicly, certain unmeasurable factors may cause two justices who occupy the same position to split on joining the majority opinion. In any event, the higher the proportion of connected coalitions that will result from using the latter definition will be compensated for by a corresponding increase in the expected proportion of connected coalitions if the method of computation described in footnote 38 is used. (We will call coalitions that are connected according to the latter definition but not connected under the stricter definition *weakly connected.*) For convenience we will follow the form we employed in the preceding chapter, and use the letter p to indicate the actual proportion of connected coalitions and the symbol π to indicate the proportion we would expect, using the formula in footnote 38.

To this point we have made no distiction between threat and non-threat situations, and we would argue that the presence of a threat to the Court affects not only the size of the opinion coalition but also whether it is connected. If a threat is present, a variable that is distinct from the policy dimension measured by the scales may be influencing the decision about whether to join the opinion coalition. We have argued that in a threat situation, some justices will refrain from publicly expressing their policy disagreements with the majority opinion in order to present a united front against the outside threat. Since, however, there is no reason to believe that the importance of a threat will be the same for all justices or will affect them commensurately with their position on the issue dimension, it

Table 9.2
Connected Coalitions in Threat and Nonthreat Situations

| | OPINION COALITIONS | | | | | | | | | |
| | STRICTLY CONNECTED | | WEAKLY CONNECTED | | ALL CONNECTED | | NOT CONNECTED | | TOTAL | |
SITUATION	N	$\%$	N	$\%$	N	$\%$	N	$\%$	N	$\%$
Nonthreat	51	49	24	23	75	72	29	28	104	100
Threat	14	40	5	14	19	54	16	46	35	100
Total	65	47	29	21	94	68	45	32	139	100

is unlikely that we will find as high a proportion of connected coalitions in threat as in nonthreat situations. Thus, in summary, we predict that opinion coalitions will tend to be connected, and that the proportion of connected coalitions will tend to be greater in nonthreat situations than in threat situations.

Table 9.2 presents the gross data on connected opinion coalitions, and Table 9.3 compares the actual proportion of connected coalitions to the expected proportion in nonthreat and threat situations respectively. From Table 9.2 we can see that more than two-thirds of all opinion coalitions are connected. This result is not dependent on our weaker definition of connectedness, for almost one-half of all the coalitions are strictly connected. There is, moreover, a fairly substantial difference present when the existence of a threat is controlled for; 72 percent of the coalitions are then connected in nonthreat situations and only 54 percent are connected in threat situations. As the data in Table 9.3 indicate, these results exceed what we would expect on a random basis. In nonthreat situations, the actual proportion of connected coalitions (p) is greater than the expected proportion (π) in every possible combination of decision and opinion coalition. (The smallest difference between observed and expected proportions is $+.15$.) In threat situations, the results are, as hypothesized, less strong and less systematic. In only six of the nine situations is the difference between observed and expected proportions positive. Furthermore, seven of the nine differences are smaller than the corresponding differences in nonthreat situations. Thus the data support the theory's predictions regarding membership in opinion coalitions.

Summary

In this chapter we considered the last of the four stages of Supreme Court decision making—the formation of the majority opinion coalition. The concept of a threat to the Court was introduced, and we argued that

Table 9.3
Connected Coalitions in Threat and Nonthreat Situations, by Size of Decision and Opinion Coalitions*

SIZE OF DECISION COALITION	8			7			6			5		
	p	π	$p-\pi$	p	π	$p-\pi$	p	π	$p-\pi$	p	π	$p-\pi$
						NONTHREAT SITUATIONS						
9	.73	.38 (11)	+.35	.67	.16 (12)	+.51	.67	.09 (6)	+.58	.80	.08 (5)	+.72
8				.63	.48 (8)	+.15	.71	.19 (14)	+.52	.67	.10 (6)	+.57
7							.60	.39 (10)	+.21	1.00	.33 (7)	+.67
6										.76	.53 (25)	+.23
						THREAT SITUATIONS						
9	.70	.44 (10)	+.26	.40	.14 (5)	+.26	.00	.07 (3)	−.07	.00	.56 (1)	−.56
8					(0)		.50	.14 (2)	+.36	1.00	.21 (1)	+.79
7							.33	.48 (3)	−.15	.75	.30 (4)	+.45
6										.67	.53 (6)	+.14

SIZE OF OPINION COALITIONS*

*Numbers in parentheses refer to the number of cases in each cell.

when the Court faced a threat and decided to persist in the policy direction that produced the threat, at least some of the justices would suppress their disagreements with the policy in the majority opinion, and opinion coalitions would tend to be larger than minimum winning size. In the absence of a threat, on the other hand, opinion coalitions would tend to be minimum winning.

We then considered two threat situations in detail. In both the 1954 School Desegregation cases and the 1974 Watergate Tapes case, despite initial disagreement among the justices over the policy to be made, the Court produced a completely unanimous result.

Finally, we discussed the pattern of agreement in opinion coalitions. We argued that if justices were motivated by their policy goals in the bargaining over the Court's opinion, then opinion coalitions should include justices who were adjacent to each other on the policy dimension in question. We also argued that this tendency should be more pronounced in nonthreat situations than in threat situations. Using data on civil liberties cases decided by the Warren Court, we found that the theory's predictions with regard to both the size of opinion coalitions and the pattern of agreement within them were supported.

Notes to Chapter 9

1. This was the Court's ruling in *Wells* v. *Rockefeller*, 22 L Ed 2d 535 (1969). The Burger Court has ruled that the same stringent standard does not apply to the apportionment of state legislative districts. See *Mahan* v. *Howell*, 35 L Ed 2d 320 (1973).

2. Robert Alexrod, *Conflict of Interest: A Theory of Divergent Goals with Applications to Politics* (Chicago: Markham, 1970).

3. *Ibid.*, p. 5.

4. The "single-peakedness" requirement "simply means that of two policy positions on one side of a political party, the party prefers the closer one." *Ibid.*, p. 168.

5. *Ibid.*, pp. 169, 167.

6. These properties are discussed in detail in *ibid.*, p. 169 ff.

7. *Ibid.*, p. 169.

8. See David W. Rohde, "A Theory of the Formation of Opinion Coalitions in the U.S. Supreme Court," in Richard G. Niemi and Herbert F. Weisberg, *Probability Models of Collective Decision Making* (Columbus, Ohio: Charles E. Merrill, 1972), pp. 165–178.

9. *Ibid.*, p. 170.

10. See the Appendix to Chapter 8.

11. The other 185 cases fell into issue areas with fewer than 10 cases, and hence they were considered unacceptable for scale analysis.

12. Two of the issue areas (search and seizure, and racial discrimination) were divided into two parts, the dividing line being the end of the 1961 term of the Court. This was done because a substantial change in behavior was exhibited by Justice

Black between these two periods, moving from very liberal to very conservative. Separate scales were constructed for each period. Thus we actually have 27 scales. The policy areas in the scales are as follows (the number of cases in each scale is in parentheses): obscenity (23), speech and press (22), religion (14), internal security (90), association (11), protest (31), voting rights (24), civil rights acts (13), reapportionment (28), immigration and naturalization (13), deportation (25), courts martial (12), racial discrimination (46), search and seizure (53), counsel (27), indigents (20), bugging (15), retroactivity (13), double jeopardy (23), contempt (15), jury trial (18), self-incrimination (44), confrontation of witnesses (13), involuntary confessions (33), discovery and inspection (10).

13. That is, coefficients of reproducibility (*CR*) and scalability (*CS*) were computed for each scale. In each set, the minimum levels of .9 for *CR* and .65 for *CS* were met, and usually the values were substantially higher. For the method of calculating *CR*, see the Appendix to Chapter 7. A description of the meaning and method of computing *CS* may be found in Glendon Schubert, *The Judicial Mind* (Evanston, Ill.: Northwestern University Press, 1965), p. 81.

14. The Court's response to the threat in this area is discussed in detail later in this chapter.

15. See Richard M. Johnson, *The Dynamics of Compliance* (Evanston, Ill.: Northwestern University Press, 1967); and William K. Muir, *Prayer in the Public Schools* (Chicago: University of Chicago Press, 1967).

16. Rohde, *op. cit.*, fn. 8 *supra*, pp. 169–170. The analysis by Schubert noted in the text may be found in Glendon Schubert, *Quantitative Analysis of Judicial Behavior* (New York: The Free Press of Glencoe, 1959), pp. 192–210.

17. Quoted in Walter Murphy, *The Elements of Judicial Strategy* (Chicago: University of Chicago Press, 1964), p. 193.

18. The cases were: *Beecher* v. *Alabama*, 389 U.S. 35, 19 L Ed 2d 35 (1967); *Sims* v. *Georgia*, 389 U.S. 404, 19 L Ed 2d 634 (1967); *Brooks* v. *Florida*, 389 U.S. 412, 19 L Ed 2d 643 (1967); *Johnson* v. *Massachusetts*, 390 U.S. 511, 20 L Ed 2d 69 (1968); and *Smith* v. *Yeager*, 393 U.S. 122, 21 L Ed 2d 246 (1968).

19. This is not meant to imply that attempts at evasion do not occur. Often, however, evasion, to the degree it is successful, springs from the latitude given to lower-court judges by the relative vagueness of a policy reached through bargaining. The point of the argument is that when the Supreme Court gives a clear and direct order it is usually obeyed, and that there is an important distinction between attempts at evasion and outright disobedience.

20. Cf. Murphy, *op. cit.*, fn. 17 *supra*, pp. 65–66.

21. Canon 19 states: "It is of high importance that judges constituting a court of last resort should use effort and self-restraint to promote solidarity of conclusion and the consequent influence of judicial decision. A judge should not yield to pride of opinion or value more highly his individual reputation than that of the court to which he should be loyal. Except in case of conscientious difference of opinion on fundamental principle, dissenting opinions should be discouraged in courts of last resort." Quoted in *ibid.*, p. 177n.

22. For example, Pierce Butler once wrote on the back of one of Justice Stone's slip opinions: "I voted to reverse. While this sustains your conclusion to affirm, I think reversal would be better. But I shall in silence acquiesce. Dissents seldom aid in the right development or statement of the law." Quoted in *ibid.*, p. 52.

23. Henry Abraham writes: "There are many legal scholars who hold to the firm conviction that whereas dissenting opinions are both eminently justifiable and necessary, concurring opinions are neither—that they are frequently nothing more than ego-manifestations and/or 'quibbling,' which would more profitably be confined to footnotes in the body of the majority opinion." Abraham, *The Judicial Process*, 2d ed. (New York: Oxford University Press, 1968), p. 207.

24. The reason that the number of cases in Table 9.1 totals only 508 instead of 636 (the number of cases on which the scales are based) is that 124 of the cases were decided *per curiam*. In addition, for convenience of presentation, four cases that resulted in four-member opinion coalitions have been omitted. The existence of four-member coalitions is of little concern since only 13 of the 636 cases were decided by fewer than eight justices.

25. By "information effect" we mean that the opinion writer may be uncertain about the behavior of other members. For example, the opinion writer will, when drafting his opinion, attempt to take into account the preferences of other members of the majority in order to secure their agreement. It may turn out that he has made his policy broader than was necessary and thus gains the assent of more than the minimum number of justices.

26. 347 U.S. 483 (1954). The argument also included cases from three other states.

27. See S. Sidney Ulmer, "Earl Warren and the Brown Decision," *Journal of Politics* 33 (Aug. 1971): 692–696. Most of our discussion of this case is based on Ulmer's research, which in turn is based on an analysis of Justice Harold Burton's papers.

28. See *ibid.*, pp. 696–697.

29. *Ibid.*, pp. 694, 695.

30. See *ibid.*, p. 699.

31. Another interesting example may be drawn from a later School Desegregation case. In September 1957, the schools of Little Rock, Arkansas, were to begin desegregation under a plan approved by a federal district court. On the first day the plan was in effect, however, Governor Orville Faubus declared a city high school off limits to black students and stationed National Guard troops at the school to enforce his order. The federal government entered the case and secured an injunction against Governor Faubus to prevent him from interfering with the black children. The children again tried to attend school, but they were met this time by a violent mob. President Eisenhower then sent federal troops to the city and the children were admitted to the school.

The school board petitioned the federal district court for permission to return to segregated schools for two and one-half years because of the violence. The district court agreed, but the Sixth United States Court of Appeals reversed. The state appealed and the Supreme Court met in special session. The Court unanimously upheld the Appeals Court in a unique opinion that was announced by the Chief Justice and signed individually by each of the nine justices (*Cooper* v. *Aaron*, 358 U.S. 1 [1958]). This was a most extraordinary show of unity in the face of violent resistance to the Court's policy of desegregation.

32. 41 L Ed 2d 1039 (1974).

33. *Washington Post*, July 9, 1974, p. A14. Emphasis supplied.

34. See *Newsweek*, July 22, 1974, p. 18.

35. 41 L Ed 2d 1039, at 1062.

36. We should also note that in both cases the Chief Justice wrote the majority opinion himself, which is consistent with our discussion in the preceding chapter.

37. A justice who voted with the majority on the merits has three options: he may join the majority opinion and do nothing more; he may join the majority opinion and write or join a concurring opinion; or he may refuse to join the majority opinion and simply concur separately in the result. Since our discussion focuses on justices who exclude themselves from the majority opinion because their policy preferences are not satisfied, we define a reduced opinion coalition as existing only in those cases which have one or more separate concurrences in the result.

38. The probabilities could be computed by assuming that every justice was equally likely to exclude himself from an opinion coalition. Thus, for any decision coalition of size n and any opinion coalition of size r, we could use the combinatorial formula

$$\binom{n}{r} = \frac{n!}{r!\,(n-r)!}$$

to compute the number of possible opinion coalitions (call this number y). We could then count the number of those y coalitions which would be connected (call this number x). Then the expected proportion of connected opinion coalitions of size r resulting from decision coalitions of size n would be x/y.

For example, there are 9 possible 8-member opinion coalitions that can result from a 9-member decision coalition. Only 2 of these would be connected (i.e., if the member at either end of the issue dimension excluded himself). Thus we would expect, on a strictly random basis, 22 percent of such coalitions to be connected.

This formula then gives us a yardstick, like the one we used in the preceding chapter, against which we can measure our theory's prediction.

Epilogue

By positing a theory and applying it, we have attempted in this book to explain systematically the decision-making process in the United States Supreme Court. In doing so, we have relied primarily on our own work throughout. The theory, as presented, is original (although it has obvious roots in the work of many researchers who preceded us), and most of the data to which the theory's predictions are applied were gathered and analyzed firsthand. This procedure was necessary because the results of much of the other research cannot be assessed directly in terms of our theory. The reader should not infer, however, that we think the work of our predecessors to be without value. The many references in the preceding pages to the work of others demonstrate both how valuable that work has been in the formulation of our own ideas, and the variety of other perspectives from which the decision-making process in the Court can be viewed—indeed, *should* be viewed to obtain a complete picture. We encourage the interested reader to seek out those works; they will greatly enrich his or her understanding of the Court. Science is a cumulative process in which the work of one person merely builds on that of others.

Furthermore, we recognize that our presentation has not been all-inclusive. Were we to consider fully all matters relating to the Supreme Court, this book would have been many times its present length. In focusing on the actual decisions of the justices, we have devoted little attention to those activities that precede or follow the formal stages of the Court's decision making.

Thus, for example, a considerable amount of recent research has been aimed at finding out what happens after the Court announces its decisions. These have come to be known as "impact studies."[1] Although most of the Court's rulings appear to be readily and automatically complied with, some—such as those concerning school prayer and other church-school relationships,[2] the rights of criminal defendants,[3] and school desegregation[4] —have not.

In addition, although we dealt with the opinion-writing stage of the process in Chapter 9, our focus there was primarily on the justices' decisions concerning whether or not to join the majority opinion. Thus we have largely not considered the details of the bargaining process,[5] or the evolution of the Court's policy making in a given issue area over time.[6]

At the other end of the process, we have not considered how litigation is generated, the involvement of interest groups,[7] the use of class actions and test cases, or the filing of briefs *amicus curiae*.[8] Also, we have not considered in great detail the Court's relationship with the President[9] and Congress.[10]

Nor, for that matter, is our discussion of some aspects of the Court's decision-making process as complete as it might have been, partly for the reasons just noted. Knowledge of which cases the Court accepts or rejects for decision, and the reasons why it does so, remains rather speculative. In our analysis of voting on the merits in Chapter 7, the influence of certain other factors (such as background characteristics[11] and roles[12]), which have been the subject of considerable research, was not considered. Finally, the discussion of opinion assignments and the formation of the opinion coalitions in Chapters 8 and 9 is far from the last word on the subject. These analyses reflect initial research efforts. It is hoped that other students of the Court will focus on these stages of the Court's decision making, thus furthering our understanding of them.[13]

In summary, we have offered a theory of one aspect of the judicial process in the Supreme Court—the decision making of the justices. We have tried to explain that aspect of the process in light of the theory, and we have examined data on the justices' decisions to assess the accuracy of our theory's implications. In doing so, our goal has been to provide the reader with a means of understanding how the justices make decisions and why. To the degree that the reader believes he or she better comprehends this process, we will have been successful in our endeavor.

Notes to Epilogue

1. See, in addition to the works cited in subsequent notes, Stephen L. Wasby, *The Impact of the United States Supreme Court: Some Perspectives* (Homewood, Ill.: Dorsey Press, 1970); and Theodore L. Becker and Malcolm M. Feeley, eds., *The Impact of Supreme Court Decisions*, 2d ed. (New York: Oxford University Press, 1973).

2. Gordon Patric, "The Impact of a Court Decision: Aftermath of the McCollum Case," *Journal of Public Law* 6 (Fall 1957): 455–464; Frank J. Sorauf, "*Zorach v. Clauson*: The Impact of a Supreme Court Decision," *American Political Science*

Review 53 (September 1959): 777–791; William Beaney and N. Edward Beiser, "Prayer and Politics: The Impact of Engel and Schempp on the Political Process," *Journal of Public Law* 13 (1964): 475–503; Robert Birkby, "The Supreme Court and the Bible Belt: Tennessee Reaction to the Schempp Decision," *American Journal of Political Science* 10 (August 1966): 304–319; Richard Johnson, *The Dynamics of Compliance* (Evanston, Ill.: Northwestern University Press, 1967); William K. Muir, *Prayer in the Public Schools* (Chicago: University of Chicago Press, 1967).

3. Otis H. Stephens, Jr., "Police Interrogation and the Supreme Court: An Inquiry into the Limits of Judicial Policy Making," *Journal of Public Law* 17 (1965): 241–257; David Manwaring, "The Impact of *Mapp* v. *Ohio*," in David Everson, ed., *The Supreme Court as Policy Maker* (Carbondale: Public Affairs Research Bureau, Southern Illinois University, 1968); Richard J. Medalie *et al.*, "Custodial Police Interrogation in Our Nation's Capitol: The Attempt to Implement Miranda," *Michigan Law Review* 66 (May 1968): 1347–1422.

4. J. W. Peltason, *Fifty-Eight Lonely Men: Southern Federal Judges and School Desegregation* (New York: Harcourt, Brace and World, 1961); Reed Sarratt, *The Ordeal of Desegregation* (New York: Harper & Row, 1966); Wasby, *op. cit.*, fn. 1 *supra*, pp. 169–185.

5. See especially Walter Murphy, *The Elements of Judicial Strategy* (Chicago: University of Chicago Press, 1964); and J. Woodford Howard, "On the Fluidity of Judicial Choice," *American Political Science Review* 62 (March 1968): 43–56.

6. For a perspective on the study of policy making in the Court, see Richard Wells and Joel B. Grossman, "The Concept of Judicial Policy Making," *Journal of Public Law* 15 (1966): 286–307. For an empirical application, see Joel B. Grossman, "A Model for Judicial Policy Analysis: The Supreme Court and the Sit-In Cases," in Joel B. Grossman and Joseph Tanenhaus, eds., *Frontiers of Judicial Research* (New York: Wiley, 1969), pp. 405–460.

7. Walter F. Murphy and C. Herman Pritchett, *Courts, Judges, and Politics* (New York: Random House, 1961), chap. 8.

8. Samuel Krislov, "The Amicus Curiae Brief: From Friendship to Advocacy," *Yale Law Journal* 72 (1963): 694–721.

9. Robert Scigliano, *The Supreme Court and the Presidency* (New York: Free Press, 1971).

10. John R. Schmidhauser and Larry L. Berg, *The Supreme Court and Congress: Conflict and Interaction, 1945–1968* (New York: Free Press, 1972).

11. John R. Schmidhauser, "The Justices of the Supreme Court—A Collective Portrait," *American Journal of Political Science* 3 (1959): 1–57; Joel B. Grossman, "Social Backgrounds and Judicial Decisions," *Harvard Law Review* 79 (1966): 1551–1564; Joel B. Grossman, "Social Backgrounds and Judicial Decisions: Notes for a Theory," *Journal of Politics* 29 (May 1967): 334–351; Sheldon Goldman, "Backgrounds, Attitudes, and the Voting Behavior of Judges: A Comment on Joel Grossman's 'Social Backgrounds and Judicial Decisions,'" *Journal of Politics* 31 (Feb. 1969): 214–222; Joel B. Grossman, "Further Thoughts on Consensus and Conversion: A Reply to Professor Goldman," *ibid.*, pp. 223–229; S. Sidney Ulmer, "Dissent Behavior and the Social Background of Supreme Court Justices," *Journal of Politics* 32 (Aug. 1970): 580–598; and John R. Schmidhauser, "*Stare*

Decisis, Dissent, and the Background of the Justices of the Supreme Court of the United States," *University of Toronto Law Journal* 14 (1962): 194–212.

12. Walter Murphy, "Courts as Small Groups," *Harvard Law Review* 79 (1966): 1565–1572; S. Sidney Ulmer, *Courts as Small and Not So Small Groups* (New York: General Learning Corporation, 1971); Dorothy James, "Role Theory and the Supreme Court," *Journal of Politics* 30 (Feb. 1968): 160–186; Joel B. Grossman, "Dissenting Blocs on the Warren Court: A Study in Judicial Role Behavior," *Journal of Politics* 30 (Nov. 1968): 1068–1090; Joel B. Grossman, "Role Playing and the Analyses of Judicial Behavior: The Case of Mr. Justice Frankfurter," *Journal of Public Law* 11 (1963): 286–309; and Harold J. Spaeth, "The Judicial Restraint of Mr. Justice Frankfurter—Myth or Reality," *American Journal of Political Science* 8 (Feb. 1964): 22–38.

13. Recent research on these stages includes: S. Sidney Ulmer, "The Use of Power in the Supreme Court: The Opinion Assignments of Earl Warren, 1953–1960," *Journal of Public Law* 19 (1970): 49–67; Gregory J. Rathjen, *A Theory of Intracourt Influence* (unpublished Ph.D. Dissertation, Michigan State University, 1972); and Gregory J. Rathjen, "An Analysis of Separate Opinion Writing as Dissonance Reduction," *American Politics Quarterly* 2 (Oct. 1974): 393–411.

Table of Cases

NOTE: The number in parentheses following a page number indicates the number of separate footnotes in which the case is cited on that page.

Index

KF8742 .R63   CU-Main

Rohde, David W./Supreme Court decision making / Da

3 9371 00002 3879